Guide to Estonia

Guide to Estonia

Ilvi Jõe Cannon and William J H Hough

Bradt Publications, UK
The Globe Pequot Press Inc, USA

First published in 1995 by Bradt Publications, 41 Nortoft Road,
Chalfont St Peter, Bucks SL9 0LA, England
Published in the USA by The Globe Pequot Press Inc, 6 Business Park Road,
PO Box 833, Old Saybrook, Connecticut 06475-0833

British Library Cataloguing in Publication Data
A catalogue record for this book is available from the British Library
ISBN 1 898323 18 6

Library of Congress Cataloging-in-Publication Data
Hough, Bill
Guide to Estonia / I J Cannon, W J Hough : editor, Inara Punga.
p. cm. — (Bradt guides)
Includes index
ISBN 1-56440-811-6
1. Estonia—Guidebooks I. Punga, Inara. II. Title
III. Series.
DK503.22.H68 1995 95-13699
914.7'41—dc20 CIP

Research by Ilvi Cannon, Bill Hough, Ināra Punga
Technical assistance by William Wickersham, Karin Ruus and Liivi Jõe
Drawings Rebecca de Mendonça
from photographs by Ināra Punga and Mirek Szepietowski
Maps *Inside covers:* Steve Munns *Others:* Hans van Well
Cover photographs Mark Wadlow (Russia and Republics Photo-Library)
Front: View of Tallinn *Back:* Estonian patriots
Typeset from the author's disc by Patti Taylor, London NW10 1JR
Printed and bound in Great Britain by The Guernsey Press Co Ltd

ACKNOWLEDGEMENTS

Appreciation is expressed to those who put together the first guide to the Baltic states when the three countries were still occupied by the Soviet Union. The Baltics had become more accessible to travellers under Mikhail Gorbachev's regime and since no tour book existed, Bill Hough encouraged the publication of one. Under Kārlis Cerbulis's initiative *Inroads* published *A Guide to the Baltic States* in 1990. In the following year, the Soviet regime collapsed and the book lost much of its relevance. However, it provided a basis for the development of the present edition. Bill Hough worked as a co-author this time.

We are grateful to Krista Areng, Liivi Jõe, Ojars Kalniņš (who has since become the ambassador of Latvia to the United States), Liina Keerdoja, Maria Pedak-Kari and Toomas Tubalkain for having written the Estonian section of the 1990 publication and thereby preparing the path.

We are most grateful to all those individuals who have supported us during the writing of this book, including Ambassador Ernst Jaakson; Consul of Estonia, Dr Aarand Roos; Juta Ristsoo; Dr Heino Ainso; Lilja Kostjuk and family; Igor V Kostjuk; Tiit Beeren and family; Marek Pavlov; Hannes Valliskivi; Aiki Alabert; Jaak Treiman; Paul and Endla Luedig; Ÿlo and Tiiu Anson; Enn Kōiva; The Baltic American Committee of Greater Cleveland; Alar Oljum; Margus Kuuskman, Ignar Fjuk; Dr H B Schmidt; Adrian de Graffenreid; Michael Kelly; Kate Naughton; Boris Cooper; Marie McCarthy; Marti Penjamm, Imanta Hütt, Michael and Eve Tarm, Arvi Jurviste, and Peet Kask.

Relatives and friends, too numerous to mention, in Estonia and the United States have assisted with this edition. But two people must be singled out: Henno Uus for giving us access to valuable literature from his considerable library, and Virginia Wickersham for having the interest to come to Estonia and to give advice from the perspective of a mainstream American abroad.

This book is dedicated to Kati and Ben.

This book is also dedicated to Kārlis Cerbulis, born in Pennsylvania; graduate of Pennsylvania State University and Harvard University School of Business; principal organizer of the Baltic Youth Congress (USA) and the Baltic Peace and Freedom Cruise; President of the Rīga Stock Exchange, and long-time supporter of the re-establishment of Baltic independence. Without his commitment, this book would not have been written.

INTRODUCTION

For decades, Estonia, like the other two Baltic countries, Latvia and Lithuania, had apparently disappeared from the world map. Invaded and occupied by the former Soviet Union from June 1940, the peoples' travails and suffering went almost unheard of in the West. That changed when the Soviet Union collapsed in 1991 and the countries of the Baltic re-emerged as independent nations.

Today, Estonia is a curious blend of old Soviet ways and new Western features. While women stroll down the streets of Tallinn in heels and Calvin Klein jeans, some Estonian farmers still work their fields with a horse and plough An odd mix at times, this small country is a land of serene beauty with long seacoasts, rolling farmlands and peaceful valleys dotted with tall white birches. Here, the north's long, dreamy summer twilight lingers from May to September; here, thick winter snows cling to small cobblestoned towns.

Changes are occurring at a frenetic pace. Inert for decades, it seems as if Estonia is trying to make up for lost time in a few months, which makes it difficult to keep track of political, economic and social developments. Truly, what is fact today is history tomorrow. New shops open frequently, businesses close down or change addresses. In this book we've made every attempt to obtain the most up-to-the-minute information possible, but changes to some of it are inevitable.

Despite the sometimes accompanying confusion of today's rapid economic metamorphosis, we believe that it is exactly these invigorating times that will add spice to your trip to Estonia!

CONTENTS

ESTONIA FACTBOX

Location:	Northern Europe, south of Finland and north of Latvia
Size:	45,215 km^2
Population:	1,574,955 inhabitants (1990): 61.5% Estonians, 30.3% Russians, 3.1% Ukrainians, 1.8% Belarussians, 1.1% Finns, 2.2% others
Government:	Parliamentary democracy
Capital city:	Tallinn (446,000 inhabitants)
Larger towns:	Tartu (115,400 inhabitants) Narva (82,300 inhabitants) Kohtla-Järve (76,800 inhabitants) Pärnu (54,200 inhabitants)
Administrative division:	15 districts (*maakond* in Estonian), 193 townships (*vald* in Estonian)
Currency:	Kroon and sent (1 kroon=100 sents)
Language:	Estonian, a member of the Finno-Ugric group
Alphabet:	Latin
Religion:	Predominantly Lutheran
Weights & measures:	The metric system
Electricity:	220 volts, 50 Hz
Legal holidays:	January 1 (New Year) February 24 (Independence Day) Good Friday May 1 (Vernal Day) June 23 (Victory Day) June 24 (St John's Day) December 25 and 26 (Christmas)
National flag:	Blue-black-white (horizontally)
National anthem:	*Mu isamaa, mu õnn ja rõõm* (My fatherland, my joy and happiness)
National flower:	Cornflower (*Centaurea cyanus*)
National bird:	Barn swallow (*Hirundo rustica*)

Part One

Background

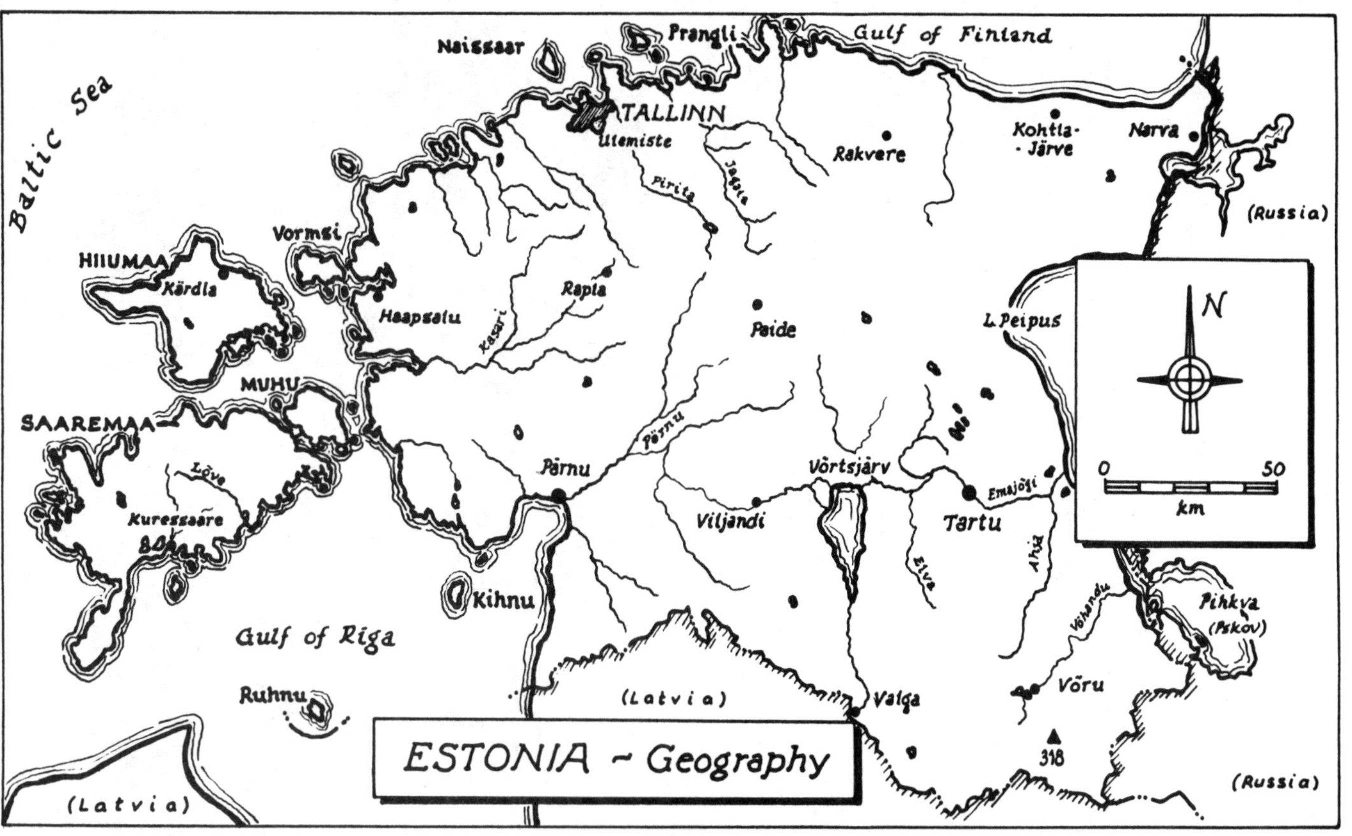
Baltic Sea
Naissaar
Prangli
Gulf of Finland
TALLINN
Ülemiste
Pirita
Jägala
Rakvere
Kohtla-Järve
Narva
(Russia)
Vormsi
HIIUMAA
Kärdla
Haapsalu
Rapla
Kasari
Paide
L. Peipus
N
0
50
km
MUHU
SAAREMAA
Lõve
Kuressaare
Pärnu
Pärnu
Võrtsjärv
Viljandi
Emajõgi
Tartu
Elva
Ahja
Kihnu
Võhandu
Pihkva
(Pskov)
Gulf of Riga
Ruhnu
(Latvia)
Valga
Võru
318
ESTONIA ~ Geography
(Russia)
(Latvia)

Chapter One

The Country and its People

GEOGRAPHY

Northernmost of the three Baltic republics, Estonia lies on the east coast of the Baltic Sea. It is bordered by the Gulf of Finland on the north, Russia on the east, Latvia on the south, and the Baltic Sea on the west. Estonia covers 45,215km^2, which is approximately the combined size of the states of New Hampshire and Vermont, and is larger than either Denmark or the Netherlands. Included in this territory are over 1,500 coastal islands. The largest of these is Saaremaa (2,710km^2), followed in size by Hiiumaa, Muhumaa and Vormsi.

Estonia is part of the great East European plain and can be divided into two distinct regions. The higher part of the plain runs north to south through the eastern part of Estonia, and consists of the Pandivere plateau in the Virumaa district, the Otepää plateau in the Valgamaa district, and the Haanja plateau in the Võrumaa district. The average elevation is 50m (164ft) above sea level, with only 10% of the territory reaching over 100m. Nevertheless, the highest point in the Baltic states is found within Estonian territory on the Haanja plateau at Suur Muna Mägi (The Large Egg Hill) with an elevation of just over 317m (1,040ft). Thanks to retreating glaciers, the landscape is quite varied and the soil is fertile.

The lower portion of Estonia encompasses the western and northern coastal regions, including the islands, and also the areas around Lake Peipus and Lake Võrtsi (which, by the way, are the two largest of Estonia's more than 1,400 lakes — Peipus is also the fourth largest lake in Europe). These areas tend to be mostly flat, often marshy, and strewn with boulders, especially in the north.

Numerous rivers run through Estonia's limestone, dolomite and sandstone plains, including the Ema River (209km), the Võhandu (159km), the Pärnu (153km), the Kasari (99km), the Piirita (98km) and the Narva (78km). Forests cover approximately 40% of Estonian territory. Pine forests dominate along the Baltic coast and the Gulf of Finland, while inland forests are mixed, with pine, spruce and birch species dominating. Northwestern Estonia (including the islands) is characterized by meadows and juniper forests. Marshlands cover almost 50% of the land.

Climatically, Estonia falls in the temperate zone. Winters are milder than in corresponding latitudes due to the Baltic Sea and an arm of the Gulf Stream. The coldest month is February, with an average temperature of -5°C (23°F). It is generally warmer in the western coastal regions and islands than in the eastern part of the country. July is the warmest month, averaging 18°C (64°F). Annual precipitation ranges between 80 and 100cm (31-39 inches).

The most important resources of Estonia are forest, peat and minerals — the latter consisting largely of oil-shale, phosphate, limestone, gypsum and various clays. Oil shale reserves may be more than 5,000 million metric tons with an oil content of 20%. Before World War II the forests of Estonia covered 897,000 hectares, of which 70% were coniferous and 30% deciduous.

FAUNA AND FLORA

The last Ice Age receded from Estonia 10,000 years ago, not leaving the fauna of this region much time to develop and branch out. There are about 18,000 different species of wildlife and more than half of this number are insects. About 60 are mammals.

Estonia's forests contain elk, deer, wild boar, badger, fox, squirrel, and beaver. The brown bear, wolf, and lynx are much rarer, but still seen. Over 300 species of birds call Estonia home, among them migrating geese, swans, ducks and storks. The national bird is the graceful barn swallow. It is believed that good fortune will follow if one decides to nest in your rafters. Other birds you'll find in Estonia are the house sparrow, blackbird, white stork, woodcock and golden eagle.

The country's inland and coastal waters boast over 80 species of fish. Although Estonia's economic history as well as social lore is closely linked with fishing, the present polluted state of the Baltic Sea has forced the Estonian fishing industry to send its ships to points all over the globe.

Estonia has 2,100 species of higher plant life. The country's once extensive forests (Estonia was once nearly covered with woodland) were thick with broad-leafed trees but today mostly abound with spruce. The most common tree is the pine, followed by the birch, spruce, aspen, oak and alder. During the first independence era, a great deal of land was used for farming and the forest made up only 20% of the country. After the Soviet takeover, many farms lay abandoned and reverted back to the wild, which is why today forests claim 40% of the country. Twenty-two per cent of the country contains marshlands and bogs.

ECONOMY

Estonia has traditionally had a rural economy. *Maarahvas* is the term used over the ages to refer to native Estonians. Literally, it means 'people of the land', but depending on the context and historical circumstances, it could also mean 'native population', 'the people that work the soil', or 'the serfs'. As late as the 20th century and before the beginning of World War II, Estonia was an overwhelmingly rural country. Nearly two-thirds of its population were engaged in agricultural pursuits.

The major industrial sectors by the end of the 1930s were textiles, foodstuffs, metallurgy, chemicals and paper. The rise in the chemical industry was based on the increased exploitation of oil-shale deposits in northeastern Estonia and the production of oil.

Farmers resisted collectivization, and an estimated one in five Estonian farmers were deported to the USSR. By 1949, Estonia's 140,000 farms had been transformed into 2,300 *kolkhozes* and 124 state farms. Later, this number decreased to 833 *kolkhozes* and 123 *sovkhozes*.

By the end of the 1940s, sovietization of agriculture and industry had been added to the war-ravaged economy of Estonia. During the Soviet occupation all property was nationalized. Estonia was fully integrated into the centralized Stalinist economic system, and its assigned major role was to supply energy to the northwestern USSR from its vast oil-shale deposits. The socially and ecologically devastating results of that policy can be seen to this day.

The rebuilding of a market economy after five decades of a Soviet command economy is in process. The oil-shale industry will continue to play a major role in heavy industry, Estonia depending on it for industrial energy and fuel supply. Estonia's large phosphorite deposits will form the base for commercial fertilizer manufacture. Forestry is a large part of Estonia's wealth, covering about 40% of its territory. Its exploitation will produce timber, pulp and paper goods. Considerable engineering skills exist in the country and are expected to play a large role in the manufacture of machinery and equipment. Light industry will continue to be led by textiles, and leather goods should follow closely.

In June 1992 Estonia successfully introduced the Estonian kroon to replace the Soviet ruble. The kroon is pegged to the German mark at a rate of 8 to 1. The kroon is backed by hard currency reserves and gold, and has been remarkable steady since 1992. However, given Estonia's 45% inflation rate in 1994, and the reported 3.4% drop in the Gross Domestic Product in the first nine months of 1994, pressure may mount on the Government to devalue the currency so as to make Estonian exports more competitive.

Privatization in Estonia moved forward between 1992 and 1995. By early 1995, more than 1,000 objects had been privatized to Estonia's population through auction, and 200 by tender, many to international bidders. Among the huge firms purchased were the *Kreenholm Textile Manufacture* in Narva (by Swedes), the *Sangar Textile Company* in Tartu (the city's largest employer), the *Viru Hotel* in Tallinn (to Finns and Estonians), the *Saku Beer Company* (80% to Swedes and Finns), *Tartu Brewery*, the *Leibur Bread Company* in Tallinn (to Finns), and others. Such giants of Estonian industry as *Estonian Air, Kalev Confectionery Co, Mootor Bus Co* and *Estonian Shipping Co* were scheduled for sale in 1995.

Agriculture is changing. Both privatization and re-organization are helping to strengthen family farming though lack of money and suitable farming equipment is slowing down the process. Meat and milk are the country's leading agricultural products.

Agriculture will still be an integral part of Estonia's economy. *Maarahvas* is an inalienable part of being Estonian and working close to the land is in its soul.

THE PEOPLE

While the first independence period (1918-1940) saw a reassertion of economic, political, and cultural rights for the nation's Estonian majority, these rights were quickly suppressed during the Soviet occupation. The Soviet period witnessed a large immigration of non-Estonians, such that by 1990 nearly 40% of the population was made up of nationals of other lands of the former USSR.

Beginning in 1989, Estonia's foremost national political movement, the *Popular Front*, fought for the re-establishement of the Estonian language as the country's official tongue. This was not welcomed by many of the country's Russian speakers who had not learned Estonian during the Soviet period. Today, there are more than 400,000 non-Estonians living in the country, many of them Russian, Ukrainian, Finnish or Byelorussian. Estonian citizenship is barred to all who cannot prove descendancy from a pre-World War II Estonian citizen. If one isn't a direct descendant, one can become a citizen if one passes a strict naturalization test proving a strong knowledge of the Estonian language and history. Non-Estonians often claim these demands are too difficult to meet.

The most often heard comment about the Estonians' character is that they are reserved, almost frighteningly so. Nor do they walk around with smiling faces. They are strongly individualistic and frank, which is not always appreciated, but they are also friendly and helpful, and once they get to know you the bonds last.

They are very sociable and when gathered around a table, which is the usual way for entertaining guests, alcohol features: their hospitality will want to keep filling your glass, but you should feel free to impose a limit on yourself. Under their new market economy they produce a variety of alcoholic beverages of reasonable quality — but good luck with *Vana Tallinn*, known to give a potent headache the morning after. Tourists often take it back home as a souvenir. Their *Saku* beer, the 'Original' label, is excellent.

Upon meeting, they greet each other with a handshake and gentlemen tip their hats. Hugs and kisses and public displays of affection by adults are seldom seen. Giving cut flowers when paying a social call is almost universal. Hence you see a large number of flower vendors, allowing you to pick up a bouquet on your way.

Their strong identification with nature and love of solitude takes them to the countryside and their *suvila* (cottages) or farms in the summers. As an extension of this quality, they keep large gardens. Should you get an invitation to the country, accept it. In the country, very likely, you will go to *saun*, the most fundamental of Estonian institutions.

Language

Estonian, a Finno-Ugric language related to Finnish, is the official language of the country. Since the occupation, Estonians also speak Russian and use it to communicate with their Baltic neighbours, but most prefer not to use it. There was a time when some Estonians bristled if you addressed them in the language of their occupiers. English, the most popular foreign language, is spoken where tourists are sure to come: well-to-do hotels, restaurants, and shops. However, on buses, trains, at corner food stands and outside the major cities, you won't find many who speak English. German is the next most popular foreign language. German tourists abound in Estonia, as do Finnish tourists. Many Tallinners also speak Finnish.

Religion

Pre-Christian

Early Estonian religion centered around animism, the belief that all things in nature have a spirit. Thus trees, rocks, fields, fire and such were powerful forces to be respected and worshipped. Sacred fields and forests could not be disturbed. To gain the attention and favour of nature's many spirits, various sacrifices were routinely performed. Awed by the forces of nature, people had to reckon with the world of the dead as well. The dead were often controlled by evil forces, but could be placated and one could turn to them for help. Long ago, the dead were set unburied in a sacred grove of trees. Special wise-people could leave their bodies and commune with the dead, gathering wisdom from them.

In pagan times the winter solstice was the most important festivity of the year for it was a time when the light of day began to win over the North's long dreary night. This victory was seen as a celebration of fertility and the coming of life after the harshness of winter.

Christianity

Christianity was well established in middle Europe before it came to Estonia. When it arrived it was thrust on the nature-worshipping populace with brutal force. In the 1220s, the German Knights of the Sword conquered the area using fire and the sword. Terrorized, the Estonian tribes succumbed to the German crusaders and, one by one, the Estonian tribes were baptized. Catholicism ruled for the next 300 years, losing control to the Lutheran Church with the advent of the Reformation in 1520.

Despite the Church's power, pagan customs and rituals were not so quickly stamped out. They often blended together with Christian rituals. Saints' Days were celebrated with pagan traditions. The old ways held fast until the 18th and 19th centuries when various religious sects grew in popularity.

In 1686 an Estonian edition of the New Testament was published. A full bible translated into Estonian was published in 1739. By this time the language of religion was Estonian, not Latin or German. Because the village school was now becoming a permanent fixture throughout the country, more and more people could read and they turned to what was available in print — mostly religious works.

After the Northern War (1700-1721) Estonia fell under Russian control and the Russian Orthodox Church grew in power. It attracted many of the peasantry whose lives were full of misery and suffering — up to 20% were Russian Orthodox Church members. Czar Alexander III (1860-1896) had several Russian Orthodox churches built throughout Estonia. Perhaps the most famous — or infamous to some Estonians — is the one that sits it Tallinn's Old Town on historical Toompea Hill. Controversial, there was a time in the 1920s when Tallinners debated whether or not to modify the building and turn it into a museum. The building was finally left alone as a testament to history.

During Estonia's first independence period 80% of the populace was Lutheran — the country's official church. During the Soviet occupation religious practices of all denominations were banned socially, church property was confiscated and theological schools shut down. Less than 10% of the population described themselves as Christians.

Today, not only Lutheranism but several other religious denominations are blossoming. The Russian Orthodox Church is back, along with Baptists and Roman Catholics. Tallinn has a Jewish synagogue. Other faiths include Methodists and Seventh Day Adventists. But though the church in its various forms is doing well, the majority of the population does not consider itself as keepers of the faith. Polls show less than a quarter of the people believe themselves to be religious.

Estonian and Baltic events

MIDSUMMER NIGHT'S EVE, June 23 and **ST JOHN'S DAY**, June 24, celebrates the longest day of summer and is a national holiday in all three Baltic countries. Many midsummer night traditions go back to pagan days. Locals gather around a blazing bonfire to sing and dance, drink beer and wear oak or flower wreaths, or stroll through the fragrant bonfire-dotted countryside in a nearly endless summer twilight.

SONG AND DANCE FESTIVAL. All three Baltic countries stage massive song and dance festivals every few years during the summer. These events attract thousands of Balts living abroad, as well as other guests, who enjoy the immense choirs and colourful folk dance displays. Art exhibitions, theatres, concerts, musicals and other forms of Baltic performing arts (mostly in the native tongue) fill the week-long celebrations. Each year, smaller regional song and dance festivals are also held.

BALTICA ANNUAL FOLKLORE FESTIVAL. This festival is staged annually in a different Baltic country every summer. It shows the culture and tradition of different countries and smaller ethnic groups. Folk dancers and singers gather from Estonia, Latvia, Lithuania, Sweden, Denmark, Finland, Norway, Spain, Russia and Germany.

Music

In the latter part of the 1980s, as Communism began to collapse in Central and Eastern Europe, the political world discovered Estonia by its singing, and the movement for freedom was dubbed 'The Singing Revolution'. But Estonians have always sung.

Folk songs probably took form in the first millennium BC, as runic verse — short tunes with a small range, but rich in variations. The accompanying musical instrument, when not singing *a cappella*, is usually the *kannel*. The *kannel*, a member of the lyre family, consists of taut gutstrings pulled over a wooden sounding board. The *kannel* is the musical symbol of the Estonian soul in folklore. Other instruments played include primitive, but sonorous fiddles, and whistle pipes.

The rhymed folk song with a wider range was introduced in the 18th century and in the 19th century Estonians began to participate in choral music. In 1869, the first song festival was held in Tartu. That developed into a national tradition with the festivals being held every five years in Tallinn. The first festival featured male choirs and brass bands. Later festivals also included mixed, women's, children's and boys' choirs. While the first festival had 800 music makers and an audience of 4,000, the festival in 1990 — the first truly non-Soviet flavoured festival since World War II — had 30,000 music makers and an audience in excess of 300,000.

In addition to the large national song festivals, school children's festivals have been held since 1961, and university students have organized song festivals with colleagues from Latvia and Lithuania since 1956.

The first Estonian compositions were chiefly choral works, written in the latter part of the 19th century. As a matter of fact, the first two original choral pieces, written by Aleksander Kunileid, were performed at the first song festival in 1869. Other well-known composers were Johannes Kappel, Miina Härma, Konstantin Türnpu and Aleksander Läte. Läte founded Estonia's first symphony orchestra in 1900 in Tartu. The first Estonian symphonic work appeared in 1896, written by Rudolf Tobias, who also wrote the first piano concerto (1897) and oratorio, in 1909.

During the independence period between the two world wars, the Higher School of Music was founded in Tartu and the Conservatory in Tallinn. Artur Kapp, who studied with Rimsky-Korsakov at St Petersburg Conservatory and taught at Tallinn Conservatory, and Heino Eller at the Higher School in Tartu are the two teachers who have greatly influenced the development of music in Estonia to this day. Not only did they themselves compose, but their students with their varying artistic expressions, have added to the storehouse of Estonian music. The first prominent Estonian opera, *Vikerlased* (The Vikings), was written by Evald Aav, a student of Kapp's.

Eduard Tubin, who fled to the West during the closing days of World War II and became a citizen of Sweden, wrote the first Estonian ballet, *Kratt* (The Goblin), in 1943. However, he is best known for his symphonic works.

A well-known figure in the choral music and conducting world was Gustav Ernesaks, who taught in the 1930s. Before the war ended he founded the State Academic Male Choir (RAM) and served as its conductor. After the war he was the chief organizer and leader of the national song festivals and wrote many choral works and operas.

After the war, a new generation of composers appeared. Veljo Tormis's choral compositions, using traditional themes from Estonians and other Finno-Ugric peoples, have attracted attention beyond his homeland. However, the composer best known in the West is Arvo Pärt. He has composed widely in orchestral, vocal and chamber forms, his early work showing the influences of Prokofiev and Shostakovich. A deeply religious man, he began to study the music of the Middle Ages and in the 1970s his artistic expression revealed characteristics unacceptable to the Soviet authorities. The most famous compositions of this period are: *Calix, St John Passion, Cantus,* and *Tabula rasa.*

Pärt emigrated to the West and has lived in Berlin since 1980. His compositions are widely performed and in 1988, *The New York Times* picked a recording of Pärt's *St John Passion* by the Hilliard Ensemble as the year's best new disc for its 'mystically compelling, profoundly religious' quality.

Another emigré musician who has become well known in the West is the conductor Neeme Järvi. After emigration in 1980, Järvi served as musical director of the Scottish National Orchestra and principal conductor of the Göteborg Orchestra, and guest conductor of major orchestras in the United States. Currently, he is the musical director of the Detroit Symphony Orchestra.

For almost a decade Tallinn has hosted the International Organ Festival every summer for ten days. Concerts are given by the world's premier organists in the city's beautiful, historic churches.

Rock music festivals have also become established as part of summer festivities. Likewise, folk music festivals are almost a common occurrence, often held together with fellow Baltic peoples, the Latvians and the Lithuanians.

Art

For today's viewers, the oldest remaining works of art are some gravestones from the 13th century and wood carvings from the 14th and 15th centuries. The oldest secular representations of the latter are the benches in the Tallinn Town Hall. Except for the stonemasons, who were Estonians, the artists of the Middle Ages were foreign masters.

The Tartu University drawing school, founded in 1803, was the first art school in Estonia and its most noteworthy teacher was the graphic artist and painter, Karl Senff. In 1832, a lithographic workshop followed and three years later a woodcut workshop was founded.

It is quite natural that Estonian national art was born during the national awakening. Johann Koler, Amandus Adamson, and August Weizenberg are the recognized founders of Estonian art. However, the first general exhibition of Estonian artists' work was not until 1906 in Tartu. In 1914, the Tallinn Arts and Crafts School opened. Interest in modern art increased. This period produced Kristjan Raud, whose portrait the Bank of Estonia put on the one kroon note when restored independence brought back Estonia's own currency. Raud's style was Symbolism and National Romanticism.

During the independence period between the wars Estonian artists divided into many schools: portraits, landscapes, neo-impressionism, expressionism, abstract expressionism, cubism, and so on. The most prominent Estonian graphic artist of this era is Eduard Wiiralt. After graduating from Pallas, the art school founded in Tartu in 1919, he continued his studies in Dresden. Then he went to live in Paris until war drums beat across Europe. He died in exile.

Sculpture was a popular medium. Amandus Adamson and August Weizenberg were sculptors. Their noteworthy successors were Jaan Koort and Anton Starkopf, who also taught at Pallas.

Artistic development was stopped by World War II and the Soviet occupation. Many artists fled to the West and the only ones who were given official approval were the artists who had retreated with the Soviets to Russian hinterlands during the war. The 'thaw' in the 1960s allowed for development of diversity in the arts. By the 1970s, there was a veritable profusion of artists. Generally speaking, their work is marked by constructive clarity of the application of form, as well as technical mastery of the aesthetic features of the material. Among the many people who fled to the West when the Red Army returned to Estonia in 1944 were the parents of the young American artist, Mark Kalev Kostabi. Kostabi's paintings, distinguished by amorphous, 'everyman' figures, have become, in the opinion of some art critics, cultural icons. His paintings are included in the permanent collections of the Metropolitan Museum of Art, the Guggenheim, and the Museum of Modern Art in New York. His works have been exhibited globally in more than 500 shows.

And finally, particular note should be made of the very distinctive leather work in Estonia. Imaginatively designed and carefully crafted leather products, such as books, albums, wallets, ornaments, speak of talented artists. There is even leather sculpture — very original!

Literature

Although Estonian literature is relatively modern, going back only to the mid-1800s and the time of the national awakening, there is nonetheless an extraordinary wealth of folk poetry dating back to ancient times. Through the years of foreign occupations, Estonian folklore imbued the Estonian people with a sense of national identity. As the only outlet for poetic imagination, the Estonian oral tradition remained strong.

In 1525 the first Estonian text appeared, a Lutheran catechism. This was followed by an Estonian language New Testament in 1680. Then, the Bible was first printed in Estonian in 1739. The first known example of secular literature written by a native Estonian is a poem by Käsu Hans. Written in 1708, the poem bemoans the destruction of Tartu and the deportation of its citizens by the Russians in the great Northern War. Kristjan Jaak Peterson (1801-1822), whose life was cut short by tuberculosis, is considered the first real Estonian poet. This gifted young man, who proudly wore native garb and walked from Rīga to Tartu to attend the university, delved into Estonian mythology and helped to set the scene for the national awakening, which was not to blossom until some 40 years after his death.

The two men considered most instrumental in advancing the development of Estonian literature in the 19th century were Friedrich R Faehlmann (1798-1850) and Friedrich R Kreutzwald (1803-1882). Both were physicians with great interest in Estonian folklore. Faehlmann started to collect verses in the countryside and after his untimely death in 1850 his friend Kreutzwald finished the work. The result of this effort was the national epic, *Kalevipoeg* (Son of Kalev), 1857-61. The epic consists of 19,023 runic verses and tells the story of Kalevipoeg, the mythical founder of the Estonian nation.

The first Estonian language newspaper, *Perno Postimees,* was published in 1857 by Johann Voldemar Jannsen (1819-1890), another significant figure of the national awakening. However, Jannsen's daughter, Lydia, was perhaps his greatest issue. She wrote the major poems of the awakening period under the pen name Koidula (Land of Dawn). The depth of sentiment and power of expression in her verse are unsurpassed in their patriotic evocations. Married to a Latvian physician, Koidula spent many years living outside Estonia, which only served to inflame her passion for her homeland. She died abroad of cancer at an early age and her remains were later brought home to rest at Metsakalmistu (Forest Cemetery) in Tallinn, where numerous other prominent Estonian cultural figures are also buried.

Romanticized historical novels as well as socially critical realism came into vogue at the end of the 1800s. The best example of the former is Eduard Bornhöhe's *Tasuja* (The Avenger). Written in 1880, it depicts the Estonians' struggle against German invaders. The most prominent writer of the realism genre was Eduard Vilde (1865-1933). A novelist of great stature, Vilde had a profound political as well as literary influence on his contemporaries. In his writings he touched upon all aspects of national life, from the ridiculous to the tragic. *Külmale maale* (Banished), written in 1896, was a landmark in the development of Estonian realistic fiction. Vilde was also a playwright. Two of his finest works in this genre are *Tabamata ime* (The Unattained Miracle), written in 1912, and the comedy *Pisuhänd* (The Fire Dragon), written the following year.

At the turn of the century, Juhan Liiv (1864-1913) emerged as another great poet. Although he struggled with schizophrenia, his subtleties, intensity of feeling and imagery established him as a great Symbolist poet ahead of his time.

At the same time the foundations for modern Estonian literature were laid by a group known as *Noor Eesti* (Young Estonia). They sought to emancipate Estonian culture from its parochialism. Chief among them were the poet and literary scholar Gustav Suits (1883-1956), Friedebert Tuglas (1886-1971), who established modern Estonian literary criticism, and Johannes Aavik (1880-1973) who modernized the Estonian language and expanded its range of expression. The independence era saw the emergence of another literary group, *Siuru,* which took its name from a mythical songbird. Members of this group shocked conventional tastes by exploring sensual and erotic themes in Estonian literature. Without a doubt, the most gifted member of this group was Marie Under (1883-1980). She is also considered Estonia's greatest poet. She burst on the scene with a powerful, exciting, highly emotional impressionism that had heretofore been unknown in the world of Estonian literature.

This period also produced A H Tammsaare (1878-1940), considered to be Estonia's greatest novelist. His greatest work, a five volume prose saga, *Tõde ja õigus* (Truth and Justice), was written between 1926-1933. This epic work explored three generations of Estonian social and political life from the 1870s to the 1920s. The story weaves realistic details about rural and urban life within the framework of philosophical issues and the human condition.

The most popular playwright of this era was Hugo Raudsepp (1883-1952). A master of cynical comedies, his best works included *Mikumärdi* (Mikumärdi farm, 1929) and *Vedelvorst* (Lazybones, 1932).

By the time World War II broke out, Estonian literature had attained a high standard. Its citizens had one of the world's highest literacy rates, over 98%, and the country ranked second only to Iceland in per capita books published. The Soviet invasion and occupation abruptly ended that era. Many writers fled to the West, some were deported to Siberia, and those that remained were not allowed to publish their works. Post-war literature reflected Soviet-style socialist realism.

After Stalin's death, a 'thaw' occurred and something akin to a rebirth of prose and poetry took place. Poets like Betti Alver (seen as inheriting the laurels of Marie Under, who had fled to Sweden), August Sang, Ain Kaalep, and Artur Alliksaar began to give expression to their art. Among the noteworthy prose writers were Arvo Valton, Mati Unt, Enn Vetemaa, Juhan Smuul, Paul-Eerik Rummo and Mats Traat. Jaan Kross has written many books of prose and poetry and several have been translated. They are readily available in Great Britain and the US as he grows more popular.

With its restored independence, the country is poised to produce a new generation of literary figures.

Theatre

Estonians did not have a native theatre until the national awakening, that is, in the second half of the 19th century. It was born in the music societies. The Tartu music society, *Vanemuine,* staged the first Estonian play, Lydia Koidula's *Saaremaa onupoeg* (The Cousin from Saaremaa). At the end of the century, the *Vanemuine* theatre group was formed and by 1906 they moved into their own building, designed by A Lindgren, and became a professional theatre group.

Estonia, a society in Tallinn, became a professional theatre group in the same year and in 1913 moved into their own building, *Estonia*, also designed by A Lindgren. In 1911, the professional theatre, *Endla*, was established in Pärnu.

In 1907, *Estonia* began staging operettas, operas in the following year, and in 1922 brought ballet to its stage. A ballet troupe was formed at *Vanemuine* in 1935.

Tallinn's second professional theatre, *Draamateater*, was founded in 1926. Theatres were also founded in Viljandi and Narva. There were eleven professional and semi-professional theatres in Estonia by 1940.

After the Soviet occupation in 1940 the theatre, as well as other institutions, came under Communist Party censorship and were used for the advancement of Soviet policies. Theatres had to stage mainly Russian plays. The 'thaw' era that arrived after Stalin's death brought innovative theatre with Voldemar Panso. In 1957, Panso founded a drama school at the Tallinn Conservatory and in 1965, together with his students, he founded *Noorsooteater* (Youth Theatre) in Tallinn. By the end of the 1960s, avant-garde theatre had been introduced by Evald Hermaküla and Jaan Tooming. Improvement of standards took place in opera during this period. Many singers had the opportunity to be trained in Italy, the best known among them being Anu Kaal, Mati Palm and Ivo Kuusk. Also, ballet dancers Kaie Kõrb and Tiit Härm developed their artistry by performing on stages abroad with world-class dancers.

Cinema

Before World War II, film making consisted of documentaries and newsreels. During the Soviet occupation, films of artistic merit did not emerge until the 'thaw'. First was Kaljo Kiisk's *Hullumeelsus* (Lunacy) in 1968, which dealt with social problems. His later release, *Nipernaadi* (Happy-go-Lucky) in 1983, was a popular feature film. Leida Laius's *Naerata ometi* (Smile, Please), 1985, and *Varastatud kohtumine* (A Stolen Meeting), 1988, have received international recognition.

Despite political censorship, remarkable achievements in documentary film making were realized by Mark Soosaar, Peeter Tooming and Rein Maran in their respective subjects.

However, puppet and animated films have enjoyed greatest international recognition. Rein Raamat and Priit Pärn are the most talented of the animated film makers. Puppet film making started in 1957 with Elbert Tuganov, and developed with talented colleagues such as Heino Pars, Rao Heidmets, Riho Unt and Hardi Volmer.

Photography

Photography exhibitions have been organized in Estonia since the 1890s. During the early independence period, many amateur photography clubs were established. Johannes and Peeter Parikas were the most gifted members of this activity. Nikolai Nylander's photographs received many international awards. Among the well known photographers are the documentary film makers Peeter Tooming and Rein Maran. The 1980s ushered in variety and artistic maturity with photographers like Tõnu Noorits, Malev Toom, Anu Tenno, and Tõnu Tormis receiving awards at international exhibitions.

Architecture

At the end of the Bronze Age permanent settlements appeared in the form of villages with their buildings made of logs. After Christianity was introduced during the 13th century, churches and monasteries constructed of stone became part of the landscape. Scandinavian and German building masters incorporated their own ideas into the architecture and Gothic design dominated from the 13th to the 18th century. Limestone was the principal building material in northern Estonia, and brick in the southern part. The oldest churches are very simple and pleasantly proportioned. Karja Church in Saaremaa is an example of that period, and Jaani Church in Tartu is unique among northern European brick Gothic structures. One of the best preserved 14th century fortifications is the Kuressaare Episcopal Castle in Saaremaa. Tallinn completed its city wall in the 16th century — one of the largest and strongest in northern Europe. The old town of Tallinn within the walls is one of the best preserved towns dating from the Middle Ages. Its numerous churches, guild halls, merchants' and craftsmen's residences and the Town Hall date mainly from the 15th century.

The most noteworthy example of Renaissance architecture is the Blackheads' Fraternity Building (1597), the work of Arent Passer from Holland. The city of Narva contained many examples from the Baroque era, but World War II did extensive damage to Narva, and the only evidence of that era is the restored Town Hall, originally built in 1671 and designed by Jurgen Teuffel. The Kadriorg Palace, built in the 1720s (Niccolo Michetti, architect), is a rich example of late-Baroque in northern Europe. The best example of Classicism can be found in Tartu's Town Hall (1789, Johann Walter, architect), the University's main building, and the numerous manor houses built by the nobility in Estonia. The architecture of the 19th century was dominated by Baltic-German architects who received their education at the Rīga Polytechnic and in St Petersburg. However, after the national awakening period preference for the national-romantic designs of Finnish architects emerged and the first professional native Estonian architects started to appear. In the 1920s, architects were educated in Tallinn. Art-Nouveau influence is evident at first (the Parliament Building in Tallinn on Toompea, 1922, Eugen Habermann and Herbert Johanson, architects), followed by functionalism. Most noteworthy examples of the latter are Tallinn Art House (1934, Edgar-Johan Kuusik and Anton Soans, architects), the Pärnu Beach Hotel (1937, Olev Siinmaa and Anton Soans, architects), the elegant beach café (1939, Olev Siinmaa, architect), and school buildings in Tallinn, Rakvere and Pärnu. Narva experienced the greatest destruction during World War II, but much of Tartu also lay in ruins when the war ended, and sections of Tallinn, which included the *Estonia* theatre and concert hall (1913, Armas Lindgren, architect), were left in ruins by the Soviet bombing raid in 1944.

During the Soviet occupation period emphasis was on cheap industrial housing construction: pre-fab developments of monstrous proportion clamp themselves to the metropolitan centres as a consequence. Examples of architecture that combine utility and sensitivity to the environmental setting can be found, however. The Song Festival Amphitheatre, the Piirita Flower Pavilion, the Piirita Sailing Centre, Tallinn's City Hall and the National Library represent such effort. There is a young crop of architects that have competed well in international competitions, Vilen Künnapu and Ain Padrik for instance, and restored independence should, in time, produce singular architectural structures.

EDUCATION AND SCIENCE

The development of elementary education in Estonia was started in the 1680s by virtually one man, Bengt Forselius. Forselius was born in northern Estonia, the son of an immigrant Finnish Lutheran pastor. He established many schools himself and before the end of the century the Swedish state ordered a school to be established in each parish. A great majority of teachers by this time were Estonians, trained in Forselius's schools. Academies were founded in Tartu (1630) and Tallinn (1631) for the training of administrators and clergy. In 1632 King Gustavus II Adolphus of Sweden elevated the Tartu Academy to the level of a university. However, records do not show that Estonians were able to attend the university at this time.

The Northern War at the beginning of the 18th century had a devastating effect on the country and education suffered a set-back. In stark contrast, the ideas of 18th century Enlightenment grew in the West while serfdom for native Estonians dug deeper roots under the rule of Russian Czars. However, rudimentary literacy made strides, largely due to the missionary work of Moravian Brethren which emphasized the teaching of reading to children in peasant homes. By the end of the 18th century a large percentage of the adult peasant population, *maarahvas,* was literate. Throughout the 19th century reading ability among the native people continued to improve, and it is estimated that by 1850 close to 90% of the Estonian population over the age of 10 could read.

When Estonia became an independent nation in 1918, compulsory primary education in the mother tongue was established. Secondary education was voluntary and based on the payment of a modest tuition fee.

Before independence, very few native Estonians could attend Tartu University, but in 1919 the University was reorganized as an Estonian institution. A second institution of higher learning, the Tallinn Technical Institute, was established in 1918. It was the predecessor to today's Tallinn Polytechnical University.

When the Soviets occupied Estonia in 1940 educators were among those arrested and deported. Educational institutions had their administrators changed, and instruction was to be based on Marxist-Leninist principles. However, implementation could not be carried out completely because of Nazi Germany's invasion in the summer of 1941.

During the German occupation, 1941-44, the authorities did not have enough time to carry out planned colonization nor the transformation of educational institutions along German nationalistic lines.

When the Soviets returned in the fall of 1944, the Marxist-Leninist curriculum was reintroduced. A major task was reconstruction, because about a quarter of the school buildings had been destroyed or damaged by the war, and many in the teaching profession had been either killed, deported or had fled to the West. Less than half of the pre-war faculty remained at Tartu University and many of them were considered unreliable by the Soviet regime. The importance and quality of Tartu University declined in general as a new Estonian Academy of Sciences was established, according to the Soviet model, and in 1952 the Tallinn Pedagogical Institute was founded. The primary training of specialists in sciences and technology was transferred to the new institutions. Other institutions of higher learning of this period are the Tallinn Polytechnical University, the Tallinn State Conservatory, and the State Art Institute in Tallinn.

One can make the assumption, based on the orientation of the people, that Western standards of scholarship and research will be reinstated by the restored republic and that Tartu University will again function as the centre of classical higher learning. Its background makes the university most suited for it. In the 19th century, Tartu's scientists were among the leading figures in Europe: the founders of modern biology were Tartu University's graduates Christian Pander and Karl Ernst von Baer; in the area of geography important achievements were made by Adam Johann von Krusenstern's group; astronomy was advanced by work done on stellar astronomy and cosmology by Wilhelm Struve, Johann Heinrich von Madler, Ernst Õpik and Jaan Einasto.

Tartu University also developed a considerable reputation in the field of medicine. Best known is Professor Ludwig Puusepp's pioneering work in neurosurgery. A new branch of science — physical chemistry — started development here under Professor Carl Schmidt. His most celebrated student, Wilhelm Frederick Ostwald, a Nobel prize winner, may be considered the founder of this new research direction. Significant successes were also realized in oil-shale technology, largely because oil-shale is a major industry in Estonia.

SPORT

'Sport in Estonia begins with Georg Lürich' is a common remark in Estonia. Lürich's strength and skill as a wrestler was already legendary at home when he won the Greco-Roman wrestling world professional championships in Hamburg in 1901. Thereafter, he had a string of victories all over Europe and the United States. In the United States he learned free-style wrestling and eventually defeated America's Frank Gotch.

Lürich was also a champion weight lifter, setting 28 different world records. His legendary achievements inspired Estonian men to become active in wrestling and weight lifting, and athletics clubs were organized throughout the country, even in small towns. As a consequence, many Estonians won individual and team world championship titles. The best known among them are Kristjan Palusalu, 1936 Olympic gold medals in Greco-Roman and free-style wrestling, and Johannes Kotkas, another Olympic gold medalist (1952) and legendary wrestler.

Besides Estonian athletes' prominence in heavy divisions of world sports, Estonian marksmen achieved excellence rapidly, their first shooting competitions being held in 1926 in Tallinn. They went on to gain experience at international competitions with modest results until 1935 in Rome, when the Estonian team captured second place and won the competition for the *Copa Argentina*. At the world championships held in Helsinki in 1937, they repeated their performance and took the *Copa Argentina* home again. Two years later, in Luzern, where the competition has its origins, the final tabulation of the world tournament placed Estonia in first place and, in addition, the team brought home the *Copa Argentina* again.

During the Soviet period, competitors in marksmanship remained strong and basketball matured to the degree that the Olympic medallist USSR basketball team included Estonian players, the best known among them being Tiit Sokk.

In track and field, the most popular summer sport, Heino Lipp was on top of world listings in this discipline during his peak years, but the Soviets never allowed him to compete in the Olympics for political reasons: Lipp never embraced the Soviet Communist rule forced upon Estonia. Thus Lipp could not compete in the 1948 Olympics, although *The Track and Field News* actually rated Lipp first in the world because his scores were so much superior to those of Bob Mathias, the eventual winner. Lipp did attend the 1992 Olympic Games in Barcelona as a member of the athletic team from independent Estonia and he carried his country's flag at the opening ceremonies. Estonian athletes during the Soviet occupation considered it no easy task to make the Soviet teams: politics played a large role in the selection process.

Estonians are a seafaring people and sailing has always been popular. As an organized sport, sailing got great impetus when Moscow became the designated host city for the 1980 Summer Olympics and Tallinn hosted the sailing competitions. In anticipation of the 1980 Summer Games more and more sailors from Europe began to participate in regattas at Tallinn Bay. The Olympic medallists, the twins Tõnu and Toomas Tõniste, are a product of this development. They won a silver medal at the 1988 Summer Olympics in Seoul, and in 1992, in Barcelona, they won a bronze.

Cycling has origins in the 19th century, but competitive cycling did not get organized until after World War II when a group of enthusiasts turned it into one of the strongest sports in Estonia. They competed in USSR tournaments and joined competitions world wide. Aavo Pikkuus developed into Estonia's leading rider, winning the USSR road racing championships in 1975 and in 1976. Pikkuus was a member of the USSR gold medal winning team at the Olympic Games held in Montreal.

The most famous female cyclist is Erika Salumäe, who won a gold medal in Seoul as a sprinter in the Soviet team. Four years later, at Barcelona in 1992, she again won a gold, but this time competing under her native country's blue-black-white flag.

Estonia is a northern country and Estonians are people that cannot live without snow. However, the country has no mountains and, therefore, has not produced downhill skiers of any real note. Cross country skiing is popular. But in all-Union and international competitions for winter sports no world-class athlete emerged until Allar Levandi captured a bronze medal in Men's Combined Nordic skiing at Calgary's 1988 Winter Olympics.

Cooperating with the dictates of weather has given Estonia's ice skaters endless frustrations. The one exception has been the speed skater Ants Antson who won a gold medal at the 1964 Winter Olympic Games at Innsbruck.

No story about Estonian sportsmen and competitors would be complete without the name of Paul Keres. He appeared suddenly on the world chess scene in the mid-1930s, and he startled that world with his originality, sharpness and brilliance. After the Soviet occupation of Estonia, Keres was three times all-Union chess champion, but in international competitions he missed out by the narrowest of margins and earned the title 'the Eternal Second'. Between 1935 and 1975, the year he died, Keres played in 66 international tournaments and finished or shared first place 30 of those times. He competed in 11 chess Olympics, winning seven gold medals and one bronze. Altogether he played in more than 3,000 games and many of them are considered unforgettable. His writings on chess are extensive and read world-over by those learning to play chess; particularly, he contributed a great deal to opening theory and was a recognized master of endgame. As a tribute to his accomplishments, Keres's portrait appears on the five kroon note issued on June 20 1992, by the re-established Bank of Estonia.

Chapter Two

A Brief History

ANCIENT HISTORY

The Ice Age retreated from the northeastern Baltic region in the Mesolithic Period between 8,000 and 4,000 BC, and the first human settlements date from 7,500 BC. These first inhabitants were probably hunters and fishermen from the south who were later overwhelmed by the invading eastern Finnish tribes, which included the Finns, Estonians and Baltic Finns (Karelians, Vepsa, Vadja and Livonians).

From 1,500 BC to the first century AD, the tribes gave up nomadic hunting and fishing for agriculture. By 500 BC, the Balto-Finns dominated the area north of the Daugava River; to the river's south lived the ancestors of today's Latvians and Lithuanians. The geographer Herodotus writes of the 'Ests' as inhabitants of the extreme north in the 5th century BC. In the fifth century AD, Slavic peoples first appeared on the southeastern border of present-day Estonia. At the same time, the ancestors of today's Latvians were pressing the Finno-Balts north to the present Estonian-Latvian border.

In the ninth century AD, Estonia became an important link in the Viking trade routes through Russia to the Byzantine empire. Estonians built fortified villages, or *kihelkond*, led by chieftains or elders; some were called 'kings,' but there was no central power base. During war with foreigners, the elders united several *kihelkond* and on occasion the entire country formed a single whole. In western Estonia and Saaremaa villages were circular; elsewhere, villages in a row along one side of a road were standard.

The ninth century also saw agricultural improvements. Households owned cultivated land which they divided into irregular patches, while the fields, pastures and woodlands surrounding villages were common to all. The traditional dwelling, a *rehielamu* and *rehetare*, had three parts all connected with one another: a threshing room, which also served as a granary, and a stable for livestock in winter; a drying room in the middle of the building; and living quarters.

Estonia was a patriarchal society. Men controlled property, family and decided marriages. Some practised polygamy. Estonians also owned slaves — mostly non-Estonians. The male victims of conquests were killed, the women and children became slaves. There was no nobility or aristocracy. Elders or anyone of wealth controlled society.

By the 13th century, major districts (*maakond)* had developed in Saaremaa, Läänemaa, Harjumaa, Rävala, Virumaa, Järvamaa, Sakala and Ugandi.

THE GERMAN CONQUESTS

In the 12th century, northern Germany witnessed the appearance of the Hanseatic League, an association of city-states designed to protect maritime commerce against Viking attacks. After the association's armadas defeated the Baltic Sea brigands, the alliance dominated the region's commerce and extended its commercial activities to the Russian cities of Novgorod and Pskov. The Hansa's interest in trade routes through present-day Latvia along the Daugava River led the merchants of northern Germany to support the Catholic Church's efforts to convert the Baltic tribes, and in 1193 the Pope proclaimed a Baltic crusade.

In 1200, Albert von Buxhoeveden of Bremen landed at the mouth of the Daugava with 23 ships and 300 soldiers. The following year, Rīga was established as a city, and in 1202 the German knights founded the Order of the Schwertbrüder, or Knights of the Sword. They subdued the Livonian tribes in 1206, and the Latgalians to the east in 1208.

The Germans then turned north, and from 1208 to 1227 they fought bloody battles against the Estonians. Estonia's lack of a centralized government and a unified army weakened the populace, and Bishop Albert was able to enlist the Livs and Latgalians of present day Latvia to help the Germans. A great Estonian military leader, Lembitu, organized a defence against the Crusaders, but he was killed and the regions of Sakala and Ugandi surrendered in 1215, followed by Järvamaa in 1217, and Läänemaa in 1218.

In 1218, Denmark's King Valdemar II sided with Bishop Albert, and the Danes invaded northern Estonia the following year. The city of Tallinn, or Taanilinn ('Danish fortress') received its name from this period. In 1220, the Swedes tried to seize Saaremaa island, but the Estonians resisted them. The Swedes, however, also landed in Läänemaa, captured the Estonian fortress at Lihula, and baptized the local population. They then sailed for home leaving a small garrison of 500 soldiers behind which was later attacked by an Estonian army from Saaremaa. Lihula fortress was captured and the Swedish garrison killed. The Danes then seized the opportunity and advanced from Tallinn to capture Läänemaa.

By the winter of 1220, all of Estonia was under German and Danish control, except for Saaremaa. In 1227 the Baltic froze, the Germans invaded the island, subdued the locals, and annexed Saaremaa to Livonia.

In 1236, the Knights of the Sword were defeated at the battle of Šiauliai, Lithuania. They sought help from the powerful German Order in Marienburg, East Prussia (today Malbork, Poland). In 1242, Alexander Nevsky of Russia stopped further German expansion eastwards by defeating the Knights at the famous 'Battle on the Ice' of Lake Peipus. Subsequently, Estonia was ruled by the Order and the Bishops of Rīga, Dorpat (Tartu) and Saaremaa-Läänemaa (Osel-Wieck). In the 1238 Treaty of Stensby, Denmark became master of Tallinn, and the regions of Rävala, Harjumaa, and Virumaa; the Livonian Order received Järvamaa. Danish control was not strong — only 20% of the vassals were Danish — the majority being German.

At the beginning of the 1200s Estonia's population was 150,000-180,000 and grew to about 250,000 by the 1500s. At the end of the 13th century German landlords placed more burdens on the peasantry, including a tithe which grew to 25% by the 16th century. Soon, the peasantry began to fall into debt and poverty.

On St George's Night, April 23 1343, the peasants rose against their Danish and German landlords, unable to bear any longer the foreign yoke, and besieged Tallinn. In Harjumaa, Läänemaa and Saaremaa, nearly all Germans were killed. The knights slaughtered thousands of Estonians in revenge and treacherously invited the Estonian army's leaders to the Castle at Paide where they were murdered. The revolt was the last uprising for more than 200 years. Denmark was unable to hold the country and King Valdemar sold northern Estonia to the Knights of Marienburg in 1346. German domination of the eastern Baltic coast was to last for 200 years. The following year, Estonia passed to the Livonian Order, based in Cēsis in Latvia. The Order offered land to German vassals if they would fight for the Order. The bishops of Saare-Laane and Tartu were the Order's most powerful vassals; both were princes of the Holy Roman Empire.

The 14th century rural economy of Livonia was grain-based — rye, barley, oats and wheat. Less than 6% of Livonia's population was urban; and the peasantry was completely Estonian and Latvian. In Estonia's cities, German merchants held most of the wealth and power by controlling commerce and city councils. By the late 1300s, Tallinn's German artisans banned Estonian membership in the city's guilds and restricted their property rights.

The Livonian Order had already experienced systemic administrative problems by the early 1300s. Perhaps most significant was the difficulty in recruiting German knights to enter into dangerous demanding service in far-off lands where life-spans were significantly shorter than in Germany. The recruitment pool was also substantially diminished by the fact that the Knights were only accepted from the ranks of the nobility. In 1410, the power of the Order was dramatically reduced after the epic battle of Tannenberg in East Prussia in which 600 of the 1,000 knights who rode into the fight fell victim to the armed might of the Lithuanian and Polish armies. After Tannenberg, it became the Hanseatic League, which succeeded to the role of organizing the commercial and administrative life of the Baltic region. The ascendancy of the merchant class led to a series of conflicts between the Order and the burghers living in the region's cities.

In 1454, the Baltic merchants appealed to Poland-Lithuania for assistance and war was declared on the Order. The war ended in 1466 with the Treaty of Thorn (today, Torun, Poland) in which the Order agreed to cede West Prussia to Poland (the region between Danzig and the Vistula), and the King of Poland became the Order's suzerain — the Grand Master of the Order became a Polish prince and royal counsellor to King Casimir (the Lithuanian Grand Duke).

In 1519, war again broke out between the Order and Poland after Grand Master Albert, nephew of the Polish King Sigismund, attempted to avoid Polish control. During this war, an important historical event occurred which was to have lasting effects on future church-state relations in East Prussia, Latvia and Estonia. Grand Master Albert, having travelled to Germany, met Martin Luther, who advised him to eschew the Order's allegiance to Rome and secularize the Order's vast estates such that the Order would profit from the saving of religious tithes and taxes. Luther's advice was heeded and the war with Poland came to an end in 1525. The Order was suppressed and its possessions transformed into the hereditary principality of Prussia, a vassal state of Poland. The Order was dissolved in Germany and in Livonia it was placed under the control of Grand Master Walter von Plattenberg, who strongly advanced the cause of the Protestant Reformation in his dominions. (A magnificent stained glass window in Rīga Cathedral depicts von Plattenberg proclaiming freedom of faith on September 21 1524.)

In 1524, Tallinn's church synod adopted the principles of the Reformation, and other towns and cities in Livonia and Estonia followed. The people living in the countryside, however, remained largely indifferent to the developments in the church given the purely German composition of the clergy.

It was the struggle between the Catholics and Protestants which spurred the development of written Estonian: in 1535 the first Estonian text, a catechism, was written and published by Simon Sanradt and Johann Koel.

The end of the order (1558-1561)

Livonia had two great Powers for neighbours — Poland-Lithuania to the south and the Duchy of Moscow to the east. In 1478, Moscow conquered the Duchy of Novgorod and it appeared that the Russians were preparing for a further move to the West. In 1502, the Knights defeated the Russians at Smolina, south of Pskov, but in 1558 Czar Ivan the Terrible invaded Livonia with 40,000 men and devastated eastern and central Estonia in what came to be known as the Livonian Wars. In 1559, the Bishop of Kurzeme and Saaremaa-Läänemaa sold his lands to King Frederich II of Denmark, who gave them to his brother Duke Magnus of Holstein. The Danes invaded northern Estonia in 1560, and in 1561 the last ruler of the Order in Cēsis, Latvia, Gottfried Kettler, became a vassal of King Sigismund August II of Poland-Lithuania. In June 1561, Tallinn submitted to the new Swedish king, Erik XIV.

In the 1560s, Poland and Sweden fought for control of Estonia and in the 1570s Russia joined the fray, besieging Tallinn for seven months in 1570-1571 and for seven weeks in 1577. Both times Tallinn held firm. King Stefan Batory of Poland-Lithuania won a series of military victories over Russia such that in 1579 Ivan's armies retreated and later Russia signed a peace treaty with Poland at Ian Zapolsk, near Novgorod. In 1584 Sweden emerged as the dominant power in northern Estonia while Poland kept southern Estonia. The Danes continued to rule Saaremaa until 1645, when Sweden took over.

The 25-year Livonian Wars had devastated Estonia, Latvia and Lithuania — cities such as Pärnu and Rakvere were totally destroyed, plague broke out, and normal life ceased. Tens of thousands had died.

In 1592 Poland's King Sigismund III, a Swede by birth, inherited the Swedish throne. His position was precarious and in 1599 Poland-Lithuania and Sweden went to war to try to resolve the issue of Royal succession. Again, Estonia was ravaged — in some parts famine, plague and battle killed more than 75% of the population. By 1629, Sweden controlled much of the area north of the Daugava River.

The Swedish era (1629-1710)

After the Armistice of Altmark in 1629, the Swedish empire dominated the Baltic Sea —Estonia, Livonia, Finland, part of Ingria, Western Pomerania, Wismar and Bremen were all subjects of the Swedish crown and King Gustav Adolphus II. The Swedish kings gave land generously to Baltic barons to win them over. With the land went the peasants and the local people were heavily overtaxed. Contrary to current popular belief, Sweden did not interfere with increasing German control of the peasantry. In 1671, Swedish King Charles XI confirmed the binding of the peasant to his birth place: peasants were sold with the land from one lord to another. Rebellions were not successful and many peasants ran away to escape serfdom — often to Russia.

Swedish rule introduced parish level education for peasant children and in the 1630s the first books in Estonian appeared. In 1631 and 1653 printing shops appeared in Tartu and Tallinn respectively. A Finnish pastor, Bengt Forselius, began training teachers in Tartu from 1684 to

1688. In 1688 there were 38 schools with 800 students in Estonian-Livonia and eight schools with 200 pupils in Estonia. In 1632, Swedish King Gustavus Adolphus converted the Tartu gymnasium to a university. Most of its students were Swedes, Germans and Finns — indeed, it is not known whether any Estonians attended the university in the 1600s.

The Great Northern War

In 1697, Sweden crowned the young and inexperienced Charles XII as king. Peter I of Russia, along with Denmark and Poland-Lithuania, decided the time was right to push Sweden out of the eastern Baltic, and the Great Northern War ensued. Charles XII defeated Russia at Narva in November 1700, but nine years later his army was destroyed by the Russians at the battle of Poltava in Ukraine in 1709. With Charles' army in Ukraine and Poland, the Russians invaded the Baltic region, capturing Narva and Tartu in 1704. A three year hiatus in fighting ended in 1707 when Peter I ordered a scorched-earth policy so that Sweden could not reconquer Livonia and Estonia. In 1708, every major building in Tartu was destroyed and Tallinn surrendered in September 1710. According to an old saying, 'no dog barked and no cock crowed from Tartu to Narva'. The Estonian population was slashed by a third. On the heels of battle came the dreaded plague of 1710, which killed nearly 80% of Tallinn's population. Finally, in 1721, as a result of the Nystadt Treaty, Russia obtained full control of Estonia, Livonia and Karelia.

RUSSIAN RULE IN ESTONIA (1710-1918)

Like the Swedes before him, Peter I sought to win over the German landlords by giving them more power. Thus, despite the Northern War, they became stronger than ever for they basically had a free hand in the region. German control of administration, justice, police, schools, the church and finance was plenary and unfettered. Estonia (the region north of Paide and Pärnu) and Livonia (the region of southern Estonia including Tartu, Pärnu, Viljandi, and Latvia north of the Daugava) were separate administrative areas from 1719 to 1775. In the last part of the 1700s, they were governed as a unit. After Russia annexed Kurzeme (Kurland) during the final partition of Poland-Lithuania in 1795, Czar Alexander I set up a post of Governor-General for all three Baltic provinces which lasted from 1801 to 1876. The German Baltic elites ruled the region via diets of Estonia, Livonia and Saaremaa, run by a twelve councillors elected for life. The diet met every three years and could deal with any local matter the councillors wished to consider.

Serfdom reached its height in 1739, with the so-called Rosen Declaration written by Baron O F von Rosen, chairman of the Livonian diet. It completely enserfed Livonia's Latvian and Estonian peasantry. Masters decided marriages, sold peasants with the land, enforced corporal punishment, and broke up families to sell individuals to other landlords. There were 1,050 large estates in northern Livonia and Estonia, yet the Germans constituted only 1% of the population. In 1764 Czarina Catherine II travelled through Livonia and was shocked at the condition of the peasantry. The Livonian Diet in Rīga ignored most of her suggested reforms, except to the extent that the barons agreed to no longer sell their serfs in open markets and to cease the sale of spouses to different owners.

Since the Baltic barons held all political, economic and judicial power, the 1816-1819 formal emancipation of Estonia's peasants brought no major changes. Though peasant unrest in Lithuania was more unruly than in Estonia and Livonia, there were disturbances in 1805, 1817, 1820-23 and 1858. Rural life improved gradually. Chimneys and glass windows appeared in farm dwellings; boots replaced leather or bark sandals.

In 1864, Czar Nicholas I ordered the formation of the Baltic Committee in St Petersburg. On July 9 1849, after three long years of discussions, the Czar adopted a proposal which was designed to permit the peasants to pay money rent for their lands (instead of rent-in-kind) and to permit the peasants to sell their land. The German revolution of 1848, and the subsequent conservative reaction in Europe, led the barons to block the 1849 reform, but in 1860 Czar Alexander II reinstituted the reform law's principal ameliatory provisions. The Czar later confirmed abolition of the former right of the barons to inflict corporal punishment on the peasants.

The first half of the 1800s saw the birth of Estonian industry with the manufacture of paper, glass works and textiles. The Kreenholm factory, the largest cotton finishing factory in Europe, opened in Narva in 1857. From 1782 to 1862 Estonia's and northern Livland's urban population went from 23,500 to 64,000. Tallinn's population grew to 20,680; Tartu to 13,800; Narva to 8,140; and Pärnu to 6,690. By the mid-19th century, Estonians were the majority population in all urban centres.

Along with manufacture came the growing National Awakening movement. An Estonian language position opened at Tartu University in 1803, and in 1838 the Estonian Learned Society began to research Estonian folklore. In 1857 Friederich Kreutzwald (1803-1882) used the Society to help write the classic Estonian saga, *Kalevipoeg,* and the newspaper *Pärnu Postimees* first coined the term *Eesti rahvas* or 'Estonian people.' Intellectuals began to identify themselves as Estonians. 1869 witnessed the first national song festival in Viljandi.

The reforms of Czar Alexander II (1855-1881) and the abolition of serfdom gradually changed Estonia. Industrialization transformed cities; Estonians became wealthier. Social mobility increased though the Baltic barons' diets remained the source of political power until the end of the century.

After Czar Alexander II was assassinated and Czar Alexander III came to the throne, Russification increased and German power was reduced since Germans lost their judicial and police powers to Russian control. The new Russian police officials usually dealt more fairly with the Estonian population. In 1865 owners and tenants were given the vote in local government elections. Now Estonians could elect township assemblies which chose a township administrator, his aides and judges. These officials began to administer taxes, schools and the police, and to deal with the sick, the old and jobless. In 1876, Estonia, Livonia and Kurzeme received their own governors. On July 9 1899, a new judicial system took effect, whereby justices of the peace became the tribunal of first instance, and a conference of judges became a court of appeal. A High Court of Appeal began sitting in St Petersburg. This removed extensive legal powers from the German aristocracy.

Six all-Estonian song festivals were held from 1869 to 1896 — with an audience of 50,000 for the 1894 performance. The Estonian language underwent a change in 1870. The northern Estonian dialect became standard Estonian and written language was introduced based on a Finnish model. Local music, literature, theatre societies and clubs appeared during the 1860s, and a real Estonian intelligentsia began to emerge with a non-German identity. Newspapers helped spread a sense of national identity. By 1869, 2,600 subscribed to the paper *Eesti Postimees*; by 1891, the Tartu paper *Postimees*, edited by Jaan Tõnisson, became Estonia's first national daily.

Estonian authors, Kreutzwald's spiritual heirs, wrote of a profound love of country. Among the foremost authors of the generation was Lydia Koidula (1843-1886), whose most important work was *Emajõe ööbik* (The Nightingale of the River Ema — 1867). Estonians consider her emotional prose unequalled in its expression of national patriotism. In the 1880s, romantic historical novels such as Eduard Bornhöhe's *Tasuja* (The Avenger — 1880) chronicled the struggle of the ancient Estonians against the German invaders. The novels of Eduard Vilde (1865-1933) criticized the condition of the urban and rural poor.

St Petersburg's Russification policies barely influenced Estonian-language publications. Between 1860 and 1900 the annual production of Estonian language books and other titles increased six fold — from 55 in 1860 to 312 in the year 1900.

Education made a rapid advance. Schools increased from 230 to 461 from 1860 to 1872. Estonia's school system was as large as Livonia's by the early 1880s. In 1887, the official language in school had to be Russian in the third year of instruction. In 1892 this changed to the first year of schooling. Angered German barons withdrew their financial support from provincial schools. Many closed. Teachers found it difficult to abandon German or Estonian for Russian. But within a few years the school system bounced back and Estonian again predominated (if unofficially). In 1897, 96% of Estonians aged ten or older could read;

thus Estonia and Livonia were the most literate regions of the Russian empire. From 1857 to 1900 the number of children in secondary schools surged from 1,282 to 5,000. In the 1860s more Estonians began to attend universities in St Petersburg and Rīga, and Estonian enrolment at Dorpat (Tartu) University increased from five in 1860 to 41 in 1880 and more than 100 in 1890.

In the early part of the 20th century, Estonian was again permitted as a language of school instruction and by 1917 more than 400 Estonians were enrolled at Tartu University.

The revolution of 1905

At the beginning of the twentieth century several writers and politicians appeared who exerted great influence on the country's destiny. Jaan Tõnisson (1868-1940), an 1892 graduate of Tartu University law school, became editor of the newspaper *Postimees* (The Postman) in 1896, worked to promote Estonian patriotism, and asserted the right to nationhood. The paper's credo was complete equality between Estonians and Germans in the economic, national and political spheres. The paper also argued against Russification measures. Tõnisson believed Estonia was too small to influence Russia, and therefore advocated allegiance to the Czar so as to force change from within the imperial system. In 1901, Konstantin Päts (1874-1956), became editor of the newspaper *Teataja* ('The Herald' 1901-1905) in Tallinn. Born on a farm near Pärnu, and a graduate of Tartu University law school, Päts was assisted by his collaborators, Jaan Teemant and Otto Strandman (attorneys); Edvard Vilde, the writer, and Mihkel Martna. A man with similar ideas, Peeter Speek (1873-1968), took over the paper *Uudised* ('The News' 1903-1905). Unlike *Postimees,* which espoused the views of Estonia's elite, *Teataja* and *Uudised* stood for the lower classes and implicitly supported anti-Czarist politics. Their journalistic voices rapidly loosened Estonian loyalty to St Petersburg, and brought about popular support for quick social and economic changes. Päts believed that support for Russian democrats would benefit Estonia's own national aspirations. These views were shared by several Tartu, Tallinn and Narva revolutionaries sympathetic to the Russian Social Democratic Workers' Party and other non-Russian minority social democratic movements.

Although the failure of Russia to cope with defeat by Japan in the Russo-Japanese War (1904-1905) was the spark that ignited the revolution of 1905, the underlying cause was intense popular dissatisfaction with widespread political and economic problems which began with the rapid industrialization in the 1890s and a growing urban working class. On Bloody Sunday in January 1905, Czarist police shot dead hundreds of St Petersburg workers and their family members who had marched on the Winter Palace to petition the Czar for reforms. The massacre ignited revolutionary movements throughout the empire. There were sympathy strikes in Tallinn, Pärnu and Narva in January and February 1905. Students in Tartu protested against the killings. Czar Nicholas II issued a decree, granting the population a right to propose changes to the system — thus legalizing protest. By early spring 1905, the Estonian countryside was alive with rebellion. German manors and properties became the targets of arson. Speek's *Uudised* called for an elected state parliament, suffrage for women, and autonomy for non-Russian regions.

In early October 1905, a railway strike broke out in Moscow and a general strike in Tallinn began on October 14. On October 16 Czarist forces opened fire on a crowd of protesters in the Market Square in Tallinn, killing at least 60 and wounding 200. A huge statue of a woman with her hand raised over her dead child and the marking '1905' now stands on the spot of the massacre behind the present-day *Estonia* theatre in Tallinn. The following day, Nicholas II issued the October Manifesto promising civil and political rights to the population, including the convening of a State *Duma* or parliament.

An All-Estonian Congress took place in Tartu on November 27-29 1905. The Conservatives, led by Tõnisson, demanded an Estonian Constitution, land reform and democratic elections. The radicals, led by Jaan Teement, called for the nationalization of large estates. Both radicals and moderates wanted Estonian autonomy, a halt to Russification, and unification of the Estonian-speaking areas of Latvia with Estonia.

There were other radical plans and a workers' Soviet was being prepared for Tallinn, when Czarist authorities declared martial law in Tallinn and Harjumaa. Most of the Russian Social Democratic Workers' Party's local committees were arrested and Päts fled to Finland after being sentenced to death in absentia. Enraged, workers went to the country and destroyed many German estates and farms. The Czarist government sent troops to Estonia and nearly 300 people were killed; another 600 were flogged or beaten and 650 revolutionaries were sentenced to death in the three Baltic provinces. Tõnisson's Estonian Progressive Peoples' Party remained the only political group permitted to exist. But even Tõnisson became radicalized after the Czar dissolved the First Duma in 1906. Tõnisson later signed the so-called 'Vyborg Manifesto' in protest, calling on the population to boycott taxes and military service, and he thereafter lost all his political rights.

Estonian participation in the third Russian Duma in St Petersburg (1907-1912) and the fourth Duma (1912-1917) declined with the introduction of a reactionary electoral law. In the first two Dumas they had five representatives, but after 1905, only two, and the reform measures prepared by the Estonian and Latvian deputies were blocked by German deputies.

Economically, Estonia developed rapidly after 1905. As the Estonian population grew wealthier, it gained control of local government. In 1904 Estonians gained control of Tallinn and Võru in 1906, and Pärnu in 1913. Tartu, Paide, Viljandi and Kuressaare remained in German control until 1917.

From 1900 to 1914, the number of Estonian industrial workers rose from 24,000 to 46,000 and by 1914 Tallinn was the centre of a rapidly growing metal and machine industry. The co-operative movement expanded rapidly. By 1911, Estonia and northern Livonia had a population of 1,086,000. In 1917, more than 200,000 Estonians lived in other areas of the Russian empire, with nearly 50,000 living in St Petersburg. By 1913, Tallinn's population had grown to 116,130, but Tartu's population had remained the same.

World War I

The start of the World War in August 1914 did not, at first, seem important to Estonia. German war goals, however, included the conquest of the eastern side of the Baltic Sea. Before the war had begun, many German nationalists had advocated pushing Russia eastward and the establishment of 'marches' in the regions of the former Russian empire subject to German control. The marches were to provide Germany with food and to serve as land for future German settlement. The political circles harbouring these sentiments were supported by many German barons in the Baltic states, who viewed with alarm the increasingly feeble Russian state and the increasing political assertiveness of the Estonians and Latvians. It must, however, be noted that neither German nor Russian politicians in 1914 would have conceived of any likelihood that the Baltic states would attain independence within four years.

On April 5 1916, German Chancellor Bethmann-Hollweg, speaking to the deputies of the German Reichstag, rhetorically queried: 'Can it be admitted that Germany will once again deliver the people liberated by her and her allies, between the Baltic and the marshes of Volhynia, which means the Lithuanians, the Poles, the Balts or the Latvians to the reactionary Russian regime? No, gentlemen, it must not be allowed that Russia may a second time march its armies against the defenceless frontiers of East and West Prussia.'

Unlike the case in Lithuania, Latvia or Poland, no battles were fought in Estonia in the first years of the war. Indeed, many Estonians supported Russia's fight against a people who had brought so much misery to their country. Baltic Germans, however, were horrified at the thought of war against their fellow Germans. St Petersburg (later Petrograd) banned the use of the German language and closed German schools and organizations. The Russian army mobilized nearly 100,000 Estonians; perhaps 12% or more were killed between 1914-1918. By the beginning of 1915, the German army had occupied Kurland and southern Latvia. Unlike Latvia, no Estonian ethnic units were formed to fight the Germans.

As the war wore on into its third year, social unrest grew, due to inflation and the lack of consumer goods and food. The Czarist government collapsed quickly in Tallinn in the first days of March 1917, since the army refused to defend the old order. As in Petrograd, a system of two power centres emerged in Estonia — the Soviet communist forces and those politicians who supported the Kerensky Provisional Government.

On March 26 1917, a demonstration of 40,000 Estonians (including 15,000 soldiers), carrying the national flag to the Tauride Palace in Petrograd, led the Kerensky Government to decree Home Rule for Estonia on March 30. Kerensky himself came to Tallinn in April 1917 to stress his support for Estonian autonomy. The new decree permitted all districts with an Estonian population to unite into a single province with a democratically elected National Council. The Council was permitted to impose taxes, and to set up an executive branch. Jaan Poska (1866-1920), the mayor of Tallinn, became Commissar of Estonia. On July 1, he opened the temporary National Council; Otto Standman was elected speaker and Konstantin Päts chairman of the executive committee. The old Baltic German diets were abolished.

Estonian fears of German invasion grew after German forces captured Rīga on August 21 1917. An Estonian regiment formed in Petrograd in July 1917, a second one in September. In October, German forces landed on Saaremaa and captured Kuressaare. German occupation of Hiiumaa and Vormsi followed.

On October 27 1917, after the Bolshevik Revolution in Petrograd, Viktor Kingisepp (1888-1922) took power in Tallinn with the Estonian Military Revolutionary Committee. Jaan Anvelt (1884-1937) headed an Executive Committee of Estonian Soviets, but when German troops advanced on Tallinn in February 1918, the Bolsheviks were forced to flee and the National Council went into hiding.

Shortly before the German's arrival, on January 27 1918, the Bolsheviks moved against their political opponents, arresting and deporting 500 Germans to Russia. Non-Bolshevik leaders were also sought out. On February 24, with the German forces advancing, Konstantin Päts and the underground executive of the National Council declared Estonia's independence in the Bank of Estonia building on Estonia puiestee in Tallinn. Equal rights were guaranteed to all Estonian residents, regardless of their nationality, beliefs or political opinion. The independence declaration read:

> 'In this fateful hour, the Estonian Diet, as the legitimate representative of the country and the people, having made its decision unanimously with the democratic political parties and other organizations, and in accordance with the principle of self-determination of nations, has deemed it necessary to take the following steps to determine the future of the land of Estonia: from

this day, Estonia is declared an independent Republic within its historical and ethnographical boundaries.'

The following day, the German army entered Tallinn. In April German occupation forces set up a puppet assembly for both Estonia and Latvia in Rīga which asked to unite with Germany. Estonian societies were closed, military units dispersed, and all political activity banned. German became the official language, and schools and courts were ordered to use German in their proceedings. Lieutenant General von Beckendorf ordered the reinstatement of mayors replaced by Estonians by the Kerensky reform decree of 1917. In Tartu, a curfew was imposed from 6.00pm to 6.00am with violators to be shot on sight. On March 28 1918 three peasants were executed for carrying weapons.

German occupation, however, may have saved Estonia, for it ended Bolshevik power and allowed the pro-independence forces to gradually organize power bases for the day when germany would be defeated.

German occupation of Estonia was resolutely opposed by the Western Allies. British Prime Minister Balfour stated that 'the Government of His Majesty is of the opinion that the right of self-determination belongs to Estonia as well as to all other nations. His Majesty's Government takes this occasion to express its full sympathy with the national aspirations of the Estonian people and affirms that it absolutely opposes all efforts to impose on Estonia, during or after the war, a political regime which does not conform to the wishes of the population or which limits their right to self-determination.'

THE INDEPENDENCE WAR 1918-1920

On November 11 1918, an armistice ended World War I and a disorderly retreat of the 150,000 German soldiers in Estonia began. On November 22, the Seventh Army of Soviet Russia invaded Estonia in the north near Narva and in the south heading towards Võru and Tartu. 2,800 Soviet fighters faced an Estonian force of 114 officers, 481 soldiers and 150 Defence League *(kaitseliit)* homeguards. Estonia's army had only 4,000 guns and 20 cannons. Although the Germans remained in Narva, they did not fight. On the evening of the 28th, the Estonians abandoned Narva as a Soviet landing to the north, at Narva-Jõesuu, threatened to cut off the city. The Soviets were accompanied by Jaan Anvelt, who proclaimed an Estonian Workers' Commune in Narva on November 29. The city was pillaged and burned. The Estonian Government under Päts faced a seemingly impossible task. A commander-in-chief of the army, Johannes Laidoner (1884-1953), was not appointed until December 23.

The Soviets rapidly advanced, capturing the city of Rakvere on December 15, the town of Tapa on December 24 and Koeru, east of Paide, on December 25. On January 2 1919, the Soviets were only 40 kilometres from Tallinn, with the Estonians holding a line from Valkla, near the Gulf of Finland, to Priske and Vetla. The Soviet advance had also continued in the south. Without offering resistance, German authorities and troops left Võru on December 7 1918, Valga on December 17 and Tartu on December 21. The Bolshevik forces carried out massacres in the captured Estonian cities and towns — 250 people were executed in Tartu, and more than 1,000 in the Rakvere district.

Estonia's spirit was revived by British, Finnish, Danish and Swedish help. The British fleet, anchored in Tallinn on December 12, captured two Russian destroyers near Tallinn (the *Spartak* and *Avtroil*) and gave them to the Estonian Navy. The British naval squadron, under the command of Admiral Sinclair, also delivered 1,000 light machine-guns to the Estonian armed forces. Since the machine-gun was not familiar to the Bolshevik forces, their use by Estonia's army created fear and panic. Finland provided Estonia with guns, a ten million mark loan to purchase supplies, and 2,000 volunteers. The leader of the Swedish social democrats, Branting, publicly called for help to Estonia, calling it 'defence of democracy'. With reinforced lines in early January 1919, Estonia repulsed new Soviet attacks. Estonian units landed at the Bay of Hara at Loksa and forced an eastward Soviet retreat. They retook Tapa on January 9 and Rakvere shortly afterwards. On January 14 Estonian armoured trains and partisans, under the command of a schoolteacher, Julius Kuperjanov, captured Tartu. One of the largest battles of the war occurred on the Paju estate near Valga on January 31. During the battle, Kuperjanov was mortally wounded as he led the Estonians and Finnish volunteers into a charge against Bolshevik positions. He later died in Tartu. Valga was taken on February 1 and Petseri on February 4.

The Estonian offensive greatly aided Latvia as it forced the Soviets to give up their efforts to capture Liepaja. In February 1919, the Red Army again launched massive attacks on the Soviet western front, attacking Narva on February 18.

The front line stabilized by May 1, and on May 13 the Estonian-backed anti-communist Russian (White) Northern Corps invaded Russia with the aim of capturing St Petersburg. General Laidoner began an offensive to the south, and on May 26, the Estonian army captured Pskov, later handing it over to the Russian Northern Corps. The Estonian army then turned to the south so as to halt the advancing German Baltic army, or *Landeswehr*, which in April 1919 had forced the Latvian government of Kārlis Ulmanis to flee Rīga for the safety of the British fleet off the coast of Kurzeme at Liepāja. On May 26, the Estonians captured Valmiera, then Limbaži and Cēsis, Latvia. On June 5, Estonian cavalry units captured Krustpils and Jēkabpils on the Daugava River.

The *Landeswehr* advanced on Cēsis in late June 1919, leading to a battle for the town from June 21-23, 1919 in which the *Landeswehr* was decisively beaten. Estonian forces advanced to Rīga on July 2, only to have capture of the city forestalled by an Allied-brokered truce. Estonian forces were to prove decisive in Latvia once more when, on October 8 1919, the Estonians sent armoured trains to Rīga, at the request of the Latvian Prime Minister, to prevent the city's seizure by the forces of the former Russian Czarist military adventurer Bermondt-Avalov, at the request of the Latvian Prime Minister.

The Russian (White) Northwestern Army Corps had met heavy Red resistance in their attempts to take St Petersburg, and in early November the Corps retreated towards Estonia. As the disintegrating Russian army of 40,000 to 50,000 men and thousands of anti-communist Russian and Ingrian Finnish refugees, reached the Estonian frontlines, they were disarmed by the Estonian government.

On November 15, the Soviet Army attacked Estonian positions along a line from Lake Peipsi to the Gulf of Finland. 12,000 Soviet forces crossed the frozen Narva River in an area held by only 1,100 Estonians and on December 14 advanced within three kilometres of the Tallinn-Narva railway, only to be repulsed on December 17 at Vaaska and Mustjõe villages.

Another Soviet offensive began on December 28, but was again repulsed by the Estonians. On December 30, the Commander of the 7th Soviet Army reported that his units were decimated and that he could no longer continue the battle. This led the Soviet peace negotiators at Tartu to abandon their proposal that Estonia establish a demilitarized zone on the shores of the Narva River. A Treaty of Peace with Soviet Russia was concluded in Tartu on February 20 1920, in which Russia abandoned 'for all time' any claims on the Estonian people and nation.

Independence

National elections to a Constituent Assembly took place in Estonia on April 5-7 1919 with 120 seats in Parliament at stake. The election results gave 41 seats to the Social-Democrats, 30 to the Workers Party, 25 to the Democrats, and the remainder to smaller parties. In the Assembly's opening session on April 23 1919, the President of the Assembly, August Rei, thanked the people of Britain and Finland for their assistance in the independence war, and thanked the Powers of the Entente for their moral support.

De jure recognition of all three Baltic states was delayed by the persistent hope of the Allied Powers, and United States President Wilson in particular, that the Bolshevik regime might be destroyed and the Kerensky regime restored to power. Indeed, in June 1919 the Allies decided to support Russian admiral Kolchak's efforts to oust the Bolsheviks and were thereby compelled to support Kolchak's position that the Baltic borders of the Russian state were not negotiable. Eventually, Great Britain and France recognized Estonia on January 26

1921, and on September 22 1921 the three Baltic states were admitted to the League of Nations.

Early Estonian governments faced many complex problems due to centuries of foreign domination; the devastating effects of German and Russian invasion and occupation; the complete collapse of economic life; the break-down of administrative machinery; and the destruction of natural resources and manpower during the war. A new government administration, law-courts, schools, and local government had to be built from the ground up. A modern military force had to be developed. The old Russian empire's social structure had dissolved and Estonia, like its Baltic neighbours, were given the opportunity to build a new democratic order and to regulate relations between all members of their new societies.

Estonia, like its Baltic neighbours, viewed agriculture as a first priority. It therefore nationalized the vast Baltic German feudal estates and distributed them to the landless peasantry, smallholders, and veterans of the independence war.

The 1920 Constitution guaranteed freedom of religion, and its Article 11 provided that there was to be no state religion. In February 1923, the Christian Democrats proposed a national referendum that made religious instruction in schools free and compulsory. A 1925 law on National Minorities guaranteed the Russian, Jewish and Swedish minorities cultural and educational autonomy and a right to establish national minority institutions.

Communists, organized in Moscow by Stalin, attempted a coup in Tallinn on December 1 1924, in which the railway station and telephone exchange was seized. The leaders, however, were soon arrested by the police and the putsch failed. Thereafter, the Communist party was banned. Martial law was imposed for a period, and until 1940 it remained in force with respect to Estonia's frontier zones and railway lines.

In 1930, a peasant movement in southern Estonia grew in size and expressed its objection to parliamentary 'absolutism.' The organizers called for a march on Tallinn, a reduction in the number of deputies and a reduction in their salaries. Another protest movement on the far right, led by a young lawyer, Artur Sirk, was founded in March 1931. The 'War of Independence Veterans' Association' (VABS) became known as the 'Liberators.' This organization called for a Presidency with extensive powers, an electoral system based on votes for individual candidates (and not lists) and a reduction in the number of parliamentary deputies. The Estonian Social Democrats opposed the Liberators' plans on the grounds that the Party was opposed to any Presidential system whatsoever. The Liberators' reform proposals were put to a referendum on October 14-16 1933 and approved by the Estonian electorate by a landslide of 416,000 votes to 157,000. The government of Jaan Tõnisson resigned, and

Konstantin Päts formed a non-party cabinet. While the Veterans' proposals were no doubt popular, a large measure of their popularity at the time may be traced to the growing international economic depression and fear of poverty by the Estonian middle-classes.

A new Constitution came into effect on January 24 1934 and Päts formed a transition government to prepare for the first direct Estonian presidential election. The Veterans' Association candidate for President, General Andres Larka, appeared to be a certain winner in the coming election, and the Veterans began severe attacks on their political opponents. The other candidates were Päts, Johan Laidoner and August Rei.

On March 12 1934, Päts referred to a 'state of urgent necessity' in Estonia and declared martial law. General Laidoner was appointed head of the armed forces, and 400 leading members of the Veterans Association were arrested. All party activities were forbidden and the Veterans' organization was dissolved. Since the Constitution forbade postponement of elections by decree, Päts had in fact carried out a *coup d'etat*.

Some have called the years 1934-1940 in Estonia the 'era of silence.' Martial law and restrictions on civil and political rights remained in effect during the period; and only the association *Isamaa* (Fatherland), was permitted. In reaction to criticism by Jaan Tõnisson's *Postimees* in June 1935, Päts closed the paper. In November 1936, four former Estonian heads of state — Jaan Tõnisson, Jaan Teemant, Johann Kukk and Ants Piip — resorted to publishing a statement to Päts in a Finnish newspaper because they were forbidden to do so in Estonia.

A new Constitution was approved in 1937 by the National Assembly elected in 1936, but it can rightly be questioned whether the absence of press freedom or full civil rights of the time made the new Constitution legitimate. Little more than half of the population voted in the 1936 elections, and in 50 of the 80 districts only one candidate stood for election. New elections occurred on February 24-25 1938, and on April 24 the Assembly elected Päts as President.

Nevertheless, although the government had strayed from democracy it did not effect the lives of the populace as overall prosperity had increased since independence. Many public works projects were put into effect and agriculture thrived.

Estonian independence ultimately fell victim to the collusion of Nazi Germany and the Soviet Union. On August 23 1939 both totalitarian regimes signed a Non-Aggression Pact with secret protocols that assigned Estonia to the USSR. In October 1939, the USSR demanded that Estonia sign a Mutual Assistance Agreement stating it would allow Soviet troops on Estonian territory. The Pact concluded, thousands of Soviet forces entered the country and established themselves at Tallinn, Haapsalu, Paldiski, Tartu and elsewhere.

On June 16 1940, two days after the presentation of similar demands on Lithuania, Soviet Foreign Minister Vyacheslav Molotov presented the Estonian and Latvian ambassadors in Moscow with an ultimatum calling for a change of government. Soviet troops massed on the Estonian frontier, and the Estonian government gave in to the USSR's demands. At Narva, on June 17, General Laidoner signed an order permitting 90,000 Soviet troops to enter Estonia, bringing the total to 115,000. The civilian population was disarmed, and the 42,000 man *Kaitseliit* dissolved.

Andrei Zhdanov, Stalin's close advisor, arrived in Tallinn on June 19 and demanded that Päts appoint a provincial doctor, Johannes Vares (1890-1946), as Prime Minister. After a staged demonstration of communists and Soviet soldiers on Independence Square in Tallinn on June 21, Päts agreed to the new cabinet.

On July 14 and 15 1940, 'elections' took place for a new State Assembly in which the only candidates were nominated by the Estonian Communist party. All others had been intimidated into withdrawing or accused of being 'enemies of the people.' 93% of the 'votes' were in favour of the Communist list.

The puppet-legislature met on July 21-23 and proclaimed Soviet power in Estonia, nationalized banks and large industry, and called for Estonia to join the USSR. General Laidoner was deported on July 19, and President Päts was deported to the USSR on July 30, although Estonia was still nominally an independent country!

From the summer of 1940 until the German invasion of July 1941, Soviet authorities arrested, deported and murdered thousands of real (or imagined) political opponents, Estonian industrialists, officers from the army, Lutheran and Orthodox bishops, farmers, and intellectuals. A maximum of 30 hectares was established for private land ownership in the countryside. By June 1941, 85-90% of all retail trade was under state control and dwelling space limited to $9m^2$ per capita. On June 14 1941, 11,000 Estonians, mostly women and children, were deported to Siberia.

WORLD WAR II

The 1940 secret German attack on the Soviet Union, operation 'Barbarossa' called for German occupation of the three Baltic states. Germany attacked the USSR in the early morning of June 22 1941, and quickly advanced into Lithuania and Latvia. The Nazi attack led the Soviet and Estonian communist authorities to arrest and deport 33,000 Estonian men to the Soviet interior for slave labour. Most of them died there in appalling conditions or were executed. German troops entered Estonia on July 5.

Pärnu and Viljandi fell to Germany on July 8 and German forces reached the outskirts of Tartu on July 10. The Germans halted while

Estonian partisans and Soviet forces battled in the city for two weeks — causing terrible damage to the city. In the last week of July, the Germans again advanced, taking Narva on August 17, Tallinn on August 28, and the last of the islands on October 21. At first welcomed as liberators and protectors from the terrors of the NKVD, the Estonian population quickly became disenchanted with German schemes to deport Estonians eastward and settle Germans in the country.

The German authorities denationalized only a small percentage of the property taken by Soviet authorities, and murdered 6,000 people — mostly Jews and Communists or perceived sympathizers. Some members of the League of Veterans seemed to have used German rule to exact revenge on their rivals. Germany established control of Estonia by naming a general kommissar as head of the government and provincial kommissars for the country's regions. A puppet Estonian administration also existed under the control of Dr Hjalmar Mäe.

By March 1944, Estonians realised German rule had to be fought, and the former Estonian prime minister, Jüri Uluots, and other patriots organized resistance cells and the Estonian National Committee. The German police, or gestapo. soon began to arrest and imprison the members of the Estonian resistance.

Although the Germans at first refused to permit an Estonian Legion to fight against the Soviets, German defeats in the east changed Berlin's policy and in late August 1942 an Estonian SS Legion was formed on a voluntary basis. Few Estonians supported the German occupation and Nazi ideology, and by October 13 1942 only 500 volunteers had joined the unit. In March 1943, German authorities began to forcibly mobilize into the Estonian Legion men who were born between 1919 and 1924. Many young men fled to Finland, where the Finnish government permitted them to fight the Soviet Army. An entire Finnish regiment and 700 or more men in the navy were composed of these Estonian volunteers.

After the German defeat in the Battle of Stalingrad, the Red Army launched a massive offensive at Leningrad (St Petersburg) and by January 20 1944 the first retreating Germans crossed the Narva River bridges heading towards the Reich. Hitler ordered General Model, the commander of the Northern Front, to hold Narva at all costs, and Army Group Narva was formed to defend the town. In late January, all civilians were ordered to leave the city. On February 1 1944, the city was bombed by the Soviet Air Force.

Faced with the resurgent Soviet threat, Üluots broadcast an appeal to Estonians in February 1944 to enlist in Frontier Defense Units to fight beside the Germans. More than 45,000 men volunteered and were placed under Estonian command.

For six months the battle raged, with many Estonians defending the city alongside the Germans, but by late July the Soviets captured the city. The Germans fought fiercely throughout Estonia, resulting in the loss of many historic properties: the city of Narva was all but obliterated; the classical palace of Ontika on the northern coast, which had been President Päts' summer residence was destroyed; the great stone bridge and the Church of St John in Tartu were bombed, and much of Tallinn disappeared in Soviet air raids beginning on March 9 1944. The Soviet army, meanwhile, quickly advanced through Latvia, and Rīga was taken by early August, thus cutting the Germans' railway connections with the Reich. By August 25, Tartu and the southeast had come under Red Army control.

Tens of thousands of Estonians now knew they had little choice: to live under a hated foreign occupation or to flee westwards. Terrible and tragic scenes ensued in which husbands, wives, mothers, sons, daughters and grandparents were separated from loved ones often by sheer fate — a Soviet advance would leave one member of the family behind Red Army lines, while relatives sought to escape from the nation's western ports and Tallinn. Many Estonian civilians were evacuated on German army ships which thereafter were bombed and torpedoed by the Red Army's airforce and navy. Many of the refugees were sent to Danzig, only to be later relocated to Dresden where some were annihilated by the terrible British and United States fire bombing in the spring of 1945. The Soviets reached Tallinn in September and captured the last peninsula of Saaremaa, Sõrve, after a fierce battle with the Germans in October 1944.

The Red Army's advance into Estonia did not respect the rights of civilians, and as was the case in East Prussia, Austria, Hungary, Poland and elsewhere, women were raped, buildings burned, men shot on little provocation, and houses ransacked of furniture and belongings.

Estonia's economy was completely destroyed less than 25 years after the destruction of World War I. Food was scarce, railways torn up, farms burned, and farm animals non-existent in many areas. One expert has written that the nation had lost 200,000 people between 1941 and 1946 to war, deportation, and outward flows of refugees.

SOVIET OCCUPATION 1944-1990

Communist party leader Johannes Vares chaired the Presidium of the Republic's Supreme Soviet until he was murdered by the Soviet secret police in November 1946. He was replaced by Eduard Pall. The Soviet secret police, or NKVD, screened all residents twelve years of age or older and organized massive deportations of landowners, members of the pre-war establishment, intellectuals, persons connected with the German army, and religious leaders. By 1950 more than 100,000 people had been deported to Siberia or Central Asia and another 80,000 Estonians had fled west to Germany and Sweden. At the end of the 1940s, many emigrated from Germany to the United States and Canada.

A serious anti-communist guerilla movement existed in Estonia, as it did in Latvia and Lithuania, from 1944 until 1955. Thousands of men and women took to the forests to fight the forcible enslavement of the nation and the destruction of the Estonian people. Tragically, the 'forest brothers' were virtually powerless against the vast military forces of the Soviet Union, although they were able to kill possibly hundreds of Soviet soldiers, NKVD personnel and collaborators.

Estonia's economy was now placed under Moscow's direct control. The cultural and linguistic Russification that the Estonian people had endured at the turn of the century under Czarist rule, was systematically re-imposed on Estonian society. Religious activities were sharply curtailed and Estonian history rewritten. Books were ordered destroyed and national monuments, even those located in cemeteries, were smashed and removed. Estonian national symbols, such as the flag and the anthem, were outlawed and replaced by newly created Soviet symbols. The intention was to wipe out all traces of the nation's independent past. The sovereign Estonian state was transformed into one of fifteen Soviet republics and democratic institutions were replaced by totalitarian Communist Party rule.

Despite the repressive nature of Soviet rule, Estonian national consciousness remained strong. The first protest letters were concerned with civil rights and not nationalist issues, but in the 1970s two small dissident groups demanded restoration of Estonia's independence and appealed to the United Nations. Four members of these groups were imprisoned for 'anti-Soviet agitation and propaganda'. Dissent spread, and by the 40th anniversary of the Molotov-Ribbentrop Pact in 1979 contacts with other Balts resulted in the Baltic Appeal for self-determination. This was followed in 1981 by a call for a Nordic nuclear-free zone which would include Estonia, Latvia and Lithuania.

Mart Niklus, a scientist who signed the Baltic Appeal, was sentenced to ten years imprisonment. A fellow scientist, Jüri Kukk, was given a two year sentence and died under mysterious circumstances after only two months imprisonment. The arrests and political trials of Estonians continued into the 1980s, as did various forms of protest against massive russification. Fundamental questions about national and cultural survival began to supersede political concerns.

Estonians living in the West formed organizations dedicated to restoring Estonian independence. This hope was based on the position of Western governments who had refused to recognize the legitimacy of Soviet rule in the country. During the entire Soviet period, the United States Government continued to recognize the Estonian Consulate in New York as the legal representative of the independent government of Estonia.

RE-ESTABLISHMENT OF INDEPENDENCE

The long repressed Estonian desire for a return to national independence was finally released in a dramatic and public way after Mikhail Gorbachev came to power. On August 23 1987, Estonians in Tallinn held a mass demonstration to demand the publication of the Molotov-Ribbentrop Pact and its secret protocols. Simultaneous rallies were held in Latvia and Lithuania, marking the 48th anniversary of the signing of the pact that robbed the Baltic states of their independence.

Mikhail Gorbachev had opened up the possibility of free expression and reform in the Soviet Union with his policies of *glasnost* (openness) and *perestroika* (restructuring). The first thing the Estonians chose to express was their desire for freedom from Soviet rule. In January 1988, former Estonian political prisoners took the unprecedented step of forming an independent political party, the Estonian Independence Party. In addition to endorsing the restoration of a free and independent Estonia, the group, which was openly opposed to the Communist Party, called for a total reconstruction of Estonian society, including multi-party elections, the restoration of Estonian as the official language of the republic, and economic, environmental and social reforms. On April 1 of the same year, Estonian intellectuals held a two day conference in Tallinn, calling for extended Estonian political and economic rights, a halt to Moscow-directed influx of migrants, and cultural independence. On the 13th of that month, the 'Popular Front for Perestroika' was born, and in rapid succession the national flag reappeared in public, hated Communist politicians were forced to resign, national monuments were restored, and banned history revived for the populace. In September, the popular movement organized a huge all-day political rally at the Song Festival Grounds in Tallinn. 'The Singing Revolution' was born. Estonia's Supreme Council (parliament) passed a declaration of sovereignty on November 16 1988, which acknowledged the supremacy of Estonian laws over Soviet laws and declared all natural resources in Estonia to be Estonia's property.

In the years 1989-90, organizational reform and efforts to negotiate independence with Moscow intensified. Free press began to take root, multiple political parties were formed, free elections held, religious life became active, and the whole society became more open. On August 23 1989 the Popular Fronts of Estonia, Latvia and Lithuania organized a human chain from Tallinn to Vilnius — a distance of 600km — to dramatize the desire for freedom by the Baltic peoples 50 years after the Molotov-Ribbentrop Pact had snuffed it out. On March 30 1990, a newly elected Supreme Council declared Soviet power to be illegal and announced that a period of transition for the restoration of the Republic of Estonia has begun. On May 8 the flag and symbols of Soviet Estonia were abolished and the country was officially re-named the Republic of

Estonia.

But the drive for political independence met strong opposition from Moscow. The end of 1990 brought dangerous omens from the east to Estonia: hardliners replaced moderates in the Kremlin. The violent crackdown came in January 1991. Estonia did not experience the bloodshed caused by special Soviet troops in Lithuania and Latvia, but uncertainty and tension ensued. On August 19, a coup by the Soviet military and KGB occurred in Moscow. Faced once again with imminent danger, the Supreme Council declared full and complete independence from the Soviet Union on August 20. On the following day the coup in Moscow failed. One by one, thereafter, foreign capitals began to recognize the independent Republic of Estonia and on September 11 1991, Estonia became a member of the United Nations.

In October 1992, the first fully free parliamentary elections since the 1930s were held and a conservative, free-market government, headed by historian Mart Laar, came into office. The Government continued the work of the previous Prime Minister, Tiit Vähi, in privatizing Estonia's economy, building trading ties with the West, and restructuring the court system. An 'Aliens Law' was adopted in 1993 which stated anyone wishing to receive Estonian citizenship, the right to permanent residency or the right to a full passport, must pass the country's stringent Estonian language and history requirement. Many non-Estonian-speaking residents raised an outcry against the law, stating it was too strict. (Because of the former Soviet Union's policy of bringing thousands of non-Estonians into the country to help Russify the area, non-Estonians now make up roughly one third of the country's population.)

Estonia is now embarking on a new political course. On March 5 1995 a coalition of former communists and free-market reformers, let by Tiit Vähi, Arnold Rüütel and Edgar Savisaar, were elected to a new parliament.

The economic and ecological problems this new-old nation faces are immense. Nor will it be easy for the people to quickly shed 50 years of Soviet influences. However, if Estonians are allowed to rebuild their home in peace, their native stamina and resourcefulness will repair the damage done to them and their land. A visitor to Estonia can see not only the beauty of the country's landscape and objects of antiquity, but also witness the restoration of a nation that was once on the threshold of extinction.

Chapter Three

Practical Information

WHEN TO GO

The weather

Though northern in location (just south of Finland), Estonia, unlike parts of Russia, is kept relatively mild by an arm of the Gulf Stream. Summer evenings can be cool enough to need a jacket. Sunny days can quickly become overcast and rainy, though the rain doesn't usually last long. Spring and autumn are generally chilly and rainy. Winter arrives around November, with average temperatures around 15°-20°F (-10° to -7°C), although the winter of 1993-1994 saw temperatures fall to -12° to -22°F for days on end, freezing the Gulf of Finland and creating havoc for vehicle owners and public transport.

The seasons

The weather is at its best and the days at their longest during the summer. Around midsummer the sun doesn't set until after 11pm and even then it doesn't get completely dark; a silvery twilight remains in the sky throughout the night. Baltic springs are fragrant and autumn colours add a rich loveliness to the land. In winter, though the days are short (the sun doesn't appear until 9am and sets around 3pm), the stunning Northern Lights sometimes make their appearance, and one can enjoy outdoor sports such as cross-country skiing, snowshoeing, ice-skating, and some downhill skiing (not very steep though). Since regaining their independence, Estonians are once more celebrating Christmas with beautiful traditional church ceremonies.

WHAT IS THERE TO SEE AND DO?

The capital city of Tallinn has a wonderful medieval atmosphere, rich in architecture and cultural events. Enveloped by a distinctly Baltic ambience, it has, nevertheless, a feel of its own.

There are interesting seaside towns, and the country has numerous ancient churches and castle sites, many of which have been, or are being, restored. Estonian woods, lakes and nordic landscape offer a tranquility that is quickly fading from the Western world. The sparsely populated land has a refreshing openness to it as fences are few and farms are isolated in gently rolling hills. Country towns, where the pace of life is slow and the people hardy, are a part of Baltic history that may date back to Viking times and beyond.

Estonia has long seashores with powdery-white sandy beaches. On some you can still find bits of amber, that golden stone which looks like a piece of frozen sunlight, one of the Baltic states' most prized natural treasures. And for the sailor, Estonia offers its beautiful western archipelago. Tallinn built a first class yachting facility for the 1980 Olympics which is sure to delight boating enthusiasts.

RED TAPE

You must have a valid passport to enter Estonia. Travellers from many countries must also have a visa. **You DO NOT need a visa if you are a citizen of one of the following countries:** Andorra, Australia, Bulgaria, Canada, the Czech and Slovak republics, Denmark, Great Britain, Hungary, Japan, Latvia, Liechtenstein, Lithuania, Monaco, New Zealand, Poland, San Marino, the United States, the Vatican.

Single and multiple visas are good for 90 days. The former is valid for six months, the latter for a year. For a visit under six weeks you must show you have sufficient sums to cover your stay (at least US$8/day for each day shown on your visa). For a stay over 90 days you need a residential permit from the Immigration Board. For a stay longer than six weeks, you must have either an invitation from a company or institution, or a personal invitation. You may extend your visa in Tallinn at the Immigration Office (38/40 Lai Street).

For those travellers who need a visa, get one from the Estonian consulate in your country. If your country doesn't have one, you can get a visa in Helsinki or Stockholm. Also, visas for citizens of several countries are available at border control points, the Ferry Terminal, and at the Tallinn, Tartu, Pärnu, Kärdla, and Kuressaare airports. You can get a visa at the border if you are a citizen from one of the following countries: Austria, Belgium, Finland, France, Germany, Greece, Iceland, Israel, Italy, South Korea, Luxembourg, Malta, the Netherlands, Norway, Portugal, South Africa, Spain, Sweden and Switzerland. Only single-entry visas are available at the border. Border visas are subject to review and it is advisable to check first.

Visa costs (at embassies): a transit visa is US$5, a single entry visa (the one most tourists get) is US$10, a multiple entry visa is US$50. No charge for travellers under 18. Visas are more expensive at the border: transit: US$12.50, single entry: US$31.50.

To obtain a visa from the Estonian embassy in your country, you must present a valid passport, two photographs, and either a notarized invitation from Estonia or a confirmed hotel reservation. It takes up to seven working days to get a visa. The price doubles for the 48-hour rush service. While in Estonia, you must carry with you a notarized letter of invitation from an individual or business in Estonia or a hotel voucher.

For Europeans, each Baltic country recognizes the visas from the other two. A visa to Estonia will give you access to Latvia and Lithuania. If you are from a country that does not require a visa for Estonia, and you wish to travel on to Latvia and/or Lithuania, you will need a visa to enter both those countries. Americans do not need a visa to enter Lithuania.

A word about the former Soviet Union (excluding the Baltic countries): Russia and the former Soviet republics require their own entry visas. If you plan to continue your travels there, you should get the necessary visa in advance. Russian embassies in the US and other countries will be happy to provide one. Keep in mind everything takes time when doing business with these embassies. For example, it will take about three weeks to get a visa in Great Britain — and your accommodation has to be pre-booked to get one. Doing business with the Russian Consulate in each of the Baltic countries is a major headache; actually it's a major headache in any country. Unless you are fiercely determined to get to Russia, it might be easiest to just travel in eastern Europe. In the Baltics expect to pay around US$30 for a visa and US$60 if you need it in a week. You will not be able to get one on any train en route to a former Soviet republic. Without a proper visa you will not be allowed to register at hotels in the ex-Soviet Union and may be fined up to US$350. Several travellers lacking a proper visa have been deported from the former Soviet country they wished to visit.

For lists of Embassies, see *Appendix Three* and *Appendix Four*.

One way of going to Estonia is by private boat or yacht. With hundreds of islands and miles of coastline, there are many harbours available. Once in Estonia, you can do a lot of island hopping. The following are harbours with passport control and customs offices:

DIRHAMI: EE3174, Tuksi, Läänemaa, tel: (372)-37-97-240.
HAAPSALU JK: EE3170, Haapsalu, Holmi 5a, tel: (372)-47-45-582, 45-536.
KUIVASTU: EE3322, Saaremaa, Kuivastu, tel: (372)-45-56-026, 75-140; fax: 98-432.
LEHTMA: EE3200, Hiiumaa, Kärdla, Sadama 15, tel: (372)-46-96-104; fax: (372)-46-96-184.
NARVA-JÕESUU: EE2001, Lootsi 1, Narva-Jõesuu, tel: (372)-35-72-841.
NASVA: VHF 16 EE3300, Saaremaa, Nasva, tel: (372)-45-56-026, 75-140; fax: 55-257.
PÄRNU: EE3600, Pärnu, Lootsi 6, tel: (372)-44-41-879.
ROOMASSAARE: EE3300, Kuressaare, Uus-Roomassaare 12, tel: (372)-45-55-574.

TALLINN-Piirita: EE0019, Regati 1, Tallinn, tel: 238-033.
VEERE: EE3300, Kuressaare, Rohu 5, tel: (372)- 45-56-701; fax: (372)-45-57-284.
VERGI: EE2122, Vihula vald, Lääne-Virumaa, tel: (372)-32-98-650.

Customs

There are lengthy customs controls between the three Baltic countries, especially if you are travelling in a private car. The Lithuanians seem manic about searching private baggage — although their Estonian and Latvian counterparts may also take time to rummage through your personal possessions. International rules apply for Estonia. You cannot bring in drugs, explosives, poisons, or weapons including guns and gas pistols, no hormonal and blood preparations, trade marks and labels. Alcohol limits are strict. Scheduled buses are not delayed by queues of private trucks and cars. If you arrive by plane or ferry, the customs are fairly routine at the airport and harbour: wait for your turn, documents ready for presentation, and then take either the red (to declare items) or green (if you have nothing to declare) customs route.

You may bring in all the hard currency, bonds, personal things and goods you wish, though an 18% VAT is slapped on goods exceeding the established limits. Interestingly, you are not allowed to leave Estonia with more cash than you entered, but you are rarely asked how much cash you have when you enter. Work it out...

The limits are:

1. Hard currency — anything over 1000 DM must be declared.
2. Alcohol and beer — you must be 21 years or older to carry in one litre of spirits, one litre of wine, ten litres of beer. Persons aged 18-21 cannot bring in spirits, but can bring in 2 litres of wine.
3. Tobacco and tobacco products — this includes 200 cigarettes, 20 cigars or 250 grams of tobacco. Duty on larger amounts: 70% of price.
4. Cultural objects.
5. Rapeseed oil.
6. Fur and fur articles. Duty: 16% of purchase price.
7. Cars, motorcycles, snowmobiles, speedboats, yachts (duty: 10% of price).

For the latest on Estonian customs information: in Tallinn, tel: (372)-631-7761. In the US — Estonian Consulate, tel: (212)-247-1450. In Great Britain, tel: (44)-171-589-3428.

Leaving the Baltics

International customs rules apply. You cannot bring out explosives, weapons, drugs, or large quantities of any goods for profit. Large sums of money require a permit from an Estonian bank or proof that you yourself brought this money into Estonia. There are no limits on bonds or personal items or goods. You can also take out non-prohibited goods in as large a quantity as you want, as long as you can show that you have paid the VAT.

Limits on alcohol and tobacco: 1 litre of strong drink (max 58%) and 1 litre of mild drinks (max 21%) or 2 litres of mild drinks; 10 litres of beer, 200 cigarettes or 20 cigars or 250 grams of tobacco.

There are restrictions. The number of 'items' of gold and silver are limited for export. Things made before 1950 and books published before 1945 require a special export permit which can be obtained from the Cultural Values Export Board, located at Sakala 14 in Tallinn, tel: 448-501 or 446-578. The process takes a few hours. For customs information, in Tallinn: 631-7761; in the US, Estonian Consulate: (212) 247-1450, in Great Britain — Estonian Embassy, tel: 44-171-589-3428.

GETTING THERE

During the Soviet era you couldn't get to Estonia without a travel agent who worked with Intourist, the former Soviet office of tourism. Though Baltic travel is much easier now, it's still wise to go to a travel agent experienced with the Baltic countries. Many tried and true Baltic travel agents get special airfare discounts you won't find elsewhere. They can also help you book less expensive rooms with hotels and private families and give you helpful pertinent information.

Estonia had been isolated from the West for so long that now, it seems, the travel industry is scrambling to make up for lost time. New plane, train, ferry and bus routes open up frequently so that reaching Estonia today is getting easier all the time.

In brief you can fly, sail, or ride from the following cities to Tallinn: Stockholm (daily flights, sailing every other day); Copenhagen (six flights a week), Frankfurt am Main (six flights a week), Warsaw (bus twice a week, daily train routes), Amsterdam (flights twice a week), Hamburg (flights twice a week, bus once a week), Munich, Berlin, Cologne (bus once a week), Sofia (train once a week)

By air

Ever since Estonia obtained independence, there has been a proliferation of airlines offering flights. Most fly from cities in Scandinavia and elsewhere in Europe. When returning to the US, an overnight stay in the connecting European city (included in the airfare) may be necessary. If you are booking a flight through an American travel agent, your ticket's itinerary page may carry a warning: TRAVEL ADVISORY EXISTS FOR: ESTONIA. The US State Department has issued this statement because health care in the Baltics is not comparable to that in the United States.

ESTONIAN AIR is not a member of the International Airline

Association. This means you can only book a flight with it in one of the cities it services on continental Europe, not from North America, Australia or Great Britain.

BALTIC INTERNATIONAL AIRLINES (BIA) — A Latvian-American joint venture. Based in Latvia, one third of its stock is owned by Baltic International USA located in Houston, Texas. Smaller than Latvian Air and in direct competition with it, Baltic International flies between Rīga and Berlin, Frankfurt, and London's Gatwick airport. It is a member of the prestigious International Air Transport Association, (IATA) and charges relatively high prices (travel agencies get discounts). In the US, tel: (713) 651-8730, (800) 548-8181. BIA in Rīga: 327-269. BIA in London: (0171) 828-4223.

ESTONIAN AIR — Estonian Air has taken over the former Estonian division of Aeroflot's planes and routes. Locally, prices are competitive with other airlines. SAS trains the cabin crew, so service is good. Flies daily to Helsinki. Also flies to Amsterdam, Copenhagen, Frankfurt, Hamburg, and Stockholm. Serves Vilnius daily (816 EEK one way for Baltic citizens and residents; US$258 one way for others! Seven day advance return ticket costs US$190). Also serves Moscow, Kiev, Minsk, and St Petersburg. Will fly to London in 1996. Not a member of IAA. In Tallinn: Vabaduse väljak 8, tel: 440-295, 446-382; fax: 211-624, or Bureau of *Estair*, Endla 59, tel/fax: 490-679.

FINNAIR — Regular flights between Tallinn-Helsinki. The flight takes about a half hour. Flights between Tallinn-New York, Tallinn-Miami require a change of planes in Helsinki. Good connections to London and Manchester, England. Liivalaia 12, Tallinn, tel: 683-771, 6-311-455; fax: 682-290. Airport office tel: 423-538.

LOT — This Polish airline offers flights between Okecie International Airport in Warsaw and Tallinn, Rīga, and Vilnius. There's also a link to Kaliningrad. Tel: in NYC (212) 869-1074; Los Angeles (213) 658-5656; Miami/Ft. Lauderdale (305) 731-3711. TOLL FREE: (800) 223-0593. LOT in Rīga: 630-095, In Tallinn: 218-127.

LUFTHANSA — Frankfurt to Tallinn on Wednesdays, Saturdays and Sundays. Flight time under three hours. Extensive onward connections to Western Europe and the USA. In Great Britain they serve Birmingham, Manchester and Glasgow. Agents in Tallinn: Pärnu mnt 10, tel: 44-037, Mündi 2, tel: 448-862, 215-557. International Direct Dial: 358-49-348098.

SAS — Daily flights between Tallinn-Stockholm, Tallinn-Copenhagen. Flight time one hour. Extensive onward connections to Western Europe and the USA. In Great Britain they serve Birmingham, Manchester and Glasgow. In Tallinn, Roosikrantsi 17, tel: 312-240, 312-241, 212-553; fax: 312-242.

Flights in Estonia

Aeroco is supposed to fly between the western Estonian islands and the mainland three times a week but service is on-again, off-again. You can't plan on it being available.
ELK (Estonian Air Company) flies between the mainland and the islands.

Airline tickets can be purchased at:
Viru Hotel Travel Agency, Viru väljak 4, tel: (372)-2-650-875.
Olümpia Hotel, Liivalaia 33, tel: (372)-2-602-434.
Airline tickets agency, Kaubamaja 11.

By train

Although trains in the former Soviet Union are slow, they can be an interesting way to travel, and prices are reasonable. From Tallinn to Rīga (9 hours) an overnight couchette is 164 EEK (US$15); from Rīga to Vilnius (10 hours) a couchette costs 3.60 Ls (US$7). However, Estonian railways, in particular, have been increasing their prices at a rapid rate, and these prices may change.

For overnight trips, rent sheets, which are clean and cheap, otherwise your sleep won't be very comfortable. Keep in mind second class service is not up to Western standards and trains stop frequently. It's best to bring along food for longer trips as it's not easily obtainable on the train (although the daily Vilnius-Tallinn trains have a dining car).

A faster alternative is the Baltic Express train, operated by the state-owned Estonian Railroads. It links Estonia, Latvia, Lithuania and Poland. The trip from Tallinn to Warsaw takes 19 hours, with stops in Tartu and Valga, Estonia; Rīga, Latvia; and Kaunas and Sestokai, Lithuania. If you wish to continue to Poland, you must change to waiting trains at Sestokai on the Lithuanian-Polish border.

Baltic Rail passes are sold in Sweden, Finland, Denmark and Norway. You cannot buy train tickets in the United States for travel in the Baltics. You cannot use Eurail, German Rail, or Eastern Europe Rail passes on Baltic trains.

You will be lucky if you find any officials who speak English or German. Though the station's phone number is given here, you may have a problem communicating if you don't know any basic Russian or Estonian. **Balti jaam** (Baltic Railroad Station) in Tallinn is located at Toompuiestee 39; tel 446-756, 624-058, 624-851. International service info tel: 456-058. Open daily 8am-8pm.

NOTE: Whenever you travel outside the Baltics, you will need a transit visa to enter the country your train is passing through. To avoid headaches, get your needed visas before leaving home. Trying to get one at night on a train in the former Soviet Union is tough and officials are often less than polite. Also, watch out for con artists!

Principal trains to and from Tallinn

From	Departure	Arrival
Vilnius	4.07pm	8.10pm
Rīga (from Vilnius)	11.38pm	8.10am
Brest	4.05am	8.10am (1 day later)
Warsaw	3.20pm	1.10pm
Moscow	3.00pm	11.05am
	4.25pm	9.55am
St Petersburg	8.28pm	5.35am
	10.25pm	8.45am
Minsk	10.47am	8.10am
Tartu	7.05am	10.26am
	3.30pm	7.19pm
	6.58pm	10.50pm
Narva	8.15am	12.20pm
	12.35pm	4.30pm
	5.00pm	8.35pm

To	Departure	Arrival
Rīga (178 EEK) Baltic Express	11.30pm 5.10pm	7.50am 12.05am
Vilnius (290 EEK) coffee/tea: 4 EEK	11.30pm	4.00am
Kaunas Baltic Express (375 EEK)	5.10pm	6.12am
Moscow (291 EEK) Tallinn Express (335 EEK)	4.10pm 6.25pm	1.17pm 10.31am
St Petersburg (154 EEK)	8.10pm 11.00pm	6.15am 8.45am
Minsk	11.30pm	10.01pm
Warsaw (554 EEK) Arrives in Rīga 12.05am Change at Šestokai, Lithuania station	5.10pm	4.50pm
Brest	11.30am	5.30pm (+ 1 day) Even dates from Tallinn, odd dates from Brest

By ferry

This used to be the budget way of getting to the Baltic states, but not anymore unless you are coming from Helsinki. If you are flying via SAS or FINNAIR, it is far less expensive to purchase a through fare with a change of planes in Helsinki than to end your flight and board a boat. Once all marine transportation to the Baltics were called ferries, but now most rides from Scandinavia and Germany are booked as cruises with matching prices. Even if you get a low rate, food and drink are expensive. The runs between Tallinn and Helsinki are made with ferries that have ferry prices.

If you have the time, this route is a leisurely way to travel. Many enjoy day trips to Estonia from Scandinavia. Ferries depart from Stockholm, Sweden and Helsinki, Finland to Tallinn; and Mukran, Germany to Klaipeda. More ferry lines are being added and current schedules keep changing. Check information directly with the ferry service.

There are five lines offering shuttle service daily between Tallinn and Helsinki. (Tallink, Estonian New Line, Kristina Cruises, Viking and Silja). You can catch an early morning hydrofoil and arrive in Helsinki as businesses open. A ferry will cover the distance between Helsinki and Tallinn (80km) in 3½ hours, a faster hydrofoil in 1½ hours. Hydrofoil service halts during periods of high wind and in winter due to the ice in the Baltic Sea.

Tickets for all ferries can be purchased at the harbour terminal: Sadama 29, open daily 9am-6pm, tel 427-009. The harbour is about a 15 minute walk from the Old Town. Tickets are also available from travel agents around town. Most ferries use the Tallinn's Main Terminal, which was opened in the summer of 1994. Spacious, it has a left-luggage room, café, bar and shops. Tallinn Harbour Information: 6-318-550.

EMINRE CO 'TALLINK SERVICES' *Tallinn-Helsinki*

Serves Tallinn from Helsinki daily taking 3½ hours. Prices for non-Estonians on most ships are 280 Estonian kroon one-way deck class. Cabins cost more. Estonian citizens pay 180 kroon. The fare on the smallest vessel is 180 kroon for Estonians and non-Estonians. This boat is not currently scheduled to stay in service in 1995. All the ferries operated by AS Eminre have restaurant facilities, bars and lounge chairs open to all passengers. A one-price 'Swedish table' sitting in the restaurants of the Tallink vessels currently costs approximately 120 kroon. Tel: 442-440.

ESTLINE *Tallinn-Stockholm*

Offers ferry service between Stockholm and Tallinn. Sadama 29, tel: 449-061, 6313-636; fax: 425-352. There is also a ticket office located on Aia 5a. In Stockholm, Sweden: tel: 46-8-667-0001. Leaves Tallinn from its terminal next to the Main Terminal — practically the same place as you have to use the same road to reach it. Both Estline and Tallink serve their passengers here.

ESTONIAN NEW LINE *Tallinn-Helsinki*
Has daily hydrofoil sailings from Helsinki to the port of Piirita, Regati pst 1, in Tallinn. A bus line takes passengers to city centre. In Helsinki (booking): Yrjonkatu 23A, tel: 90-680-2499. Ticket office at Olympia Terminal: 90-669-193. In Tallinn: Harbour Terminal, tel: 428-382 or 601-906.

FINNISH VIKING LINE *Tallinn-Helsinki*
Offers a catamaran. Will get you from Finland to Estonia faster than by plane (including check-in time). At the time of writing the company is having labour disputes which may be resolved by summer 1995.

KRISTINA CRUISES *Tallinn-Helsinki*
Offers service to Helsinki daily (2½-4hrs). In the summer of 1994, the fare for one-way passage started at 180 kroon, deck-class. In Tallinn, tel: 6-318-700; fax: 6-318-703. Tickets may be purchased at the harbour office of Kristina Cruises. In Helsinki, the company's office is located at Korkeavuorenkatu 45, tel: (90)-629-968.

SILJA LINE *Tallinn-Helsinki*
Offers sailings between Tallinn and Helsinki every day of the week. The Monday, Tuesday and Wednesday sailings from Tallinn, and the Thursday, Friday and Saturday sailings from Helsinki have an overnight on the ship, so the voyage is in effect a 'mini cruise.' Fares with a tourist-class cabin range from 390 kroon to 1,050 kroon per person for a 2-bed seaside cabin. Daytime sailing fares begin at 370 kroon. Silja Line's office is located in Tallinn's harbour terminal.

VIKING LINE *Tallinn-Helsinki*
Offers two catamarans between Helsinki and Tallinn. The vessels will make a total of five round trips a day. The larger catamaran will operate as a car ferry in the summer. Tickets start at 130 Finnish marks or 350 EEK, one way (US$28). Tickets may be purchased at Wris Reisibüroo, Pääsukese 1 in Tallinn, tel: 6-312-056; at Estonian Holidays Office in the Viru Hotel, tel: 6-301-942; or at the harbour in Tallinn, tel: 6-318-623. In Helsinki: Mannerheimintie 14, tel: (90)-12351.

EURO-CRUISES works with: Kristina Cruises, Tallink, Estonian New line and Estline. For more information: in New York tel: (212) 691-2099; fax: (212) 366-4747.

By bus

BUS FIRM MOOTOR — Offers quick service between Tallinn and Warsaw. A 44-seater bus leaves Tallinn on Monday morning and arrives in Warsaw at midnight. En route bus stops in Pärnu and Rīga. Estonia is the only Baltic country with a regular bus link to Germany. Buses run between Tallinn and Cologne, Munich and Hamburg. Stops include Pärnu, Rīga, Berlin, Hannover, Essen and Nürnberg.

International transport to/from Tartu

Tartu is served by two daily trains to Rīga, including the *Baltic Express* (which continues on to Jelgava, Šiauliai, Kaunas and Warsaw) and a night train which continues to Vilnius and Minsk. The *Baltic Express* arrives in Tartu from Tallinn at 7.44pm and departs for Rīga and Warsaw at 7.50pm. The same train arrives in Tartu from Warsaw and Rīga at 10.42am and departs for Tallinn at 10.45am. The *Baltic Express* leaves Warsaw for Tartu daily at 2.20pm, leaves Kaunas for Tartu at 12.15am and leaves Rīga for Tartu at 6.25am. The night train to Rīga and Vilnius arrives in Tartu from Tallinn at 2.23am and therefore does not present a very comfortable alternative to the *Baltic Express*.

TARBUS, at Ringtee 14, tel: 475-316, offers a new international bus line from Tartu to Berlin in a sleek, modern coach. The bus leaves Tartu on Mondays at 5.30pm, arrives in Valga at 6.45pm, arrives in Rīga at 10.20pm and Berlin at 9.30pm on Tuesdays. The bus departs Berlin at 5.30pm on Thursdays, arrives in Rīga at 6.50pm on Friday, at Valga at 10.15pm and in Tartu at 11.30pm.

A bus of the MOOTOR company leaves Tartu once a week for Stockholm and Uppsala in Sweden with Oslo, Norway as the final destination. Departing Tartu at 2.00pm and arriving in Stockholm by ferry the following day at 9.00am, over two hours later it reaches Uppsala at 11.40am and Oslo at 7.30pm. Return bus leaves Oslo at 7.00am, Stockholm at 4.00pm, arriving in Tartu the next day at 1.00pm. Tickets to Stockholm are 600 kroon, and 900 to Oslo. A connecting bus, using the Tartu-Stockholm ferry link, takes passengers on to Copenhagen from Stockholm arriving there at 20 minutes after midnight. Tickets are 1,100 kroon to Copenhagen. Information in Tartu can be obtained from the office of Lõuna-Eesti Turismikeskus, Turu 2, tel: 476-357 or 474-553. In Tallinn, tel: 410-100.

Buses from Tallinn to other European cities

From Tallinn		To	Arrival/ Duration
9.40am 12.45pm 3.00pm 11.40pm	via Pärnu	Rīga (95 EEK)	3.45pm 6.55pm 9.05pm 5.40am
9.30pm	via Rīga	Vilnius (135 EEK — Lithuanian bus)	9.20am
12.30am (Arrives in Rīga 5.30pm, departs 5.40pm)	via Rīga	(Estonian bus)	10.30pm
7.00am (Thurs) Departs Pärnu 9.00am Departs Rīga 12.10pm Departs Panevežys 3.15pm Departs Warsaw Sundays 8am, arrives Rīga 9.50pm, arrives Tallinn 3am		Warsaw (480 EEK) (Bus Station Al Jerozolimskie #144)	midnight
7.00am (Tues, Sun) Departs Pärnu 9.00am Departs Rīga 12.20pm Arrives in Berlin 11.10am Wed; arrives in Nürnberg 6.50pm Wed Departs Munich Wed 11.00am, dept Nürnberg 1.30pm Departs Berlin 9.00pm, dept Stuttgart 8.45am Mon/Thurs Costs: Berlin 1040 EEK, Nürnberg 1200 EEK.	via Berlin	Munich (1,280 EEK)	9.30pm (Wed, Mon)
4.50pm (4-5 days a week) Departs Copenhagen 1.00am, arrives Tallinn 10.20am		Copenhagen (1,100 EEK)	11.00pm
Departs Tartu 2.00pm Departs Tallinn 4.30pm Departs Oslo 7.00am, Uppsala 2.50pm, Stockholm 4.00pm Arrives Tallinn 10.10pm, Tartu 1.00pm Costs: Uppsala 600 EEK, Oslo 900 EEK Service available 4 days a week		Stockholm, Uppsala, Oslo	Arrives Stockholm 9.00am Arrives Uppsala 11.40am Arrives Oslo 7.30pm
7.00am (Wed, Sat) Departs Cologne 11.00am Tues/Sun		Cologne (1,280 EEK)	9.30pm (Sun, Thurs)
9.45pm		St Petersburg (82 EEK)	6.35am
6.25pm (Sat)		Kaunas (132 EEK)	6.50am
7.45pm		Kaliningrad (154 EEK)	11.00am

WHAT TO TAKE

CLOTHES — Since laundromats outside hotels are few and far between, it is advisable to bring clothes you can wash yourself. You'll also be doing a lot of walking (often over cobblestoned streets), so a pair of comfortable walking shoes is a must. In summer, a lightweight jacket or sweater will come in handy, as will an umbrella and raincoat. Rain gear is especially helpful during the spring and autumn, as is warm layered clothing. In winter, warm clothing is advisable: a warm coat, gloves, hat, scarf and boots are essential. You will not need formal attire. However, people do appear dressed up in public (suits and dresses) and that includes concert halls and theatres. Jeans and sportswear are unacceptable in some restaurants and night clubs.

MEDICINES — Aspirin, prescription medication, antacids, etc. Though these over-the-counter medicines are now available in Tallinn (for a high price), out in the countryside they aren't so easy to find. Best to bring along what you need. Cotton, gauze, bandaids, asthma medication, penicillin and prescription drugs are in short supply. *If you have any prescription medications, bring an adequate supply to last you through your trip*. See the 'Pharmacy' section for a list of available pharmacies.

MOSQUITO REPELLENT — Essential! The Baltics' many bodies of water and swamps can make some places a mosquito nightmare. Baltic mosquitoes are big and hungry.

BATTERIES — Shops carry them but it is advisable to bring any kind that you may need.

CONTACT LENS ESSENTIALS — Solutions, cleaners, heaters are difficult to track down in the Baltics. The only place to get hard contact lense solution is the firm A/S Lens in Tallinn at the eye hospital.

GLASSES — A second pair. If you break your first, you will have to spend a considerable amount of time getting replacements. Best to avoid this scenario.

FEMININE NAPKINS — Throughout the Soviet occupation, Baltic women got by without pads or tampons. Many still do. Though supplies are available in stores, it is more convenient to bring your own along.

ALARM CLOCK — Don't expect an alarm call in most Estonian hotels. Best to bring along a small battery-run travelling clock.

LAUNDRY DETERGENT — In small packets. What soap you get in hotels is too small to wash out clothes effectively. The better hotels offer laundry and dry-cleaning services.

FILM — Western film is available. For convenience bring your own stock along. You can have your film developed in Estonia for a reasonable price and at many locations.

TOOTHPASTE — Tallinn has all kinds of brands available. Less so out in the country.

SPICES AND SUCH — There are good restaurants in Estonia, but you may want to be prepared in case you don't always find them. Bringing along small bottles of your favourite seasoning such as tabasco sauce or ketchup might not be a bad idea. Some travellers slip in old standbys like a jar of peanut butter.

TOILET PAPER — This was a rare commodity in the Soviet days. Things have changed, especially in Tallinn and the larger cities, but out in the country most public restrooms offer cut-up newspapers at best, while it is not unusual to be offered nothing at all.

FINANCIAL CONSIDERATIONS

What will it cost?

For the Western tourist, travel and most of the cost of living expenses in Estonia are reasonable. The exception may be hotel rooms for the walk-in client. If you book on your own, you will encounter high prices. However, travel agents and tour operators abroad are given rooms at about 20% less than that quoted at the desk. Most major hotels give large discounts to wholesalers. The time of year makes a difference, too. De luxe hotels discount when there is less business traffic — during July and August and on winter weekends. Tourist hotels discount during the winter. All told, a pre-booked package will get you better hotel rates.

Private lodgings are inexpensive compared to the West, as are restaurants and transportation. If you make private arrangements with the many Bed and Breakfast type establishments that have now sprung up throughout the Baltics, your nightly lodgings will cost you a great deal less.

Most lower priced hotels aren't up to par with Western-style courtesy and service. Though there are several inexpensive hotels, keep in mind that you get what you pay for. A US$20/night room may sound great, but don't be surprised at the rusty plumbing, cracked wall plaster, shared grungy toilets or the smell of cigarette smoke in your sheets.

During the summer, expect to pay (for a single room):

- Private Bed and Breakfast — starting from US$10/night
- Inexpensive hotel: US$20/night
- Average hotel: US$25 — US$50/night
- Above average hotel: US$75 — US$120/night
- Expensive hotel: US$100+/night.

Many charge lower rates the rest of the year, except at Christmas.

Some expensive restaurants in Tallinn are on par with Western prices, but provincial places are usually moderately priced to inexpensive. In general, prices are higher in Tallinn than in the rest of the country.

Camping

Until recently one could set up a tent wherever one wished. In many places this is no longer allowed, and, due to increased crime, not recommended. Most major recreation areas have designated camping areas. Camping facilities are numerous on the islands and it's beautiful country for it.

Local currency

Estonia was once part of the Soviet Union's ruble zone. In June 1992, Estonia issued its own currency, the Kroon, (abbreviated to EEK and pronounced krone) which is linked to the German mark. Coins are cents (sent) and 1 kroon equals 100 cents. There are approximately 12EEK to US$1; DM1=8EEK; UK£1=19EEK. All transactions within Estonia must be made in kroons, although in some places the Finnish mark is accepted. Exchange rates are set daily by the Bank of Estonia and a commission of about 2% is charged on each transaction. Get your kroons in Estonia as it is difficult to get them abroad. You'll find currency exchange locations all over Tallinn and there are always a few in other cities, all major European currencies and Australian dollars are accepted. Since the kroon is tied to the DM, exchange rates aren't fixed. Stay away from hotel exchange bureaus as they do not give good rates.

Note: In the summer of 1994, US dollar bills were subjected to scrutiny by an electronic device in most currency exchange places and banks in Tallinn, and some were rejected. No explanations given, but counterfeit bills are evidently a problem. Bills with slight tears or markings were often rejected. So, no matter what country you are from, take along clean, whole bills or you might find yourself short of kroons!

Travellers cheques and credit cards

Though modern day conveniences like travellers cheques and credit cards are beginning to catch on in the Baltics, you can't always rely on them. Some Estonian banks will take your travellers cheques, but at a hefty service charge and often after several days of delay. Though technically many outlets in Tallinn and Tartu say they will cash your travellers cheques, in reality, they won't. Your chances improve if you're carrying American Express travellers cheques. Põhja-Eesti Bank is an agent for American Express and will cash them free of charge. You can exchange your travellers cheques at the Palace Hotel in Tallinn which has a percentage charge, and the Viru Hotel which charges a flat fee. Credit cards such as VISA, American Express, MasterCard and DinersClub are honoured at most major hotels and restaurants. Quite a number of shops accept VISA cards. Tallinn's Viru Hotel has installed the Baltics' first IBM cash machine. With instructions in English and Finnish, it allows VISA International card holders to withdraw Estonian kroons.

Cash

You cannot convert your money into Baltic currency anywhere outside of the Baltics except Finland, and in Moscow and St Petersburg, Russia. So, the most convenient way to travel is to bring all your money along in cash (via a money belt). You may choose to either deposit it in a bank (but keep in mind they are not in good shape financially) or a safe deposit box. If you already have an account in a bank, you may send money via a wire money transfer through New York and Stockholm. You can also wire money to the Baltics via Western Union and an International Postal Money Order (US$3 charge for sending up to US$700 via a money order).

Don't leave cash in your hotel room. Always try to have someone you trust with you when walking the streets of the big cities wearing a money belt. Unfortunately, the crime rate is increasing as living standards drop — but it isn't anywhere near as bad as in New York City.

Tipping

Service tipping is usually not included in hotel or restaurant bills, though some establishments may include a 10% gratuity automatically. This gratuity often ends up in the hands of the management — not your server. When tips aren't included most people add 10-20% and give taxi drivers, hotel porters, etc, tips — but this should be done only if you think the service was good. It often isn't and then you shouldn't feel obliged to give anything.

HEALTH AND SAFETY

Health Insurance

Health insurance is well worth considering. Most Baltic hospitals are not up to Western standards. Doctors are well educated but are occasionally forced to work with a limited supply of medical instruments, materials and medicines. If you become seriously ill or need an operation, it's possible that you'll require a ferry to Finland or an airlift to a modern hospital in Scandinavia or Germany. If you find yourself in a medical emergency and need a doctor quickly in Estonia, call your country's embassy, which will provide you with a list of English speaking physicians in various specialties. (See *Appendix Three*.)

Pedestrians

For the tourist, keep in mind that potentially dangerous situations exist on many Tallinn streets. Everywhere construction is taking place, a lot of it on the upper floors. Don't walk near such construction sites; you never know when something loose could fall down to the street. There don't seem to be those safety features present at these sites which are standard in most Western countries.

Also, romance with newly acquired freedom combined with access to cars seems to be intense as speeding cars on the road are the norm. Many of them are not in the best state of repair. Be very careful when crossing the streets. Do not expect motorists to give you, the pedestrian, the right of way.

Vaccinations

None needed.

Drinking water

Generally, its worst quality is the taste, but some travellers get upset stomachs. To be safe, drink bottled juices and sodas instead of tap water and avoid ice in drinks. Bottled water is available. If you are living with tap water, boil it before drinking it.

Crime

Unfortunately, crime is increasing, though the major cities are nowhere nearly as dangerous as many United States urban areas. Use common sense. Single women shouldn't be out alone after dark. Don't dress in expensive clothes and jewellery or carry expensive cameras. Always try to walk with someone you trust. Pickpocketing is growing, so ladies, make sure your purse is shut and strapped securely in your hand or around your shoulder — not on your back. Consider a waist pouch. Men should be wary where they put their wallets. Don't leave cash in your hotel room. Car theft is a growing problem. In general, wear inconspicuous, practical clothing and travel in an older, inexpensive car. Stick to common sense — don't go to sleazy bars and cafés, don't make a late night rendezvous with strangers, and don't drink so much alcohol that your guard is down. It is not unusual for liaisons with prostitutes to end with the Western 'client' being robbed, even dead.

COMMUNICATIONS AND TRANSPORT

Time Zones

Estonia runs on the 24-hour timetable, not the am/pm American system. It is in the East-European time zone like Finland, thus two hours ahead of Greenwich mean time (GMT) and seven hours ahead of New York City. Daylight saving time is in effect from April to October, though the switch is made weeks earlier than in North America. When both have switched, the following time differences are in effect: when it is 10pm in Tallinn, comparable times are: 9pm — Paris; 8pm — London; 3pm — New York; noon — Los Angeles; 11pm — Moscow and St Petersburg.

Telephone — Emergencies

Dial the appropriate number below. Speak slowly and clearly. State phone number and address.

Fire	001
Police	002
Emergency medical	003

Telephone — general information

It's a rather frustrating exercise trying to communicate by phone. Although significant steps have been taken to modernize the telephone system in Estonia, there still appears to be a considerable climb ahead. There exist three systems in Tallinn and they are somewhat integrated: the old scratchy Soviet system, a new cellular (EMT) system, and a new digital system. As a consequence, some phone numbers in the city have six digits and some have seven. The rule is: dial 6 before telephone numbers starting with 3.

The situation with public phones is complicated in a different way. The new ones, which were installed after the kroon was introduced, are operated by a magnetic Alcatel card which can be purchased wherever the phones are located. Cards are worth either 30 or 250 kroons. The cardphones, which are programmed to provide instructions in Estonian, English, Finnish and Russian, have instant access to Estonia's new digital telephone exchange. The pay phones that are left from the Soviet era and are coin operated present a problem because many of them no longer work. If you find one that works and you want to make a local call, have a 20 sent coin ready. As most public phones do not take money, just pick up the receiver and dial.

To call within Estonia long distance: dial 8, wait for the dial tone, dial the two digit area code (recent modernization of the phone system in Tartu has resulted in a one digit area code and Tallinn has a one digit code, either a 2, or a 6 in front of numbers starting with a 3), then the local number.

Rarely can long distance calls be made from a public phone. Use the phone at your hotel, or go to the Central Post Office at Narva mnt, across from the Viru Hotel — calls here are less expensive than from your hotel.

Some area codes:

Haapsalu — 47
Hiiumaa — 46
Jõgeva — 37
Kihelkonna — 45
Kohtla-Järve — 33
Kuressaare — 45
Muhumaa — 45
Narva — 35
Narva-Jõesuu — 35
Otepää — 42
Paide — 38
Pärnu — 44
Põltsamaa — 37
Põlva — 30
Rapla — 48
Taevaskoja — 30
Rakvere — 32
Sillamäe — 49
Tallinn — 2 (6 for digital exchange)
Tartu — 27 (7 — if the number has 6 digits)
Türi — 38
Valga — 42
Viljandi — 43
Virtsu -47
Võru — 41

Radio

EESTI RAADIO (Estonian Radio) — 290m medium wave: 103FM: 50.6 short wave — 5.925 MHz. In English: Mon-Fri: 6.20pm-6.30pm; Mon and Thurs: 7pm-7.30pm. Also in German, Finnish and Swedish.

RADIO KUKU — Tallinn's first commercial station. Broadcasts news, ads and music programmes. Can only be heard around Tallinn. It's the most popular radio station today. On air 24-hours a day.

RADIO LOVE — Private radio station focusing on cultural issues. Offers classical oldies all day long. Hourly news.

Television

You can watch nine channels in Tallinn: Estonian TV, Kanal 2, Tipp TV, EM TM, RTV and four Finnish channels. A special aerial is needed for two of the Finnish channels. On weekdays, Estonian TV broadcasts one hour of CNN at 5pm. Three new commercial channels, Eesti Reklaami TV, Tipp TV and Kanal 2, have recently been established.

ESTONIAN TV — A boring blend of cultural items spiced up by some Western films and programme with Estonian subtitles.

KANAL 2 — A great new channel set up by Estonian director Ilmar Taska. Offers classic Estonian films and much Hollywood programming. Taska lived and worked in Hollywood in the 1980s and is a devotee of classic film.

TIPP TV — Opened in late 1994 by the entrepreneur, Juri Makarov. US programming with Estonian sub-titles and some music videos.

Newspapers

Day-old Western newspapers and magazines such as *Newsweek, International Herald Tribune* and German, Swedish, Finnish and other European news publications are carried by most good hotels and some bookstores in Tallinn. The largest selections are on the mezzanine of the Viru Hotel and the first floor of the Olümpia. You'll always find *The Guardian, Independent and Financial Times* in the main hotels. German papers tend to be more expensive.

Three good Baltic newspapers published in English are:

The Baltic Observer, 3 Balasta Dambis, Rīga, LV-1081, tel: (371)-2-462-119, 463-667. In the USA and Canada: c/o Ivars Rozentals, 558 Pilgrim Drive, Suite A, Foster City, CA 94404, USA or Sandra Slokenberga, 235 E 81st St, #6 FW, NY, NY 10028, USA, tel/fax: (212) 988 3256. In the UK: Rebecca Marshall-Clarke, Redhill House, Hope Street, Chester, CH4 8BY, England, tel: (44)-1244-681-619; fax: (44)-1244-681-617. Subscription US$85/year. Is relatively objective.

The Baltic Independent, Editor-in-Chief: Tarmu Tammerk, PO Box 45, Pärnu mnt 67a, EE0090 Tallinn, tel: (372)-2-683-074; fax: (372)-6-311-232. Subscription: US$75/year. You may want to order either of these papers for several months before your trip to get an 'up to the minute' picture of the rapidly changing Baltic scene.

ESTI ELU/Estonian Life is a bilingual weekly publication that gives news, opinion and analysis. Available at hotels, airport, harbour and kiosks. Editorial office is located at Narva mnt 5, tel: 445-466 or 422-444; fax: 449-558.

Every couple of months *The City Paper* and *Tallinn This Week* are published which give helpful information to visitors. The *City Paper* also provides fascinating in-depth articles about life in Estonia. Be sure to pick up a copy to become familiar with the latest events.

Addresses

You will frequently see street addresses containing the abbreviation 'mnt,' 'pst,' or 'tn'. 'Mnt' stands for 'maantee' — highway. 'Pst' stands for 'puiestee' — avenue. 'Tn' stands for 'tänav' — street.

Electricity

Like most of Europe, Baltic current is 220 volts, 50Hz. You will need an electrical converter if you wish to use a North American hair dryer, shaver, contact lens heater, etc. Most North American time-keeping gadgets will not work properly as they usually function with 60Hz. Your electric clock will run too slowly. Come prepared with a battery operated clock. The same goes for items that need to run at a certain speed, such as a cassette player.

Transport within Estonia

The gentle Estonian countryside is well worth a visit. Farms are isolated, people few and most fields unfenced, which gives the land an inviting openness. Signature birch groves stand in lovely clusters by lakes and meadows. Many places can be visited in day trips from the regional capitals, though you won't be as rushed if you plan to stay overnight.

Some things to keep in mind when you venture into the Estonian heartland:

- There are few hotels. Smaller towns and villages don't have any and those hotels that are available are not usually up to Western standards. Plumbing is old and rusty, and the rooms shabby looking. Some places don't have hot water or even heating.
- Country inhabitants speak, at most, very limited English. It's easier to travel with someone who knows the native language. Lacking such companionship, carry a dictionary with you; you can pick one up at any central Tallinn bookstore.
- Roads to major towns are good, but standard country roads are not normally paved. When it's dry, cars kick up a lot of dust. Avoid small unpaved country roads in the winter. The roads are not cleared after snow, and in the early Spring your car may sink in the mud.
- Most roads have no markings or numbers. Directions often entail descriptions such as: 'take the road to your left heading for the town of so-and-so.'
- Restaurants are no longer few and far between. However, their hours may often not extend beyond 9pm. Though roadside cafés and inexpensive 'shashlik' (a kind of shiskebab) stands are appearing, it's not a bad idea to bring along drinking water and food. You may have to drive many kilometres before you can find a place to eat and drink.
- Business hours: many country shops and restaurants close at 5 or 6pm.
- Toilets and toilet paper are rare commodities. Most public toilets are horrible and smelly holes in the dark are common, with squatting the norm. Balts regularly make use of their fine woods for their toilet needs during trips. The more decent public pit stops require a small fee and usually provide toilet paper.
- Prepare for Sunday travel. Just about everything outside the major cities is closed on Sundays (apart from filling stations, bars and restaurants).
- When travelling to the islands by car, bear in mind that on weekends and holidays the traffic is heavy and the wait for a place on the ferry can be *hours* long! Plan your itinerary so that you can avoid such congestion. Travellers on foot do not have such long waits to worry about.

By rail

Departure Tallinn	Destination	Arrival
1.40pm 5.40pm 7.35am 10.30am (Fri, Sun) 3.22pm	Tartu (35 EEK) Narva (35 EEK)	5.30pm 8.10pm 11.50am 2.20pm 6.55pm
6.10am 10.15am 1.50pm	Pärnu (20.40 EEK)	9.21am 1.20pm 4.58pm
10.00am	Haapsalu (14.90 EEK)	1.06pm
8.00am 3.00pm 6.15pm	Viljandi (24.90 EEK) (25.70 EEK)	11.12am 5.37pm 9.24pm

By bus

For journeys within Estonia, the bus is generally a better choice than the train. Buses run more frequently, travel faster and are more comfortable. Unfortunately, they are not equipped with toilets and luggage compartments, and though inexpensive, trips are often long, and side roads sprinkled with potholes (major roads are good though). On some routes tickets are sold after all seats have been taken, forcing you to stand in the aisle during the entire trip. If you get a seat you will have a comfortable journey as trips within Estonia are not too long — three hours from Tallinn to Tartu, two to two and a half hours from Tallinn to Pärnu.

Bus trips between Tallinn and Vilnius take 12 hours (stops in Rīga) with several customs and immigration controls along the way. This trip on an overnight bus is not fun. (In a modern car, this same trip takes eight hours.) Bus station facilities are far from being up to Western standards. If you are tall, a smoker, or have children, we recommend you consider travelling by train. It might be best to take the bus to Pärnu or Valga, stay overnight, and continue on local buses or trains. A private rental car for three or more people may also be a decently-priced alternative. The Reisibüro Travel Agency in Tallinn's Viru Hotel prebooks long-distance buses, trains and arranges private transfers.

Keep in mind the language barrier. Most officials know no English or German. If you don't know any basic Russian or Estonian, you will have a problem communicating. If you run into problems, have your hotel or a travel agent help you make reservations.

Most buses leave from the main terminal, but check, because other points of departure exist. In Tallinn, tickets can be booked at the station or the office at Pärnu mnt 19, just behind the Palace Hotel. Return tickets cannot be booked at the point of departure. If you are not fond of crowds, avoid travel on weekends in the summer. For information about inter-city buses, tel: 444-484.

Buses from Tallinn to cities in Estonia:

Departure	To	Arrives/Duration
Express: 7.30am, 8.00am, 9.30am, 2.30pm, 3.40pm, 4.30pm, 5.00pm, 7.00pm *Local:* 10.15am, 11.00am, 1.10pm, 5.00pm, 7.00pm	Pärnu (26 EEK)	2½ hours
Express 6.20am, 7.40am, 10.20am, 11.15am, 12.40pm, 1.00pm, 3.20pm, 7.50pm *Local* 6.30am, 7.15pm, 4.15pm, 4.00pm, 9.00pm	Tartu (42-50 EEK)	*Express bus* 2½ hrs *Local bus* 3 hrs
11.10am 3.00pm 7.00am	Narva (44 EEK) (via Rakvere)	3.05pm 6.15pm 10.55am
8.45am 11.30am 1.00pm 5.30pm	Viljandi (28-35 EEK)	11.20am 2.00pm 3.35pm 8.05pm
Express: 9.30am, 11.05am, 1.30pm *Local:* 2.45pm, 3.30pm, 4.00pm, 9.00pm	Haapsalu (20-22 EEK)	2 hrs
7.40am, 9.20am, 11.00am, 2.50pm, 5.00pm (Fri), 5.40pm	Kuressaare (52-56 EEK)	4½ hrs
7.00am, 9.35am, noon, 2.45pm, 4.15pm	Võru (62 EEK)	5¼ hrs

City transportation

City buses, trams and trolleys run from 5am to midnight; on Sundays 6am to midnight. For information for trams: tel: 556-903; buses: 444-484; trolleys: 491-870.

Information on city transportation: 444-493, 532-548.

By car

The M-12, a major highway in the Baltics, runs from Minsk, Belarus, through Vilnius to Rīga, Tallinn and St Petersburg. It is part of the new in-progress Via Baltica which is planned to run from arctic Finland down into Central Europe. The Finns are working on improvements to the 625 mile stretch of the Via Baltica in the Baltics by adding slip roads, signs and Western-style filling stations. This throughway is planned to connect to the 1,750 mile Trans-European Motorway that will run from Gdansk, Poland to Istanbul, Turkey.

If you come by car, come prepared. In Tallinn, you can get spare parts for just about any kind of automobile. But inland, it's not that simple and here one's own spare parts can come in handy. Cars rented in Europe include travel insurance covering travel in almost all parts of Europe — make sure it includes the Baltics. You will need transit visas for countries you plan to drive through other than the Baltics.

Car theft is increasing. Don't tempt the potential thief. Lock the doors and don't leave anything in the car. Fuel is 50% less expensive than in Western Europe and comparable to US$1.30/gallon. Western gas stations — the Finnish *Neste* and Norwegian *Statoil* — are mostly located near larger cities. *Statoil* has stations and shops near the airport and harbour terminal open 24-hours; *Neste* is at Regati 1 in Piirita, 10am-10pm; in Järve, Pärnu maantee 141, tel: 580-453, open 24-hrs. *Shell* has returned to Estonia after an absence of some 50 years. Before World War II it operated 15 stations, mostly in the Tallinn area. Today it has opened its first post-war station in Pärnu. There are petrol stations located in nearly all towns. Look for the sign on the roadside that shows a petrol pump marked below by the number of metres to its location, and an arrow if one has to turn off the road. Most are self-service stations.

Roads have no hard shoulders for disabled cars. There are no dual carriageways and traffic is generally very light. Drive defensively; there are some reckless drivers on the road.

Night driving can be difficult as roads outside cities have no lane markers and the headlights of local cars are not strong. Country roads are often unpaved. City drivers are not known for their courtesy. 90km/hr is the speed limit on country roads. If a town's name is written on a blue sign, you don't have to slow down driving through it. If the sign's background is white, you must slow down to 60km/hr. In large cities, the speed limit is generally 50km/hr. When you see a streetcar stop and open its doors, you must also stop.

Car rental

Car rentals are expensive. If you do pursue this route you can manage well with a road map. Or you may consider hiring a chauffeur. Someone with experience driving in the Baltics is an asset as, in general, Baltic drivers are not the most courteous, nor the safest drivers around. Many streets are in poor condition. For more information, see the *Tallin Directory*.

ANIMAL CARE

It is not unusual to spot a roaming, hungry stray dog or cat as you walk the streets of Tallinn. Pet population control is not yet a familiar concept. Medicines for animals have a long way to go before they catch up to Western standards and dog and cat food is still a new concept. Another problem is car accidents. Baltic drivers are not known for their courtesy to pedestrians, be they human or otherwise, so car accident rates are high. Should you run into a situation where you wish to help an animal in distress, the following list may be of help:

Agropol, Peterburi 71, tel: (372)-2-214-671. Hours: 8am-4pm weekdays.
Drugstore, Rävala 7, tel: (372)-2-440-572. Hours: 8am-7pm daily, 9am-4pm Saturdays, closed Sundays.
Interfarm, Lembitu 3-2, tel: (372)-2-441-534. Vaccines imported by Holland's Intervet. Hours 9am-6pm weekdays.
Magdalena Drugstore, Pärnu 164, tel: (372)-2-510-006. Hours: 8am-6pm.
State Veterinary Laboratory, Väike-Paala 3, tel: (372)-2-215-668, 215-548.
Tallinn Veterinary Clinic, Västriku 2, tel: (372)-2-557-250, 555-906. Hours: 8am-6pm weekdays, 9am-2pm Saturdays, closed Sundays.
Tiina Toomet Clinic, Kopli 75a, tel: (372)-2-474-739. Hours: 9.30am-5pm weekdays.

Outside Tallinn:
Eesti Zoovetvaru, Pärnasalu 31, Saue, tel: (372)-2-596-132. Hours: 8am-4pm weekdays, 9am-2pm Saturdays, closed Sundays.
EPBK Ltd, Kreutzwaldi 1, Tartu, tel: (372)-2-34-613-02.
ITC Ltd, Sipasoo, Habaja, Harjumaa, tel: (372)-2-751-456. Open 24 hours a day.
Saue Vet Ltd, Sovhoosi 1, Laagri, Harjumaa, tel: (372)-2-519-625. House calls for small animals by Dr E Pendin, tel: (372)-2-536-085.

What about pets?

Dogs and cats, together with a health certificate, can be brought into Estonia without putting them into quarantine. Estonia is not the best place to bring your dog. Veterinarians don't commonly use vaccines against parvo or hepatitis, although they do for rabies. Your dog can contract just about anything from a Baltic pooch. All things considered, it's probably best for your pet to stay at home.

Part Two

Tallinn

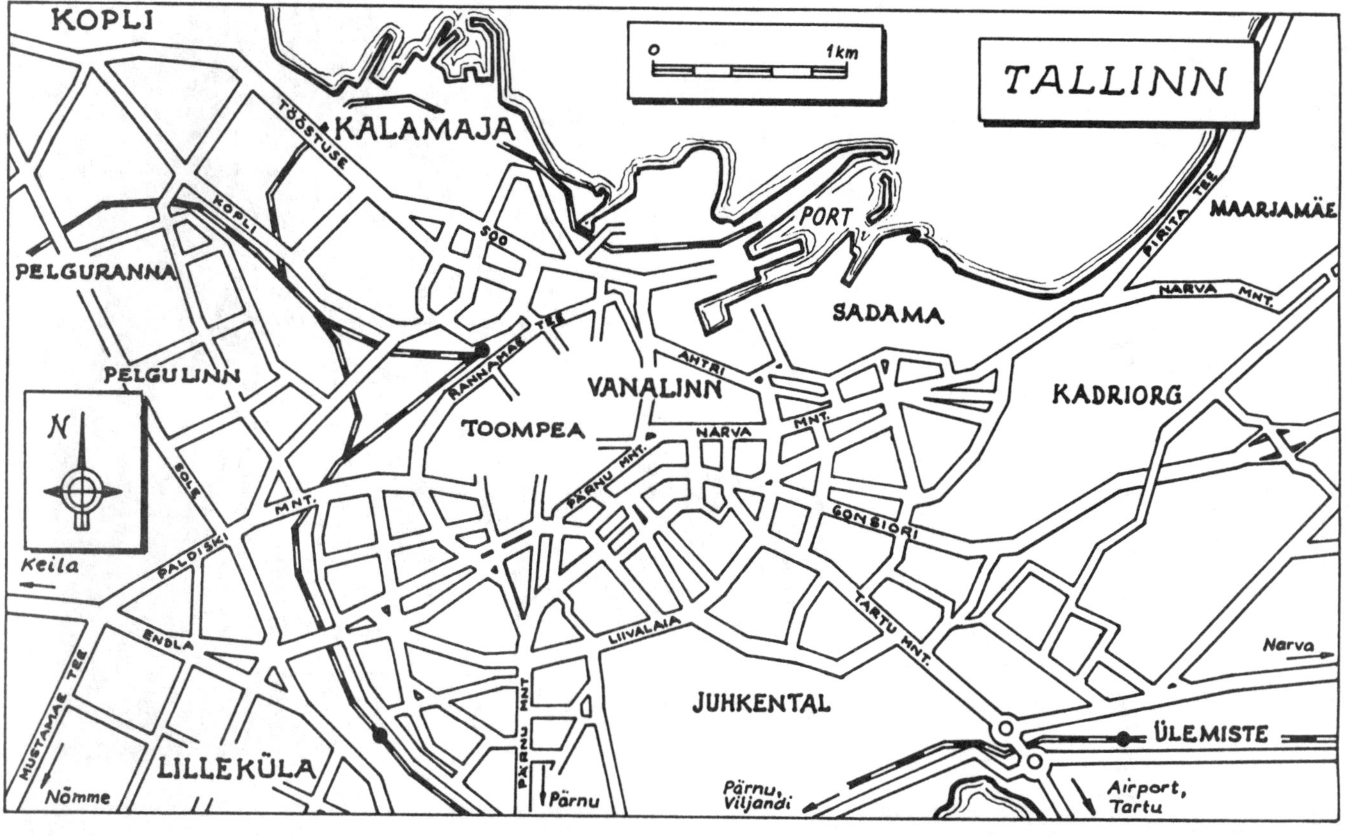
KOPLI
0
1km
TALLINN
KALAMAJA
TÖÖSTUSE
KOPLI
SOO
PORT
PIRITA TEE
MAARJAMÄE
NARVA MNT.
SADAMA
PELGURANNA
RANNAMÄE TEE
AHTRI
VANALINN
KADRIORG
PELGULINN
TOOMPEA
NARVA
MNT.
N
PÄRNU MNT.
SOLE
MNT.
GONSIORI
Keila
PALDISKI
TARTU MNT.
LIIVALAIA
ENDLA
Narva
MUSTAMÄE TEE
JUHKENTAL
PÄRNU MNT
ÜLEMISTE
LILLEKÜLA
Nõmme
Pärnu
Pärnu, Viljandi
Airport, Tartu

Chapter Four

Tallinn

HISTORY

Known in many older books as *Reval*, Tallinn is the capital city of Estonia. Its settlement goes back at least 3,500 years and, being blessed with a natural harbour, it became a port on the east-west trade route in Europe. Its bluff, not far from the water, was an excellent location for a fortress settlement. The earliest recorded mention of Tallinn is by the geographer Idrisi on his world map of 1154 AD. Some interesting legends are associated with the city. The high rock of the fortress settlement, known as Toompea, is believed to be the burial mound of Kalev, the mythical forefather of Estonians. His grief-stricken widow, Linda, built it with boulders she carried in her apron. One boulder fell out of her apron and rolled a distance. Linda, exhausted and filled with grief and self-pity, wept uncontrollably. Her tears formed Lake Ülemiste at the edge of town, and to this day you can still see Linda's runaway boulder in the middle of the lake.

Another legend says that the lake is the home of the Old Man of Ülemiste who has sworn to drown completed Tallinn with its waters. Centuries ago, the Old Man would query the builders at the end of the day's work: 'Is the city finished yet?' And the answer was always the same: 'No, not yet.' To this day you will see construction in Tallinn, because the citizens do not want the Old Man to pull the plug under Ülemiste and flood the city.

A legend is also associated with the first foreign invaders of Tallinn. In 1219 Danish King Valdemar II arrived with 1,500 ships to conquer the land for the Church. On the third day of battle things were going badly for the Danes. Only heaven could help them, so the Archbishop of Lund raised his eyes toward the sky and — lo! — a red flag with a white cross, the Daneborg, fell into his hands. In one stroke, Denmark got its national flag and Tallinn its name — *Taani linnus* (Tallinn) means Danish fortress.

The Danes built a fortress on Toompea and, in it, Toomkirik, the seat of the bishopric. The king himself was its patron until Danish rule ended in 1346. During this rule, Tallinn joined the Hanseatic League, which brought it prosperity. Gradually, a town grew at the foot of Toompea.

The Teutonic Knights succeeded the Danes. They and the bishop lived in Toompea, the merchants, artisans, and seafarers forming the town below, building around them high stone walls with red-roofed defence towers. Thus Tallinn had a dual character: the citadel on the hill housing the nobility, and below its walls the commercial community, home to tradesmen and craftsmen. Administratively, the two were autonomous until 1889 and to this day the buildings reflect this historic contrast.

In the 15th and 16th centuries Tallinn was one of the biggest North European cities. Through its port furs, hides, wax, linen and hemp were taken to the West, while salt, cloth, wine and herring were taken to the East. The great guild halls, graceful merchants' homes, and many of the churches date from this time.

During Swedish rule (1561-1710), the Hanseatic League began to break apart. A plague in 1603 greatly reduced the number of Tallinn's inhabitants. In 1684 a fire on Toompea burned most of the houses, and in 1695-97 Estonia suffered a great famine. But worst of all was the Northern War, started in 1700 by Czar Peter I of Russia in order to gain access to the Baltic Sea. Ten years later his armies surrounded Tallinn. Under heavy bombardment and with the population suffering from a plague, the city surrendered. The city's population loss from deaths caused by the war left only 1,962 inhabitants. Previously there had been 9,801.

The prosperous era had ended. In that decline may be hidden the secret that explains why Tallinn is such a well preserved medieval town. The argument goes that its people were too poor to demolish and rebuild — they had to repair and fix up what they had.

As part of the Russian empire (1710-1918), Tallinn became a provincial centre. Governmental organs remained in the hands of the German nobility. Tallinn's isolation increased as St Petersburg's importance grew. It wasn't until 1870, when the Baltic railway was opened, that the city became a centre of commercial activity again. The railroad connected Tallinn's port with Moscow and St Petersburg, and through them with other towns and cities further into Russia.

The 1917 Russian Revolution gave Estonia the long sought opportunity to become an independent nation and Tallinn became its capital. During World War II Tallinn was damaged by Soviet bombing raids, but fortunately the Old Town was spared. Under Soviet occupation, Tallinn was subjected to intense industrialization and immigration of peoples from other parts of the former USSR and the population more than doubled. Huge pre-fab housing developments that mar the city's appearance are a legacy of this period. When this frantic construction was taking place some natives began to wonder whether it was not time to tell the Old Man of Ülemiste that certain sections of Tallinn were finished. The Lasnamäe type of construction was considered a worse threat to Tallinn than a deluge.

OLD TOWN

The Upper Town, Toompea

Toompea Castle dominates the setting. The word *Toompea* is an Estonian derivation of the German word *Domberg*, or cathedral mountain. Currently, it is the seat of Estonia's government, *Riigikogu* (parliament). In the Middle Ages, it was part of *castrum minor* (small fortress), and the whole of Toompea was known as *castrum major* (large fortress). Originally, the small fortress was built by the Sword Brethren in 1227-1229 in a rectangular shape. For centuries only Estonia's German hierarchy lived on the fortress hill, which has seen much rebuilding and redesigning. Today, only the northern and western walls remain and three of the four towers are more or less intact. Two of these towers, *Landskrone* and *Pilsticker* (German for 'Land Crown' and 'Arrow Sharpener'), and the northern part of the fortress can be viewed most splendidly from the yard of the house at 13 Toomkooli Street. The third tower, *Pikk Hermann* (Tall Hermann), was built by the Livonian Order in 1371 and it is a majestic symbol for the country. The flags of many foreign powers have flown from its staff, but now Estonia's tricolors, blTues-black-white, grace the sky and once again signify home rule.

The ideal place to begin a tour of Toompea is the Castle Square, which is dominated on one side by the Castle originally begun by the Danes in 1219, and on the other side by *St Alexander Nevsky Cathedral.*

The salmon-coloured facade of the Castle which faces Castle Square dates from the year 1773, but the inner parts of the building were begun in 1219 when the Danes began construction of their fortress. Their work was continued by the German Brethren of the Sword after the Order took possession of the fortress in 1346. The 50.2m Tall Hermann Tower at the edge of the Castle was completed during the early 16th century and owes its design to similar towers along the river Rhine. At the base of the tower is a memorial tablet inscribed with the names of socialists executed by the Czarist police in 1905.

By the time of Catherine II's reign, the Castle had fallen into a state of disrepair. Catherine ordered the reconstruction of the building. In 1767 she approved a new design by the architect Johann Schultz from Jena in Germany, and the building was completed in 1773.

The St Alexander Nevsky Cathedral was begun in 1895 and was completed on November 2 1897 after a design by Professor Mikhail

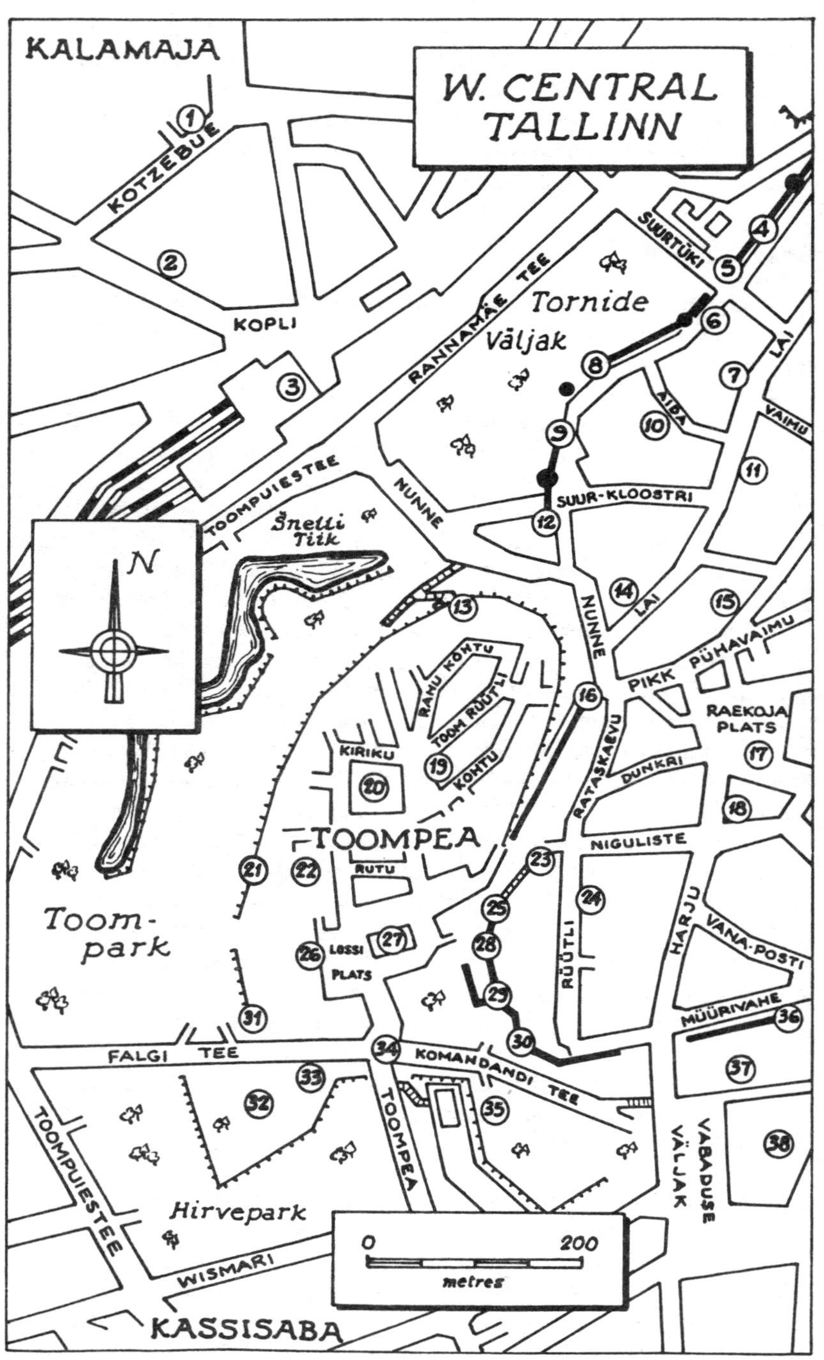

KALAMAJA
W. CENTRAL TALLINN
KOTZEBUE
KOPLI
RANNAMÄE TEE
Tornide Väljak
SUURTÜKI
LAI
AIDA
VAIMU
TOOMPUIESTEE
NUNNE
SUUR-KLOOSTRI
Šnelli Tiik
N
RAHU KOHTU
TOOM RÜÜTLI
KOHTU
KIRIKU
PIKK
PÜHAVAIMU
RAEKOJA PLATS
RATASKAEVU
DUNKRI
TOOMPEA
NIGULISTE
RUTU
Toom-park
LOSSI PLATS
RÜÜTLI
HARJU
VANA-POSTI
MÜÜRIVAHE
FALGI TEE
KOMANDANDI TEE
TOOMPEA
TOOMPUIESTEE
VABADUSE VÄLJAK
Hirvepark
WISMARI
0
200
metres
KASSISABA

W. CENTRAL TALLINN

Key to Map

1. KALAMAJA MUSEUM
2. CINEMA
3. RAILWAY STATION - Balti Jaam
4. EPPING TOWER
5. PLATE TOWER
6. NATURE MUSEUM
7. THEATRE
8. LÕEWENSCHEDE TOWER
9. GOLDEN LEG TOWER
10. APPLIED ARTS MUSEUM
11. PUBLIC HEALTH MUSEUM
12. NUN'S TOWER
13. PATKUL STEPS
14. PUPPET THEATRE
15. ART MUSEUM
16. PIKK JALG
17. TOWN HALL
18. GALLERY
19. KNIGHTHOOD HALL
20. TOOMKIRIK
21. PILSTICKER TOWER
22. LANDSKRONE TOWER
23. MUSEUM
24. MUSEUM and CONCERT HALL
25. LÜHIKE JALG
26. TOOMPEA PALACE
27. St. ALEXANDER NEVSKY CATHEDRAL
28. STABLE TOWER
29. VIRGIN'S TOWER
30. KIEK IN DE KÖK (Cannon Tower)
31. PIKK HERMANN
32. STATUE of LINDA
33. SWEDISH BASTION
34. RĪGA GATE
35. INGRIAN BASTION
36. THEATRE and MUSIC MUSEUM
37. GALLERY
38. St. JOHN'S CHURCH

Preobrazhensky of the St Petersburg Academy of Arts. The construction was initiated by Prince Sergei Shakhovskoy who was appointed Governor of Estonia in 1885. After the escape by Czar Alexander III from a railway accident on October 17 1888, it was decided that the new cathedral be dedicated to St Alexander Nevsky. The largest bell in the Cathedral weighs 976 poods (1 pood = 36lbs) and the building can shelter up to 1,500 persons.

Down the street is the modest *Toomkirik* (Cathedral), an example of late Gothic architecture. It is named the Cathedral of St Mary the Virgin and is the seat of the Estonian Evangelical Lutheran Church. A wooden church was first built here after the Danish invasion of 1219. A stone church was later built by Dominican monks from Denmark and was consecrated in 1240. It was the centre of *castrum major* and streets radiated from it. The Estonian name of the Cathedral (*Toomkirik*) is derived from the German *Domkirche*. In 1486, the Germans started to call the citadel Domberg, which was translated into Toompea in Estonian.

In the fire of 1684 that destroyed much of Toompea, *Toomkirik* suffered badly. After the fire it was rebuilt as a Gothic basilica. The western tower in the late baroque style dates from 1778-1779. The interior is impressive with its walls covered by memorial tablets and coats-of-arms, grave markers on the floor, the sarcophagi of noblemen and rich merchants, and the baroque altar and pulpit. Among those buried in *Toomkirik* are the Swedish general Pontus de la Gardie and his wife Sophie Gyllenhelm, daughter of King Johann III of Sweden, and the Estonian-born Baltic-German nobleman, Adam Johann von Krusenstern, who led the expedition for the Russian Czars' first circumnavigation of the globe in 1803-06.

Significant buildings from the 18th century include the Commandant's house at 1 Toompea Street, the office building at 3 Rahukohtu Street, and the dwellings at 2 Kiriku plats and 1-7 Lossi plats. The Commandant's house is a baroque building constructed in the mid-1600s. A plaque on the building notes that one of the commandants was Abraham Hannibal, son of an Ethiopian prince, a favourite courtier of Peter the First and the great-grandfather of the Russian poet Alexander Pushkin.

The dwelling at number 4 Lossi plats, across the street from the St Alexander Nevsky Cathedral, was used by Peter I in 1711 during his first visit to Tallinn shortly after the Treaty of Nystadt confirmed Estonia's cession from Sweden to Russia.

From the 19th century, remarkable structures are the Count's house at 8 Kohtu Street, and the Ritterschaft House at 1 Raamatukogu plats. The dwelling house at number 2 Kohtu (Court) Street was built in 1798 by Count Hans Heinrich von Tiesenhausen. The classical main building is located between the courtyard and the former gardens which descend to the narrow *Pikk jalg* street. The gatehouse of the dwelling faces Kohtu Street. The last owners of the building were the von Toll family, lords of Kukkuse manor in northeast Estonia.

Number 6 Kohtu Street was built in the middle of the 19th century by the wealthy baronical family, Ungernsternberg. Their magnificent country manor may be visited on the Estonian island of Hiiumaa. The building later housed the Estonian Literary Association, and now houses the presidium of the Estonian Academy of Science.

The Finnish embassy was located at 4 Kohtu Street before World War II. It has been restored to the Finnish government.

At number 1 Kohtu Street is located the Knighthood Hall, built in the late 1600s as a meeting house for Estonia's knights. Its facade on Kohtu Street is in the Baroque style, but the facade facing the Cathedral of St Mary was built in 1846-47 in Renaissance style. Before the World War II the building served as the Estonian Foreign Ministry. Currently, it houses the Estonian National Art Museum temporarily.

At number 8 Kohtu Street is a building built in Classic style. Indeed, many authorities consider the building to be Tallinn's best example of Classicist architecture. The building's facade displays the text *Parentum Voto ac Favore* (With ancestors' promise and favour). It is believed that the building was designed by Carl Ludwig Engel, who most notably designed Helsinki's Lutheran Cathedral and Cathedral Square. Currently, the building houses departments of the Estonian Ministry of Finance and offices of international organizations such as the World Bank and the United Nations Development Program. It was restored in 1994-1995.

At Toomkooli and Rahukohtu streets are paths to observation platforms from which one can get breathtaking views of the city below and the Gulf of Finland. At Toompea are located, also, cafés and restaurants to suit a variety of palates. Of particular interest is the café *Neitsitorn* (Virgin's Tower), located in a wall tower near Toompea Castle. The tower acquired its name in the Middle Ages when it housed the prison for women of easy virtue.

Today one can approach Toompea from several directions, but before the 17th century *Pikk jalg* (The Long Leg), provided the only entry. The distrust and animosity between the inhabitants of Toompea and the lower town is further exemplified by the *Pikk jalg* gate tower, which dates from 1380. The gate was locked every evening at 9 o'clock, and as a special precaution at times of unrest, a strong oak trellis on iron chains was lowered as an additional barrier.

The Lower Town

Leaving Toompea by *Pikk jalg* and turning right onto *Lühike jalg* (The Short Leg), which is actually a short stepped street, you arrive at *Niguliste Kirik* (St Nicholas' Church), which was built by the German merchants and craftsmen that settled in the area in 1230. The merchants were invited to Tallinn by the Knights of the Sword and emigrated from Westphalia. The Church is named for St Nicholas, protector of merchants and sailors. It was built before Tallinn was protected by walls, and therefore also had a military purpose. During 1405 to 1420 it was extensively rebuilt and the old choir demolished. A three-aisled choir was raised in its place and a new vestry erected at its end. For a while the Order halted construction of the church tower out of suspicion that it might be used for attacks on Toompea. The tower was eventually completed in 1510-1515. Virtually no structural changes of any significance were made to the Church after 1696. It is the most pleasingly proportioned late Gothic church building among Tallinn's churches. It was virtually destroyed by Soviet bombers in the spring of 1944 but was rebuilt after the war. By then, however, the German community no longer existed and the atheist Soviet state preferred to make museums out of church buildings. Thus Niguliste's more recent function has been to serve as a museum and a concert hall. South of Niguliste, you will notice Tallinn's oldest tree, called the *Kelch limetree*. Under the 300-year-old tree lies the grave of the chronicler Christian Kelch, whose 1695 *History of Livonia* records: 'Estonia is the landlord's heaven, the clergy's paradise, the stranger's goldmine, and the peasant's hell.'

At the end of *Lühike jalg* three streets go in different directions. Turning right onto *Rüütli* (Knight Street), a short walk will lead you to the town wall and an inconspicuous house next to it which was medieval Tallinn's executioner's home. His sword, which bears the inscription, 'God's mercy is renewed every morning as I raise my sword and help a sinner to enter eternal life,' is on display at the Town Hall Museum.

A short walk down *Niguliste* (St Nicholas' Street) will bring you to *Harju tänav*. In the Middle Ages the area was inhabited by metalsmiths. It was heavily bombed by the Soviets during the war, and the buildings are mostly of post-war construction.

The third street is *Rataskaevu* (The Wheel Well) which gets its name from the wheel well that has stood there since 1386 at the intersection of Dunkri tänav. On the street are located some dwellings dating from the 15th century. If you turn right onto Dunkri, you will come out at the very heart of Old Tallinn, at *Raekoja plats* (Town Hall Square).

Raekoja plats dates back at least to the 12th century. All the main streets of the town converge here. In the Middle Ages, the square was a market place surrounded by merchants' and smiths' shops and today it is still surrounded by stylish old houses. Among those of architectural significance are the Renaissance merchant's house at Raekoja plats 18, a municipal office building at Raekoja plats 15, and the chemist's shop at Raekoja plats 11. It has been a pharmacy since 1422 — the oldest in continuous operation in the Western world.

The square is no longer used as a market place — now summer

festivals and open-air concerts attract crowds. However, the best time to grasp the square's beauty is when it is deserted in the early morning light.

The most magnificent building on the square is *Raekoda* (Town Hall, 1402-1404). It is the only surviving Gothic town hall in northern Europe. The mid-17th century facade of the building rests on arches which served as a trading place in the Middle Ages. The tall tower at its eastern end has a 61.5m Renaissance spire topped by *Vana Toomas* (Old Thomas), the symbol of Tallinn: a weatherwane depicting a medieval warrior. Legend has it that he keeps watch on the horizon and warns the townsmen as soon as an enemy is in sight. The two principal rooms in the building are the Citizens' Hall, where chamber concerts are held, and the Council Hall which contains wooden benches that bear the oldest woodcarvings in Estonia.

If you take *Saiakäik* (Pastry Passage), under a vault opening on the square, you will be able to visit several different little shops. The little street got its name from a bakery that used to fill the passage and the square with its delicious aroma. On the right hand side of the passage is the 13th century *Pühavaimu kirik* (Holy Ghost Church), which in the Middle Ages was the Town Hall's chapel. It is also the church in which native Estonians worshiped. One of its pastors, Johann Koell, translated the Lutheran Catechism into Estonian in 1535. Another pastor in that era, Balthasar Russow, wrote *A Chronicle of the Livonian Province* in which, for the first time, attention is drawn to the brutal treatment of the peasants by the feudal lords. The church has several noteworthy features: its altar was commissioned from the Lübeck master, Bernt Notke, in 1483; the outside wall has on it the oldest public clock in Tallinn; and the bell in the tower, cast in 1433, is the oldest in Estonia. It is the only religious building in Tallinn that still has a 14th century appearance.

Saiakäik ends at *Pikk tänav* (Long Street). Pikk tänav starts at Pikk jalg gate and ends at *Suur Rannavärav* (Great Coastal Gate), a length of 800 metres — the longest street in the Old Town. Along the street are located homes of rich merchants who made it the centre of social life in medieval Tallinn.

Across the street from the public clock of the Pühavaimu church stands the Great Guilds' building, built in 1410 by an organization of rich merchants. It is a typical example of Gothic architecture and today houses the Museum of Estonian History.

Going down Pikk Street, at house number 20 is St Canute's Guild hall, built in 1863-64 in the pseudo-Gothic style. St Canute's Guild admitted both merchants and craftsmen. At Pikk 28 is the hall of the Brotherhood of the Blackheads, so named because the members' patron saint, St Mauritius, was a Christianized Moor. The Blackheads' house is a splendid example of Renaissance architecture in Tallinn. Next to it is the *Oleviste* (St Olaf's) Guild house, home to the oldest guild in Tallinn,

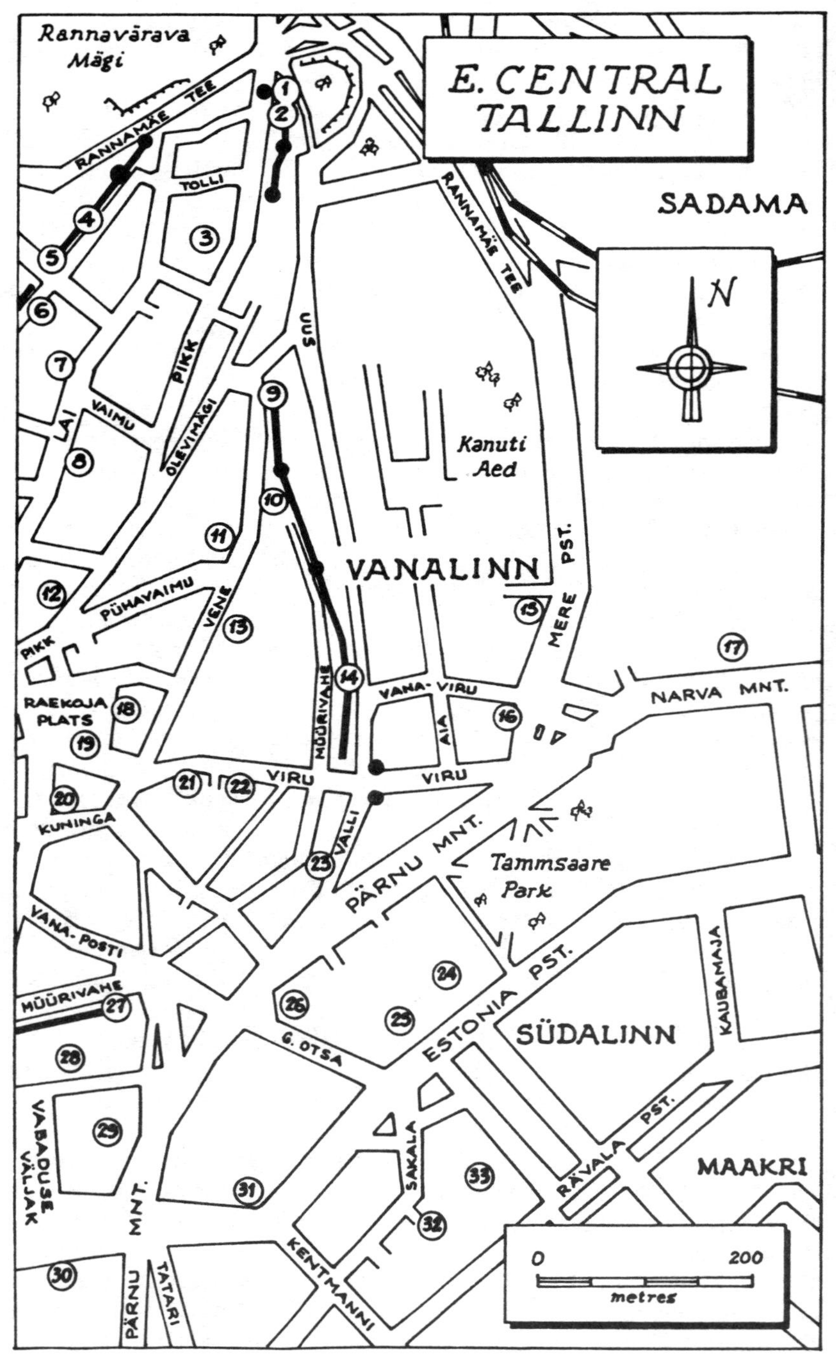
E. CENTRAL
TALLINN
Rannavärava
Mägi
RANNAMÄE TEE
TOLLI
SADAMA
N
UUS
PIKK
VAIMU
LAI
OLEVIMÄGI
Kanuti
Aed
VANALINN
MERE PST.
PÜHAVAIMU
VENE
PIKK
RAEKOJA
PLATS
MÜÜRIVAHE
VANA-VIRU
AIA
NARVA MNT.
VIRU
VIRU
KUNINGA
VALLI
PÄRNU MNT.
Tammsaare
Park
VANA-POSTI
MÜÜRIVAHE
KAUBAMAJA
G. OTSA
ESTONIA PST.
SÜDALINN
VABADUSE
VÄLJAK
SAKALA
RÄVALA PST.
MAAKRI
KENTMANNI
PÄRNU MNT.
TATARI
0
200
metres

E. CENTRAL TALLINN

Key to Map

1. PAKS MARGAREETA
2. MARITIME MUSEUM
3. St. OLAV'S CHURCH
4. EPPING TOWER
5. PLATE TOWER
6. NATURE MUSEUM
7. THEATRE
8. PUBLIC HEALTH MUSEUM
9. BREMEN TOWER
10. St. NICHOLAS' CHURCH
11. LINNAMUSEUM
12. ART MUSEUM
13. DOMINICAN CLOISTER
14. HELLEMAN TOWER
15. ADVENTIST CHURCH
16. FIRE SERVICE MUSEUM
17. CENTRAL POST OFFICE
18. GALLERY
19. TOWN HALL
20. GALLERY
21. & 22. CINEMAS
23. HINKE TOWER
24. ESTONIA THEATRE
25. ESTONIA CONCERT HALL
26. ESTONIAN DRAMA THEATRE
27. THEATRE and MUSIC MUSEUM
28. GALLERY
29. St. JOHN'S CHURCH
30. RUSSIAN DRAMA THEATRE
31. CITY LIBRARY
32. OLD TOWN STUDIO THEATRE
33. SCIENCE ACADEMY LIBRARY

founded in the 13th century.

On Pikk Street is also *Oleviste kirik* (St Olaf's Church), once considered to be the highest structure in the world. The first known record of it is dated 1267. At its heyday in 1500, its tower reached 159 metres. Even at today's height of 124 metres, it is an impressive part of Tallinn's silhouette. A relief of the church in St Mary's chapel depicts elements of the legend attributed to the building of this Gothic structure.

Tallinners had long wanted to build a church of unprecedented height, but could not find a competent builder. Finally, a young masterbuilder named Olev was found. The mighty building was almost finished when Olev looked down from the steeple and, losing his balance, fell to the ground. After his body hit the ground a toad and a snake came out of his mouth. People considered it only appropriate to give the church his name.

Pikk Street ends at one of the six gates that served as the only entrances to medieval Tallinn. The whole town was surrounded by a 2.5km long wall that was 2.5m thick and 15-16m high. Three quarters of it still stands today. Originally the wall had 48 towers and of these 20 stand today, along with parts of two gates and two fortified approaches. A massive cannon tower, *Paks Margareeta* (Fat Margaret), is located at the end of Pikk Street, beside *Suur Rannavärav*. Paks Margareeta's waist measures 24m, her walls are 4m thick and she is currently used for the Maritime Museum. The architectural and aesthetic value of these structures is enhanced by Tallinn's coat-of-arms carved in stone above the gate.

You will see the other mighty cannon tower, *Kiek in de Kök*, on Komandandi tee from Toompea to *Vabaduse väljak* (Freedom Square). The curious name is derived from Low German, 'peep into the kitchen.' From its high windows (the tower is 46m high) the soldiers could watch housewives cook. The tower withstood many onslaughts successfully, as evidenced by the six cannon balls embedded in its wall. Today the tower is a museum that exhibits photographers' works.

A walk along *Vene tänav* (Russian Street), will take you to the remains of the early 13th century Dominican monastery. Now it is a branch of the Tallinn Town Museum and, in the summer, open-air plays are staged in its grounds. Another rich merchant's house at Vene 17 is worth a visit for its splendid interior staircase in the hall.

Roaming on your own through the many other streets will reveal treasures too numerous to list. Don't hesitate to do so.

THE REST OF TALLINN

Former moats, bastions, and war ruins are today's parks and avenues around the Old Town. They are pleasant settings for walks and catching views of the city. The southern and southeastern section of the Old Town is merged with the new commercial and civic centre of Tallinn. Viru, Olümpia and Palace hotels as well as the Central Post Office, shopping districts, theatres, art galleries and other important services are located here.

To the north of the Old Town is *Balti jaam* (The Baltic Railroad Station). Also to the north is *Kalamaja*, which was the district inhabited by Estonians who were servants and labourers to the citizens living inside the walls in the Middle Ages. The northern shore meets the Gulf of Finland.

In the northeastern direction is the *Piirita* resort area and *Merivälja,* a suburb of private homes, most of them built by the owners' own hands during the Soviet occupation.

To the east lie the park of *Kadriorg* with its palace, the Song Festival Amphitheatre, and, beyond, the pre-fab monstrosity called *Lasnamäe.*

Kadriorg was built by Peter I as a summer residence for his wife, Catherine I, the Lithuanian born servant in the home of Latvian pastor Ernest Gluch. He called it Katharinenthal. The local people started calling it Kadriorg (Catherine's dale). The park and the palace were designed by the Italian architect Niccolo Michetti and construction started in 1718. An upper and a lower garden were laid out. There are groves of trees (70 species altogether), squirrels, birds, swans on the pond, and sculptures and monuments in abundance. Among them is a monument to Friedrich R Kreutzwald, author of the Estonian national epic *Kalevipoeg.* On the seashore stands *Russalka*, a statue in memory of perished sailors from the shipwreck of the *Russalka* ('mermaid') off the Estonian coast. In 1938 a government building was built in the upper garden. The Palace was the house for the Art Museum but it has been closed for the last few years for major renovations, which are not expected to be completed before 1995. The residence of the President of Estonia is also at Kadriorg. In the park is a cottage built for Peter as lodging when he came to observe the progress of the construction. It contains many of his personal effects.

At Kadriorg is the amphitheatre where national song festivals are held every five years. Other large gatherings are held here, too. Here 'The Singing Revolution' had a gathering of over 300,000 people (a third of the Estonian nation) in September 1988, to express a collective desire for freedom.

Continuing along the embankment from Kadriorg you will reach Piirita. First to catch your attention is the Piirita Hotel and Yachting Centre on the left, which was built for the 1980 Summer Olympics. Estonian New Line's catamarans from Helsinki use it as their harbour. As you cross the Piirita River, pause on the bridge to get a view of the scenic river mouth. On the eastern bank of the river are the remains of St Bridgit's Cloister. Originally built in 1436, it included a church, monastery and convent but was destroyed by fire in 1577. The ruins are among artists' favourite subjects in Tallinn. Piirita also has a two kilometre sandy beach for enjoyment of water sports in the summer.

A sacred and lovingly attended spot in the area is *Metsakalmistu* (Forest Cemetery). Here are buried the nation's loved and respected sons and daughters, among them opera star Georg Ots, novelist A H Tammsaare, chess grand master Paul Keres, poet Lydia Koidula and conductor-composer Gustav Ernesaks. The remains of the martyred last

president of Estonia before World War II, Konstantin Päts, were brought from Russia in 1990 and laid to rest here. Set in natural pine wood, the cemetery offers an interesting cultural glimpse into Estonians' customs and aesthetics.

Travelling in the opposite direction from Old Tallinn, only a few kilometres to the west, you will come to *Rocca al Mare*. The Italian name was given in 1863 by the merchant and burgermeister, A Girard de Soucanton, who had his summer house here. Today the area is an open-air museum where examples of rural architecture have been brought from different parts of Estonia and arranged to give an atmosphere of traditional Estonian village life. On Sundays, folk song and dance concerts are given in one of the farmyards.

Just past Rocca al Mare is the Tallinn zoo. Founded in 1939, it has over 5,000 exhibits and woodlands on its 215 acres. There are various places to eat. Tel: 599-855, 599-944, fax: 6-393-049.

Southwest of Rocca al Mare are nestled Soviet style housing developments, Õismäe and Mustamäe. The latter was the first such pre-fab residential housing built in Tallinn. Farther south and southwest of Ülemiste Lake, which has provided Tallinn with its drinking water since the 14th century, is the residential garden suburb of *Nõmme*, mostly built between the two world wars.

ARRIVING IN TALLINN

Airport

Tallinna Lennujaam (Tallinn Airport), located southeast of the city, on Tartu maantee, was one of the facilities built to host the Yachting events of the 1980 Summer Olympics. It has a bar, restaurant, caféteria, news-stand, souvenir shop, flower shop, post office, pay phones, information booth, car rental service, currency exchange, and ticket office. The trip from the airport to the city centre takes about 10-15 minutes to drive.

There is no scheduled limousine service, but you can get to town either by bus Nº 22 or Nº 90. For bus Nº 22, buy your ticket (2 EEK) from the bus driver. You have to validate your ticket on board. Checkers board buses at random to check for validation and you will be fined if you cannot present a validated ticket. The bus stops rather frequently. Among the stops are *Balti jaam* (Baltic Railway Station), Hotel Tallinn, *Vabaduse väljak* (Freedom Square), *Estonia* (Estonia Theatre), and *Kaubamaja* (The Department Store). Runs every 20-30 minutes.

Airport bus 90 is a shuttle that takes passengers from the airport or harbour to the bigger hotels (Palace, Olümpia, Viru and Tallinn). It also stops at the bus and train station. Tickets can be bought from the driver for 4 EEK.

If you take a taxi, make sure the taxi has a metre. About 40 EEK is a reasonable fare to the city centre. There are now official airport taxis.

Bus station

The central bus station, named *Maaliinide Autobussijaam*, is located on Lastekodu 46 just off Tartu maantee. Ten minutes by tram 2 or 4, the fourth stop after Viru väljak. It is rather dismal, Soviet-era grey, and impersonal. Few foreigners use it. If you decide to travel by bus, you will have to search for someone who can speak English. Come equipped with an Estonian dictionary and use our *Useful Phrases* section. As for local transportation services, taxis are available and city buses pull up to the area where long haul buses terminate. Tel: 422-549.

Railroad station

Balti jaam (Baltic Railroad Station) in Tallinn is located at Toompuiestee 39; tel: 446-756, 624-058, 624-851. International service info tel: 456-058. Open daily 8am-8pm. Ten minute walk from the centre of town. Trams 1 or 2, the third stop after Viru väljak. The large building got much needed repairs in 1994. Like the bus station it used to be a dismal, Soviet-era grey. City buses pick up passengers on the square in front of the station, as well as by the curb on the side of the station. A short distance from the latter is a taxi stand.

Ferry terminal

Tallinna Reisisadam, (Tallinn Harbour) Sadama 29, open daily 9am-6pm, tel: 427-009. The harbour is about a 15 minute walk from the Old Town, three minutes by car. Trams Nº 1 or 2, one stop after Viru väljak. Bus 65 from the port to the city centre runs every half hour. Most ferries use Tallinn's Main Terminal, which was opened in the summer of 1994. It is a spacious place with services such as currency exchange (cheaper in town though), restaurant, bar, left-luggage room, shops, an Information Desk, and other comforts Western travellers are accustomed to. Ferry tickets are also available from travel agents around town.

The commercial port, **Tallinna Uussadam**, is at Muuga, 16km from the city centre. Bus 54 stops at Tallinn's main department store, *Kaubamaja*.

WHERE TO STAY

For a long time Tallinn lacked moderately priced decent hotels. That's slowly changing though most of this kind of lodging is not centrally located. However, the city transit system is good and Tallinn is not huge so the distances aren't great. There is always the taxi. Perhaps more available is the city bus.

The top hotels are usually geared towards businessfolk and their wallets. The *Palace* charges out of sight prices. But you can get a double at the *Viru* for around US$80; the *Olümpia* tends to be higher.

Unfortunately, the *Tallinn* and other large hotels are run down and Soviet-era looking.

All told the hotel scene has greatly improved over the last few years. New, private establishments keep opening up that are up to par with Western standards and reasonably priced. Selections cover a wider range of choices nowadays. The prices listed below are the latest available at the writing of this book. However, they are for the walk-in client. Keep in mind you can often get lower rates if you book your Estonia trip through a travel agent or tour operator who specializes in Baltic travel. Hotels give them rooms to sell at a discount. You could save up to 20%.

Hotels

Moderate to expensive:

Noobel, Tuvi 14b, tel: (372)-2-683-713, 681-704, fax: 681-710. Once a former government minister's home, it's now a luxury hotel. Full service, double room: 2,100 EEK. Has a casino. Reputedly a base for illegitimate business types and might be advisable to avoid.

Olümpia, Liivalaia 33, tel: (372)-6-315-315, (reservations), (372)-6-315-333 (operator), fax: 6-315-325. (Singles from 800 EEK, doubles from 1,000 EEK). A high-rise close to town centre; ten minute walk from the Old Town. Built for 1980 Summer Olympics. Most improved hotel in Tallinn and still being renovated. Prices moderate except for the renovated rooms. Accepts most credit cards.

Palace, Vabaduse väljak 3, tel: (372)-2-444-761, fax: 443-098. 154 rooms (singles 2,200 EEK; doubles 2,800 EEK. Slightly cheaper rates apply on weekends). The best hotel in town. International four-star hotel. Centrally located, excellent service. Accepts most credit cards. A 'Sky Bar' on the top floor stays open late.

Rataskaevu, Rataskaevu square 7, in the Old Town, tel: (372)-2-441-939, fax: 691-458, 443-688. An old hotel with a comfortable, low-key atmosphere. The best location in Tallinn.

Viru, Viru väljak 4, tel: (372)-6-301-311, fax: 6-301-303. 458 rooms (singles, 1,100 EEK, doubles 1,430 EEK). Convenient central location, soviet-style high rise constructed in early 1970s by Intourist. Has had restoration and Westernization. Great views of the Old Town. 'Café Amigo' disco. Accepts most credit cards.

Moderate:

Burmani Willa, Kadaka tee 62, tel: (372)-2-532-085, 532-260. 8 rooms, 700 EEK. Pre-war villa. Rooms equipped with telephone, radio and TV. Sauna and small indoor pool. Two 40-seat conference rooms; bar. You need a car to stay here, unless you wish to take a taxi (US$4-5) or a bus.

Kannike, Vabaduse pst 108, tel: (372)-2-513-257. Singles 450 EEK, doubles 700 EEK. Nice new hotel in the suburb of Nõmme (ie a fair distance from the centre).

Kelluka, Kelluka tee 11, tel: (372)-2-238-811, 237-398, fax: 245-205. 500

EEK. Small, well-run hotel located in a residential district near Piirita and Lasnamäe. Nice, cosy style. Good for a long stay. You need a car.
Kungla, Kreutzwaldi tänav 23, tel: (372)-630-5325, fax: 630-5315. (Singles 400 EEK, doubles 500 EEK). Seven-storey Soviet-era, partially renovated hotel downtown. Same price range as Piirita, but shabbier.
Mihkli, Endla 23, tel: (372)-2-453-704, fax: 451-767. 28 rooms. (Single room with breakfast 430 EEK). Modest and centrally located. Good value. Has bar, café and souvenir shop.
Peoleo, Pärnu mnt 555, tel: (372)-2-771-801, fax: 771-463. (Singles 650 EEK). A Best Western, Scandinavian style, attractive hotel located outside Tallinn (15 minutes from centre by car), with fine restaurant, gift shop and saunas. A public bus passes Peoleo regularly.
Piirita, Regati 1, tel: (372)-2-238-598, fax: 237-433. (Singles from 430 EEK, doubles 560 EEK). Three-stories, 5km from town centre in the Olympic Yachting Centre (a 20-minute bus ride from the centre of town). Located in woodland by the sea. The best (and most expensive) sauna in Estonia is found at the top.
Silva, Laulu 14, tel: (372)-2-514-990. Guest house.
Hotel Susi, St Peterburi mnt 48, tel: (372)-2-215-541. Doubles 580 EEK. 42 rooms. Offers pool, sauna, restaurant and bar. Comfortable, but far from the centre.
Tallinn, Toompuiestee 27, tel: (372)-2-604-332, fax: 448-607. Well located, but has a gloomy Soviet-era presence. Price reflects its condition. Sold by the Privatization Agency in 1995.

Inexpensive:
Hotel Agnes, Narva mnt 9, tel: (372)-2-438-870. 104 rooms, 208 beds. Single and double rooms. All rooms have shower, TV and radio. Excellent central location. Bar. Affiliated to Estonian Youth Hostels.
Hotel Dorell, Kärnu 39, tel: (372)-2-435-560. Doubles 140 EEK. Two stops by tram from Viru Hotel. Off Narva mnt. Former dormitory. Good value.
EMI, Sütiste tee 21, tel: (372)-2-527-362, 521-611. Doubles 350 EEK. This inexpensive hotel, in the suburb of Mustamäe, has showers shared between rooms. By trolley bus (2 or 3) it's not far to the centre.
Hotel Kajakas, Pärnu mnt 123, tel: (372)-2-555-922, fax: 556-504. Not in the centre, but close to tram-line.
Hotel Kristine, Luha 16, tel: (372)-2-682-000. Located off Pärnu mnt.
Hotel Pääsu, Sõpruse pst 182, tel: (372)-2-520-034. Located in the suburb of Mustamäe. Take trolley-bus 2 or 3 from the department store *(kaubamaja)*.
Hotel Peedu, Võrse 22, tel: (372)-2-528-609. Near Hotel Pääsu. Bathrooms in the hall. Take trolley bus 2 or 3 from the centre (15-20 minutes).
Stroomi, tel: (372)-2-304-200, fax: 304-500. Singles 230 EEK, doubles 380 EEK. Located 3.5km from centre in the district of Kopli, but offers pleasant service and is clean. Offers a bar, solarium, sauna, barber and manicurist.
Hotel Vitamiin, Narva mnt 7, tel: (372)-2-438-585, fax: 432-271. Centrally located. 22 rooms, 45 beds. All rooms with shower, toilet. Some with telephone and TV; bar. Major renovations due for completion in 1995.

Bed and breakfast

In the US, contact: **Home/Host International**, 2445 Park Avenue, Minneapolis, MN 55404, tel: (612) 871-0596, fax: (612) 871-8853.

Baltic Bed and Breakfast, Raekoja plats 17. Organizes accommodations in private homes throughout Tallinn, Rīga, Vilnius and St Petersburg, tel: (372)-2-445-104, fax: 557-630.

Bed & Breakfast, Rasastra Ltd, Sadama 11, near Tallinn harbour, tel/fax: (372)-2-602-091. Arranges B&Bs with families and in apartments in Estonia, Latvia, Lithuania and St Petersburg. Averages US$15/night.

Family Hotel Service, Mere pst. 6, tel: (372)-2-441-187, fax: 557-630.

Estonian Farmers' League's Department of Tourism in Saku. Offers farmstays. Tel: (372)-2-683-410, fax: 771-385, 721-783.

Youth hostels

The Estonian Youth Hostel Association, Liivalaia 2, tel/fax: (372)-2-441-096 or 445-853. Offers hostels in Tallinn, Taevaskoja, Otepää, Virtsu, Klooga and Kabli. In Tallinn the YHA is loosely connected with the centrally located Hostel Agnes at Narva maantee 7, near Hotel Viru and the central post office. The hostel offers pleasant 2-4 bed rooms. If arriving by train, walk to the back of the station and take the tram (trolley) marked Kopli-Kadriorg or Kopli-Ülemiste and get out at the fourth stop. If arriving by bus, walk out the front door of the bus station and upon reaching Tartu maantee, you will see a tram stop. Take either tram going to the centre three stops and you will be minutes from the hostel. The hostel can sometimes be run-down (broken furniture, etc) but the price is reasonable at 60-120 EEK. Another hostel is located in the dormitory at Kuramaa tr 15, tel: 237-781, 327-715, but it is in a bad neighbourhood known for crime. Best to avoid.

The Barn, Viru tn 1, in the heart of the Old Town, tel: 313-853. Opened in 1994. 100 EEK a night.

Camping sites

Sites are open from June 1 to September 1. All are provided with running water, lavatories and cooking facilities.

Kalev, Kloostrimetsa tee 56 A, tel: (372)-2-238-686.

Rannamõisa, Tabasalu, tel: (372)-2-716-332.

Island of Aegna, reached by ferry. 16 cabins.

EAT, DRINK AND BE MERRY

Basic to the Estonian diet is *leib* (bread). The term includes only the wide variety of dark bread found throughout the country. Every region seems to have its own recipe. Differences originate with the grains whose quality is determined not only by the soil and climatic conditions, but also cultivation. *Leib* is served with every meal; there tends to be an almost religious association with it — not only because of the scriptural tenets, but also because deprivation has often been part of the people's history and bread was the essential food that gave some assurance of survival at times of war and plague. Hence, bread is not thrown away. Stale bread reappears as an ingredient in several recipes. For example, a very delicious Estonian dessert is *leiva supp* (bread soup).

In the West, loaves made of bleached flour are also known as bread, but not in Estonia. The variety of breads made with white flour are known as *sai*. Traditionally, *sai* is not a daily indulgence. It is consumed on holidays and special familial occasions, such as birthdays and entertainment of guests. The ultimate *sai* is the *kringel*, a large braided loaf, prepared in the shape of a pretzel and generously filled with raisins and nuts. *Kringel* is central to birthdays and festive holidays, such as Christmas.

The Estonian cuisine can be said to be of the meat and potatoes variety, generally covered with a rich gravy. Pork has traditionally been the basic meat. The peasant could not afford meat, but for Christmas he would try to have a pig to kill for the table. No parts were wasted. The blood was drained and used to prepare *verevorst* (blood sausage). Even the intestines were cleaned out and used as casings for the sausage. Bones and hooves were boiled slowly for hours and the liquid used in an aspic called *sült*. Pork is roasted and served with baked potatoes. On the side, sauerkrat is served. Again, recipes vary according to the region and, on the whole, sauerkraut on a country plate is a delicious experience.

Soups are very popular and tasty. It is safe to say it is always served with the main meal of the day, which is at noon. But the meal is generally started with a course of cold foods, which can consist of a selection from any of the following: the previously mentioned *sült*, served with either vinegar, strong mustard, or horseradish, or all of them; *rosolje*, which is a tasty mix of diced vegetables, including beets, meats, eggs, seasonings, and all of it mixed thoroughly with sour cream; and marinated or smoked eel or other fish, and the ubiquitous *leib*. Some housewives will serve *pirukas* — small pies filled with either meat, carrots or cabbage.

Among vegetables, cucumbers and cabbage dominate. Housewives often have a wonderful recipe for marinating cucumbers and the result is *hapu kurk*. Most people have garden plots so in season fresh vegetables abound.

A favourite national pastime is mushroom picking in the woods and many housewives will serve, in season, delicious dishes featuring mushrooms. They are also conserved and, again, variety is offered by the different kinds of mushrooms found and the different recipes families use.

Native desserts tend to be on the modest side. The humble but tasty *leiva supp* has been mentioned already. Then *kissell* is quite common. It is a clear sweet soup made from a variety of garden berries, usually from redcurrants, often served with *sai*. Because of the universal practice of having kitchen gardens, desserts containing berries, rhubarb or apples are most prevalent. The mouthwatering *tort* (torte), a favourite dessert at parties, is a legacy of the Baltic barons. As a matter of fact, many of the foods found in Estonia today originated in the Baltic barons' kitchens where the Estonian serf served as a kitchen hand.

Beverages traditionally consisted of ale and mead, teas brewed from flowers and plants found in the wild or from one's own garden, and milk. Today, coffee is very popular and it is as certain to be served to you when visiting an Estonian home as it is to hear 'Amen' in church. Along with coffee, the hostess likes to offer cognac or liquor, and often chocolate. All of the latter were imported products that over the years became part of the Estonian table and reflect Tallinn's historic position as a major station for trade routes. Now Tallinn manufactures some of its own, like *Kalev* chocolates and *Vana Tallinn* liquor. In this context, a bit of historical information should be included. The fried meat pattie known in Estonia as *kotlett*, and the world-over as the hamburger, originated in Tallinn at the time of its membership in the Hanseatic League. So, there you are Ronald McDonald! The circle is completed and you have returned to Tallinn!

It is the custom that before one starts to eat, one says to others at the table *Head isu!* The closest translation is *Bon appétit!*

Where to eat and drink

The following list should be used with some caution because most are not yet 'established.' In the last few years, many restaurants, cafés and bars have opened. The number is amazing if you compare the present situation in Tallinn to the Soviet era, when only a few places existed for the tourist in the hotels allocated for them. There doesn't seem to be a street in Tallinn where one cannot stop for refreshment and rest. But because private entrepreneurism is in its infancy, the result is quite uneven. Fine chefs have yet to be trained, and service, albeit greatly improved over the Soviet way of doing things, is still slow. Sometimes a waiter will even display poor or non-existent training by arguing with a customer.

Some restaurants and cafés are filled with smoke, making them intolerable to non-smokers. Ventilation is poor in many restaurants and if the weather is hot, a stop in some restaurants can be a miserable experience. A noticeable effort and improvement in many restaurants is the attention paid to bathroom facilities: no longer need one struggle with oneself should nature call.

Restaurants

Aj Sha Nj Ya, Mere pst 6. Authentic oriental-tasting food. Mid-range prices. Could spruce up its appearance. Offers take-aways. Hrs: noon-midnight. Tel: (372)-2-441-997.

Ariran, Telliskivi 35. Cozy Korean restaurant. Delicious spicy food. Hrs: 11am-10pm.

Astoria, Vabaduse väljak 5 (Freedom Square). Beautifully restored luxury à la carte restaurant but service does not match. Main attraction is the live cabaret and music performances in the evening. Casino. Hrs: 1pm-7pm, 9pm-2am. Reservations, tel: (372)-2-448-462.

Carina, Piirita tee 26. Located on the main road to Piirita, a few kilometres from the Old Town. Stylish and modern overlooking the Bay of Tallinn. Good food and service. Live music on occasion. Expensive. Hrs: noon-midnight. Tel: (372)-2-237-475.

Controvento, Vene 12. Tallinn's first Italian restaurant whose owner hails from Genoa. Has two levels; the bar has more ambience than the dining room. Ingredients imported from Italy and the chef is Italian. Large portions and there are many of them. Good service. Decent food. Reasonable prices. Pizzas start at 30 EEK. Tel: (372)-2-440-470. Hrs: 6.30pm-11.00pm. Closed Mon.

Eeslitall, Dunkri 4. Top-quality. Everyone's favourite — recommended by nearly all travel guides to Tallinn. Finnish owned, Eeslitall (the donkey's stall) is set in a medieval building in the city centre. English menu, slow service. On the third floor a cocktail bar offers drinks until late. The second floor houses a jazz café. Popular cellar bar, open until 6am daily. Reservations for restaurant are recommended. Tel: (372)-2-446-033.

Elysee. 2nd floor of the Olümpia Hotel, Liivalaia 33. Newly renovated, pleasant atmosphere; one of the best, it offers good food and service. Live music. Recommended if you absolutely need to eat in an hotel. Café downstairs has good pastries. Hrs: noon-midnight. Tel: (372)-2-631-5891.

Galaxy, top of the Estonian TV tower, Kloostrimetsa 58A. A Western venture. The Soviet army tried to seize this tower during the ill-fated putsch in Moscow in August 1991, but failed. Offers fantastic views of Tallinn, the Gulf of Finland and Piirita. Live music in the evenings. Ticket for tower 22 kroon. Hrs: 12.30pm-2am. Tel: (372)-2-238-250.

Gloria, Müürivahe 2. An elegant restaurant evoking the pre-war era in the Old Town wall near Vabaduse väljak. Offers good food and usually good service with live music. Expensive, but recommended for its atmosphere. Hrs: noon-midnight, Sun noon-6pm. Tel: (372)-2-446-950.

Gnoom, Viru 2. Located on the main street of the Old Town, it offers a meal in an elegant medieval townhouse. Hrs: noon-midnight. Tel: (372)-2- 442-288.

Juta, Kiriku plats 1, on Tompea Hill. In a vaulted cellar of the *Kunstimuuseum* (Estonia Art Museum). Great fish, good food. Only restaurant we found which plays music from 'Phantom of the Opera' and 'Les Miserables'. Tel: (372)-2-452-262. Recommended.

Karikas, Kuninga 3. Located in the centre of the Old Town, near City Hall. Continental cuisine; moderately priced. Tel: (372)-2-446-665.

Kuldne Kotkas, Nunne 2. Pleasant restaurant and bar in the Old Town. One of Tallinn's best kept secrets. Their excellent food is à la carte — dinner with soup and entree about 50-60 EEK.

Kullassepa Kelder, Kullasepa 7/9/11, off the Old Town Square. Good food and service in a vaulted cellar. Beer in cellar and on ground floor. Moderately priced. Hrs: noon-midnight. Tel: (372)-2-442-240.

Kuller, Kallaku 1 (by St Alexander Nevsky Cathedral). Here one can enjoy an inexpensive hearty meal in a wonderful old building on Toompea with a roaring fire in winter. Estonian beer served. Hrs: 11am-9pm. Good light meals in warm country-style atmosphere.

Lembitu, Kloostri tee 6. Located at the Piirita river. Beautiful, new restaurant, owned by a Canadian-Estonian firm which also operates the Motel Peoleo on the Pärnu maantee. Overpriced, but with a wonderful view and excellent service. Hrs: noon-midnight. Tel: (372)-2-237-379.

Linda, Palace Hotel, Vabaduse väljak, ground floor. Fine restaurant with an excellent assortment of wines and liqueurs. Very expensive. Hrs: noon-midnight. Tel: (372)-2-443-461.

Little China, Vene Street 30. Opened in 1994. The best Chinese food in Tallinn. Nice surroundings, exotic cocktail menu, good food and very expensive. Tel: (372)-6-313-126.

Maharaja, Raekoja plats 13. Good but pricey Indian cuisine. It was one of the first ethnic restaurants to open in the Baltics. Excellent service. Credit cards accepted. Tel: (372)-2-444-367.

Mereneitsi, mezzanine of Hotel Viru, Viru väljak 4. Has a Scandinavian interior and large windows overlooking nearby park. Food is expensive but prepared well. May be closed in winter months.

22nd Floor (of the Hotel Viru), the restaurant here has reasonably good food, but the best thing is the wonderful views of the Old Town and the harbour. Tel: (372)-2-650-1750.

Mõõkkala (Swordfish), Rüütli 16/18. A seafood restaurant in the cellar of medieval Tallinn's executioner's house. Takes credit cards. Tel: (372)-2-666-886.

Nord, Rataskaevu 3/5. Housed on several floors in an Old Town dwelling, it offers seafood on the ground floor, *Sanjay's* — Chinese and Indian on the second floor (dinner for two at around 400 EEK) and the *Rebaseurg* (Fox Lair) bar in its vaulted cellar. Hrs: 9am-midnight. Tel: (372)-2-441-152.

Nunne Kelder, Nunne 4. Located in a cellar next to the children's theatre. Offers fine food and drinks at reasonable prices. A good place for lunch or dinner. Order from the bar as you enter and your food will be brought to your table. Recommended. Hrs: noon-midnight.

Olematu Rüütel, Kiriku poik 4a. Beautifully designed Scandinavian-style restaurant on Toompea, opened in 1994. Fine service, well-prepared food. A modern sauna can be rented for parties, and a small (4 room) hotel is located on the second floor. Hrs: noon-10pm. Tel: (372)-6-313-827.

Õlletuba, Vana Turg 1. Located on the top floor of an old warehouse near Town Hall, it offers Estonian beer and local dishes served in a traditional Estonian setting. Recommended. Hrs: noon-10pm. Tel: (372)-2-443-727.

Peking, Kopli 2b. Open daily from noon-11pm. Tel: (372)-2-601-819. Poor food, mediocre service.
Piirita, Merivälja tee 5. The view of the bay gets the highest recommendation. Continental cuisine, bar, dance floor and live music. Hrs: noon-midnight. Tel: (372)-2-238-102.
Pizzeria Margareta, in the Palace Hotel, Vabaduse väljak 3. Western-style pizza hut, with reasonable prices and service. Hrs: 11am-11pm. Tel: (372)-2-666-702.
Reeder, Vene tänav 33. Good food in cozy atmosphere, downstairs bar for beer and pizza. Tel: (372)-2-446-518.
Roosikrantsi, Roosikrantsi 1; at Vabaduse väljak. Offers well-prepared dishes but service can be sporadic and disinterested. Expensive. Reservations. Not recommended. Hrs: 8am-midnight. Tel: (372)-2-446-536.
Sub Monte, Rüütli tänav 4, behind the Niguliste church. Overpriced, stuffy restaurant located in a vaulted medieval cellar. Good food in Old Town atmosphere. Hrs: noon-11pm. Tel: (372)-2-666-871.
Tiina, Nunne 18. Offers Estonian fare and will give a 10% discount to customers wearing a national costume. Has musical programs featuring Estonian singers or folk dancers. Live music after 8.30pm. Tel: (372)-2-602-371, 602-372.
Toomkooli, Toomkooli 13, by the Cathedral on Toompea. One of Tallinn's best restaurants. Offers a beautiful view, especially in the summer in the open-air café. Reasonably priced. Reservations recommended. Hrs: noon-11pm. Tel: (372)-2-446-613.
Vana Saku, Peoleo Motel, Pärnu mnt 555. Unmarked restaurant. Decent food away from the city. Pleasant surroundings and uncommonly friendly service. Live piano music sometimes. Tel: (372)-2-556-566.

Fast food

Bistro at 2 locations: Narva mnt 6 and Estonia pst 5. Swiss joint venture. Relatively good pasta, salads, soups and other light food at reasonable prices.
Hõbekass, Harju 9, Old Town. Offers substantial meals. Great for lunch but is often smoke-filled. Tel: (372)-2-443-293.
Peetri Pizza, a chain with locations at: Liivalaia 40, tel: (372)-2-446-378 (restaurant and take-away); Kopli 2c, tel: (372)-2-449-422 (restaurant and take-away); Lai 4 (Old Town, has couple tables); Pärnu mnt 22 (to go); Pargi 8, tel: (372)-2-232-077. Western style fast food. Ten types of pizza, salad, ice-cream and beer. Quick and inexpensive.

Cafés

Bogapott, Pikk Jalg 9 at Toompea. Serves Finnish coffee and delicious pastries in an historic building at the top of Pikk Jalg. Attractive with patio. Hrs: 10am-8pm. Tel: (372)-2-443-220.
Café at the Viru Hotel, Viru väljak 4. Conveniently located on the ground floor of the Hotel. Pleasant, expensive (for Tallinn) with relatively good food. Coffee, cakes, light food. Will probably close soon. Hrs: 10am-11pm.

Dominican Kohvik, Vene 16. Opened in the summer of 1994. Trendy, spacious bar/café with huge fireplace.
Fat Margaret's, Pikk 70. Sandwiches in a medieval courtyard.
Gnoom, Viru 2. Upstairs, quaint place to refresh.
Harju, Suur-Karja 4. Pleasant with tasty pastries. Hrs: 9am-9pm. Tel: (372)-2-449-960.
Maiasmokk, Pikk tänav 16, Old Town. Tallinn's oldest café. A *fin-de-siècle* coffee shop, à la Vienna, located in the building of the oldest chocolate producer in Estonia (founded in 1864). Good coffee and pastry. Often crowded. Hrs: 11am-10pm. Tel: (372)-2-601-396.
Mary, Vene 1. A pleasant new café with a fireplace. Excellent pastries and coffee. Friendly, English-speaking service. Piano music some evenings. Located at the top of Vene tänav just five minutes from Hotel Viru. Recommended.
Neitsitorn, Lühike Jalg 9A at Toompea. Mulled wine and snacks in one of the most interesting settings in Tallinn. The 'Virgin Tower' offers food and snacks on three levels in a medieval tower in the Old Town wall. In the basement there is a classic hot wine café which is a must-see for all visitors. In the summer one can dine outside the Old Town wall. Hrs: 11am-10pm. Tel: (372)-2-440-896 or 440-514.
Pärl, Pikk tänav 2. Renovated modernistic café in the Old Town. Plenty of room. Hrs: 9am-9pm. Tel: (372)-2-443-355.
Pegasus, Harju 1, Old Town. On two floors with a spiral staircase. Formerly a café for Estonian writers and continues to feature contemporary art on its walls. Offers former Soviet Union memorabilia along with its coffee and cakes. More of a hangout for forlorn youths. Hrs: 10am-11pm. Tel: (372)-2-440-807.
Restko, Lai 29. Snacks, drinks, lunch. Hrs: 10am-8pm. Tel: (372)-2-609-728.
Salvaator, Pikk 5. New, clean with well-stocked deli in front and coffee shop in back.
Vegan, Uus 22. Old Town. Vegetarian café.
Vesiveski, Suur-Karja 17/19; large windows add a touch to an otherwise ordinary place. Self-service with excellent coffee and cakes but woefully few places to sit. At a busy intersection near the cinema Sõprus.
Wiiralti Kohvik, Vabaduse väljak 8. Clean, good coffee and pastries.
Wimbledon, Karli pst 2, next to the tennis courts just minutes from Hotel Palace. Highly recommended. Burning fireplace in winter; nice view, convenient; excellent coffee and cakes. Bar in front as well. Best place to get an early coffee or tea. Full meals available.

Bars

Some have nice atmosphere, but many, especially cellar bars, can be noisy and filled with smoke and, during hot weather, stuffy inside due to poor ventilation.

Arabella, Dunkri 3. Refreshments for children.
Bonnie and Clyde, at the Olümpia Hotel, Liivalaia 33. A favourite of business folk.

Corrida, Vabaduse väljak 5, next to the Palace Hotel. For the black coffee and cognac set.

Bel Air, Vana-Viru 14. Across from the Viru Hotel. Cocktails and dancing to DJ's choices. Hrs: 6pm-midnight Sun-Thurs, 6pm-4am Fri/Sat. Tel: (372)-6-312-699

Eeslitall, Dunkri 4. Highly recommended. A cozy bar on the third floor. A vaulted cellar offers live music nightly from 10pm. Cover charge after 8pm. Tickets: 10-15 EEK depending on the band playing. Hrs: open until 6am. Tel: (372)-2-448-033.

George Brownes Irish Pub, Harju 6, Old Town. A lavish two-floor Irish style pub in the Business Centre. Wonderful piano bar on second floor. Serves Guinness and a wide variety of drinks. Expensive. Hrs: 3pm-midnight. Tel: (372)-2-443-742.

Gosser Beer Pub, Rahukohtu 2, behind the Cathedral on Toompea. A modern, pleasant bar which offers Austria's Gosser beer on draft. Also offers meals.

Harjuvärava mägi, Outdoor café. Open in the summer and located in an old bandstand across from Kiek in de Kök. Has live bands and a pleasant atmosphere.

Hell Hunt, Pikk 39. Means 'The Gentle Wolf'. A crowded, smoky Irish pub in the heart of the Old Town; burning fireplace, food served. Popular with the young crowd. Hrs: 10am-3am.

Karikabaar, Kuninga 3. Friendly atmosphere in the basement of a medieval house in the Old Town. Fri/Sat disco. Mostly Russian clientele. Hrs: 1pm-1am. Tel: (372)-2-441-780.

Karja kelder, Väike-Karja 1. Renovated by the Saku brewing company, this venerable cellar beerhall serves all kinds of Saku beer and food. In the heart of the Old Town. Hrs: 10am-midnight. Tel: (372)-2- 440-280.

Kuldne kotkas, Nunne 8. Pleasant bar; opened in 1993; a 5-minute walk from the Baltic Railway Station. Warm food served from an à la carte menu. Hrs: 8am-10pm, Sat/Sun noon-10pm.

Lucky Luke's, Mere pst 20, behind the Linna hall. Large drinking, eating and dancing place on the water in the port area. Small casino downstairs. Nice view of the Gulf of Finland. Only gets going after 9pm. Open to 3am.

Mündibaar, Mündi 3. First bar opened in Tallinn. Located in an old cellar. Popular among young Russians and Estonians. Hrs: 4pm-2am. Tel: (372)-2-446-741.

Othello, E Vilde tee, at the trolley bus stop 'Kaja' in Mustamäe. Packed with 'mafia' boys, 'businessmen', 'working girls' and more interesting real-life types; a bit like Chicago in the 1930s. Patrolled by 'Barricuda Security'. 50 EEK to get in.

Rebaseurg (Fox Burrow), Rataskaevu 3/5. The deepest cellar in town, dark and medieval. Offers an intimate bar with small disco floor. Hrs: 1pm-3am. Tel: (372)-2-448-591.

Regatt, Merivälja tee 1, Piirita. Frequented by young people, primarily for dancing; disco on weekends. Tel: (372)-2-238-359.

Shoti Klubi, Uus 31. Tallinn's Scottish bar. Beautiful surroundings — a fine outdoor café in summer. Hrs: 10am-6pm.

Sky Bar and Casino, Palace Hotel, Vabaduse väljak 3. 50 EEK entry for floor show. Hrs: 9pm-3am. Tel: (372)-2-443-461. Frequented by business folk. The head of the local Rīga *mafia* was murdered here in 1993.
Tolli Baar, Pikk 66. A pleasant, quiet bar which serves good food next to the ancient Great Coastal Gate at the edge of the old city. Estonian beer available. Inexpensive. Hrs: 10am-8pm.
Tooro Pub/Bar, Suur-Karja 18. Lively pub; cover charge for live music. Open to 6am. Unfortunately, pick-pockets are known to operate here late at night.
Von Krahli teatri baar, Rataskaevu 10. Warm beer, live music and dancing. Live bands include jazz, rock, blues, swing and folk. Many young peope. Profits from bar support the theatre upstairs. In the summer offers an outdoor café. Hrs: 4pm-1am, Fri/Sat 4pm-4am. Tel: (372)-2-446-462.

Night clubs

Café Amigo, Viru Väljak 4, in the Viru Hotel, lower level. Opened in late 1994, the 'café' is actually a beautiful nightclub which has quickly become Tallinn's most popular. Here you'll find Estonians of all ages, Russians, Finns, Scandinavians, Germans and all manner of others rubbing shoulders and dancing. Don't miss the 'Ariba Ariba' girl pouring tequila shots into unsuspecting customers who don't realize it's more powerful than vodka. The 'Marguerita' is the drink of choice. Live bands.
Eestli Tall Cellar, Dunkri 6. Live music every night of the week — rock, blues and jazz. A steady favourite since it opened five years ago.
Lucky Luke's, Mere pst 20, behind the Town Hall or Linnahall near the port. Popular disco with young people. Open until 3am.
Othello, E Vilde tee, at the trolley bus stop 'Kaja' in Mustamae. Packed with 'mafia' boys, 'businessmen', 'working girls' and more interesting real-life types; a bit like Chicago in the 1930s. Patrolled by 'Barricuda Security'. 50 EEK to get in.
Piraat, Regati 1, tel: 237-043. In the Olympic Centre at Piirita. A fun disco with live bands on the weekends. Very popular with people younger than 30. Open until 2am. You'll need a taxi to get there.
Silva, Raudtee 64, in the suburb of Nômme. Small, but popular disco for young people. Open until the wee hours. You'll need a taxi to get there.

SHOPPING

Shopping is gradually beginning to resemble the rest of Scandinavia, but the prices are lower. Opinion is expressed that, of the three Baltic countries, Tallinn's commerce is the most Westernized. Among the bargains are handcrafted goods, such as sweaters, socks, scarves, wooden implements and leather goods. Alcohol and tobacco are noticeably inexpensive.

Most of the stores are located in the Old Town and outlying streets, and new ones open almost daily. Hours are usually from 10am to 7pm. The Continental practice of closing for lunch is observed in places.

Usually this happens between 1pm and 2pm. Many shops close early on Saturday. Prices are noticeably higher in Tallinn than in other towns.

You can pick up several souvenir knick-knacks at the main Post Office opposite Hotel Viru. It carries postcards, stamps, maps and guides at prices lower than elsewhere in town. Keep this place in mind when making a phone call as it is less expensive here than calling from hotels.

If time allows you only one stop shopping, head for the Tallinn Kaubamaja (department store) behind Viru Hotel at Gonsiori 2. Formerly, under Soviet central planning it was pitifully undersupplied and overstaffed, but now it's stocked with everything, including car parts, and is clean and pleasant.

The only 24-hour store, 'Pink Panther,' Uus tän 7, is a mini-market with an extensive selection of alcohol.

Artworks and crafts

A-Galerii, Hõbusepea 8.
Art Chamber, Pikk jalg 5.
Deco, Koidula 11.
Diele Galerii, Raekoja plats 14.
Draakoni, Pikk 18; concentrates on print and graphic work, by far the strongest aspect of Estonian art.
Galerii Art Maiden, Rüütli 18.
Galerii G, Narva mnt 2.
Galerii Sammas, Vabaduse väljak 6.
Galeriis Tokko and Arrak, Raekoja plats 14.
Hansa Alt, Sauna 10.
Keraamika Ateljee, Pikk 33. Ceramics.
Kunstihoone Galerii (Art Hall Gallery), Vabaduse väljak 6; a State exhibition gallery that often shows challenging works.
Liivakell, Liivalaia 12. Sells quality native art: paintings, glass and metalwork.
Lühikese Jala Galerii, Lühike jalg 6.
Luum, Harju 13.
Matkamaja, Raekoja plats 14.
Molen, Viru 19.
Munkadetagunetorn, Müürivahe 58.
Mustpeade Galerii, Pühavaimu 9.
Russkaja Galerii, Endla 8.
Sammas, Vabaduse väljak 6.
Tallart, Aia 12.
Tallinna Kunstihoone (Art Hall of Tallinn), Vabaduse väljak 8.
Vaal, Väike-Karja 12; exhibits only the elite. Check it out.

Antiques

There are a number of antique dealers in the Old Town, including shops at Viru 16, Kohtu 6 and Rateskaevu 16. Should you buy an antique, save the sales slip. Purchases of things dated before 1950 (for books before 1945) require a special permit to leave the country. These can be obtained from the Cultural Values Export Board, located at Sakala 14, tel: (372)-2-448-501, 446-578. The process can take a couple of hours.

Books

Foreign language books are available, as are quite a variety of maps. At bookstores you will find nice postcards and posters.

Homeros, Mündi 3, tel: (372)-2-631-1059.
Lugemisvara, Harju 1.
R&E Bookstore, Pikk 2; foreign language & Estonian books, tel: (372)-2-446-275.
Rahvaraamat, Pärnu mnt 10.
Viruvärava, Viru 23. German books and maps dominate foreign issues.

Photo and film

Agfa, Narva mnt 18.
Estonia, Narva mnt 14.
Filmari, Suur-Karja 9.
Fotoluks, Vana-Viru 3.

Records

Music is a universal language and here you can buy it at bargain prices. The high regard Estonians hold for choral music is evident, and compositions by Veljo Tormis are valued.

All in 1, Pääsukese 1.
Kapellmuusika, Mere pst 20.
Lasering, Pärnu mnt 38.
Muusik, Kaarli pst 3.

Sporting goods

AG, Raekoja Plats 4.
Bensport, Tartu mnt 7.
EVO, 'Kalev' Pärnu mnt 44.
Tennis Shop, Kaarli pst 2.
West-Sport, Väike-Karja.

Other

Stockmann, the first Western department store in Tallinn. Finnish. Located in the Viru Hotel courtyard. Sells clothes, cosmetics, toys and household goods. Prices lower than in Finland.
Tallinna Kaubamaja (The Tallinn Department Store), Gonsiori 2, near Viru Hotel. This store was completely transformed in the spring of 1994 from a dingy, Soviet-era, poorly-stocked store to a modern department store that could be located anywhere in the West.

TALLINN DIRECTORY

Useful telephone numbers

Airlines

Estonian Air: 446-382, 440-295.
Finnair: 423-538, 311-455.
SAS: 212-553, 6-312-240.
Lufthansa: 6-388-888, 215-557, 444-037.

Bus station: 422-549.

Emergencies

Fire: 001.
Police: 002.
Medical: 003.

Express Hotline

Free information 24-hours a day. English spoken. Shop, hotel, taxi, transport and company information: 6-313-322.

Harbour terminal: 601-960.

Hotels

Olümpia: 6-315-333.
Palace: 444-761.
Peoleo: 771-801.
Piirita: 238-615.
Viru: 6-301-390.

Railway station: 446-756.

Tourist boards

Estonian Tourist Board: 450-486.
Tallinn City Tourist Board: 666-959 or 448-886.

Beauticians and barbers

Stylish hair care, such as in other European towns, is possible in Tallinn. Every hotel has a beauty parlour and a barber. Appointments are advisable.

Hotel Olümpia, Liivalaia 33, tel: (372)-2-602-216 (beautician), 602-288 (hairdresser).
Hotel Viru, Viru väljak 4, tel: (372)-2-650-889.
Palace, Vabaduse väljak 3, tel: (372)-2-444-761.
Tallinn Service House (*Teenindusmaja*), the huge five-storey modern structure across from the Viru Hotel car park. 2nd floor. 20 beauticians and hair cutters. All quite good and prices are very reasonable!

Beauty parlours and barbers are dispersed all over town. Unless one comes recommended, you won't know the quality of work. One way of being steered to a good stylist is to ask an acquaintance you have met, especially if she or he has hair styled to your liking.

Car rentals and driving

Cars are available at Tallinn's airport, ferry terminal, at the harbour, and major hotels with or without a driver. Advance reservation is recommended. In general, car rentals are expensive as most of them are based on German cars.

Foreigners must have a valid licence and passport and, generally, are required to be over 22 years of age. Driving is on the right hand side of the road. Speed limit on open roads is 90km/h; in populated areas it is decreased to 50km/h. Front seat belts are required to be worn by law. Never drive after drinking; no level of alcohol is tolerated by the police.

Driving in Tallinn, beware of the trams which run along the centre of the road. When trams stop to discharge their passengers, all other traffic must halt. Observe the international 'No stopping' and 'No parking' signs. Don't leave your car unlocked and never leave valuables in it. You must pay an entrance fee to drive in Tallinn's Old Town. Guard posts are set up at all entrances where you can pay.

Though Tallinn does not have parking meters, you must pay to park in the centre of town. Buy your ticket from the booth or ticket machine near the car park and place it behind the windscreen inside for all to see. If the police spot a car parked without a visible ticket they will lock its wheel. It'll be unlocked after a fine is paid. Car theft is rising. Try to park your car overnight in a paid-for car park. Some car parks: by the Harbour Terminal and airport, under the viaduct on Pärnu maantee, 64 Linnu tee, 29 Sõle, at the Hotel Peedu, Tammsaare tee and Kadaka tee.

Consult the traffic police about problems: **Tallinna Liikluspolitsei**, Lastekodu 31 (trams 2 and 4 take you there; get off at Autobussijaam), tel: (372)-2-445-450.

The following are some car rental agencies:

Avis, at Tallinn Airport, Lennujaama tee 2; tel: (372)-2-215-602, fax: 212-735. Also at tel: 6-388-222.

Balt Impex, Liivalaia 12; tel: (372)-2-683-722, fax: 683-971.

Balt Link Ltd, Tartu 13; tel: (372)-2-421-003.

Baltic Limousine Service, Vabaduse väljak 10b, 6th fl; tel: (372)-2-438-838, fax: 438-471.

Europcar Interrent, Mere pst 6; tel: (372)-2-441-637, 449-196, fax: 431-667. Tallinn Airport; tel: (372)-2-219-031.

Finest Auto, Pärnu mnt 22; tel: (372)-2-666-719.

Europcar, Tallinn Airport; tel: (372)-2-219-031, or **Refit Ltd**, Mere pst 6, EE0001; tel: 441-637, 449-196, fax: 431-667.

Hertz, Tartu mnt 13; tel: (372)-2-421-003 or 424-254, fax: 450-893.
J Mägi & Co, Veimeri 1-19, EE0038; tel: (372)-2-341-217, mobtel (372)-2-372-8-25-248-355. Offers cars with chauffeur.
Roadrunner Estring, Paldiski mnt 135, EE0035; tel: (372)-2-771-524. Offers some cars with chauffeur.

Chemists/Pharmacies

Tõnismae Apteek (Pharmacy), Tõnismagi 5. Prescriptions filled Monday through Friday, closed Sat & Sun. Night service. Has an information desk about kinds of medicine available in city pharmacies. Tel: (372)-2-441-813.
Linnaapteek (City Pharmacy), Pärnu mnt 10; tel: (372)-2-442-262.
Puiestee Apteek, Rävala pst 7; tel: (372)-2-449-572.
Vanaturu apteek (Old Market Pharmacy), Vene 1.
Suur-Pärnu Apteek, Pärnu mnt 76.

Churches

Estonia has traditionally been predominantly Lutheran and the majority of churches are, therefore, of that denomination.
Toomkirik (Dome Church), Toom-Kooli 6 at Toompea, Evangelical-Lutheran.
Jaani kirik (St John's Church), Vabaduse väljak, Evangelical-Lutheran.
Kaarli kirik (St Charles' Church), Toompea 10, Evangelical-Lutheran.
Pühavaimu kirik (Holy Ghost Church), Pühavaimu 2, Evangelical-Lutheran, English language worship service on Sundays at 3pm.
Katariina Kirik (St Catherine's Roman Catholic Church), Vene 18.
Oleviste kirik (St Olaf's Church), Lai 50, Evangelist-Baptist.
7 Päeva Adventisti kirik (7th Day Adventist), Merepuiestee 3. The Methodist Congregation worships here until their own church building is constucted.
Aleksander Nevski Katedraal (St Alexander Nevsky Cathedral), Lossi plats 10 at Toompea, Russian Orthodox.

Complaints

If service is unacceptable to you, complain to the management or to the tourist bureau, Tallinn City Tourist Office, Raekoja plats 18; tel: (372)-2-666-959 or 448-886, fax: 441-221.

Conference services

Hotel reservations, catering, transportation, simultaneous and consecutive translations, recording, minutes, and other conference-related matters can be booked with FRENS Ltd, in Tallinn; tel: (372)-2-446-987, fax: 441-932.

Florists

There are many florists downtown. Both cut flowers and potted plants can be purchased and you can order bouquets, arrangements and wreaths. Nice florist shops are located near *Raekoja plats* (Town Hall Square), on Mündi, Vene, and Vana-Viru streets as well as on Saiakäik.

A very colourful sight is provided by the flower vendors along the road to the Viru Gate and they offer a large variety of flowers. Near Tallinn Kaubamaja is another stretch of flower vendors.

Guides and interpreters

You can hire your own tour guide at:
Tallinna Turismi Büroo (The Tallinn Travel Bureau), Toompuiestee 17A; tel: (372)-2-666-007 or 451-569.
Service Bureau, Viru Hotel, Viru väljak 4; tel: (372)-2-652-080.
Service Bureau, Palace Hotel, Vabaduse väljak 3; tel: (372)-2-443-461. They also can provide interpreters and secretaries.

Laundry

Hotels offer laundry and dry-cleaning services. Coin-operated laundries are practically non-existent and service is slow in laundry and dry-cleaning establishments.

Libraries

Eesti Rahvusraamatukogu (The National Library of Estonia), at Tõnismagi. Open Sun-Fri; tel: (372)-2-444-796. It is one of the largest in Estonia. In addition to Estonian books, it has a large collection of books in Russian and other foreign languages. Foreign newspapers and magazines are available in the reading room. Exhibits are shown in the lobby.
Teaduste Akadeemia Raamatukogu (The Library of the Academy of Sciences), Rävala puiestee 10, open Mon-Sat; tel: (372)-2-443-916. The library has over 3.4 million volumes and it is the foremost research library in the country. It has sections on literature, science, history, natural sciences and technology. It also has a 500,000 item 'Baltica' collection.
A H Tammsaare nim Tallinna keskraamatukogu (The A H Tammsaare Central Library of Tallinn), Estonia puiestee 8. The Lending Department in the main building is open Mon-Sat; tel: (372)-2-443-245; The Reference Room is open daily; tel: (372)-2-441-286; The Foreign Literature Lending Department and Pelguranna Branch Library are located at Sõle 47A; tel: (372)-2-494-925; Music Library and Mustamäe III Branch Library are located at Sõpruse puiestee 186; tel: (372)-2-526-725; Pääsküla Branch Library, Rannaku puiestee 10; tel: (372)-2-518-019; Piirita Branch Library, Merivälja tee 24; tel: (372)-2-237-532; Fr Tuglas Branch Library, Õie 14; tel: (372)-2-511-142.

Lost property

Leiubüroo (Lost and Found), Narva maantee 31; open Mon-Fri; tel: (372)-2-430-795. For things left on trams and buses, ask at tram and bus terminals. The chances of recovering your lost item are slim.

Markets

Kadaka Turg (Kadaka Market), in a huge former greenhouse in the district of Mustamäe. (Trolley bus N° 1 from the Tallinn Department Store). Thousands of tourists now descend on this flea market for everything from icons and Soviet army mementos, to blue jeans and country handicrafts. A must-see!
Nõmme turg (Nõmme Marketplace), Turu plats 6; open daily except Monday.
Tööstuskaupade turg (Fleamarket), Paldiski maantee 80A; open Sat and Sun.

Medical care

Most of Estonia's hospitals and clinics are not up to Western standards, but the ones visitors go to are good and your bill will be inexpensive. Should you become ill or suffer an accident, your hotel will get you a doctor. Emergency help is available 24-hours a day. **For emergency medical help dial: 003**. For emergency care and qualified medical service, use the following facilities:

Keskhaigla (Central Hospital), Ravi 18. In the city centre. Also at Sütiste tee 10.
Kiirabihaigla (Emergency Medical Centre), Sütiste 19. Located in the suburb of Mustamäe.
Estonian Finnish Medical Centre, Ehitajate tee 137, EE0035. Buses 16, 26, 46, 47; trolleys: 6, 7. 24-hour on-call doctors. Private clinic.
Dental, Toompuiestee 4; tel: 6-311-222. Open Mon-Fri, 8am-8pm. For emergencies go to *Kiirabihaigla* listed above.
Baltic Medical Partners, at Olümpia Hotel, 4th floor, and Toompuiestee 4, 2nd floor; tel: (372)-2-602-200, 602-201, 666-009.

Museums

Adamson-Ericu Museum, 3 Luhike jalg, open Wed-Sun 11am-6pm. Opened in 1993, it displays the paintings, leatherwork and metalwork of the Estonian artist Adamson-Eric (1902-1968).
Ajaloomuuseum (History Museum), located in the Old Town, Pikk tänav 17, open Thur-Tues 11am-6pm; tel: (372)-2-443-446 and 602-163. A permanent collection of Estonia's early history based on the holdings of the Estonian Provincial Museum that was founded in 1864. It is housed in the Great Guild Hall, built in 1410, which is one of the finest examples of secular Gothic architecture in Tallinn. The collection features Estonian fine art from the 19th century to 1940.
Dominiiklaste klooster (Dominican Monastery), in the Old Town, Vene 16, open in the summer 11.00am-4.30pm; tel: (372)-2-441-829. The remains of the Gothic monastery hold a collection of medieval stone carvings.
Kiek in de Kök, in the Old Town, Komandandi tee 1, open Tue, Wed, Fri, 10.30am-5.30pm; tel: (372)-2-446-686. History of Tallinn's fortification in the tallest cannon tower in Tallinn, built in 1475-83. Its name is derived from the Low German 'peep into the kitchen'.
Kunstimuuseum (Fine Art Museum). Temporarily at Kiriku Plats 1, on Toompea, while the palace at Kadriorg is undergoing renovations. Only a small

part of the collection is exhibited at the museum's temporary home, an 18th century building that was the Foreign Ministry building 1920-1940, and the National Library 1948-1992. The Museum's hours: Wed-Sun, 11am-6pm; tel: (372)-2-449-139. For guided tours: 449-340.

Linnamuuseum (City Museum), in the Old Town, Vene tänav 17, open Wed-Mon 10.30am-6.00pm; tel: (372)-2-445-856 and 441-829. The collection, representing Tallinn's history, was founded in 1937. The building is a medieval merchant's private home.

Loodusmuuseum (Natural History Museum), in the Old Town, Lai tänav 29, open Wed-Mon 10.00am-5.50pm; tel: (372)-2-444-223. Contains a permanent exhibit of Estonian wildlife and countryside. Established in 1941.

Maarjamäe Loss (The Palace of Maarjamägi), northeastern end of town, on Piirita tee 56, open Wed-Sun, 11am-5pm; tel: (372)-2-237-071. A permanent exhibit of Estonia's modern history. Its exhibits include particularly fine portrayals of the 1905 Revolution, World War I in Estonia and the events of the independence period, 1918-1940. The neo-Gothic limestone summer palace, built for Adjutant General Orlov-Davydov in 1874, sits on a bluff by the sea. A must-see. The exhibits are good.

Meremuuseum (Maritime Museum), Pikk tänav 70, open Wed-Sun 10am-6pm; tel: (372)-2-601-803. The collection, started in 1935, is an exhibit of Estonia's shipping and fishing history. It is housed in the imposing cannon tower *Paks Margareeta* (Fat Margaret), built in 1510-31.

Niguliste Kiriku Muuseum (St Nicholas' Church Museum), in the Old Town, Niguliste 13, hours vary; tel: (372)-2-445-989 or 449-911. The most important works on display are the high altar executed by Hermen Rode from Lübeck, the fragment of the canvas *Danse macabre* by Bernt Notke, and the altar of St Anthony by Nichel Sittow.

Peetri majamuuseum (Peter I's Cottage), east of town, at Kadriorg, Mäekalda 2, open daily in the summer 11am-5pm; tel: (372)-2-425-480. Closed Monday and Tuesday. A simple Dutch cottage built to lodge the Czar when he came to inspect the progress of the palace's construction.

Raekelder (Town Hall Cellar), Raekoja plats, open Wed-Sun 10.30am-5.30pm; tel: (372)-2-441-829. Exhibit of the history of the City Council.

Raevangla (Old Town Prison), Raekoja tänav 4/6, open Thu-Tue 10.30am-5.30pm; tel: (372)-2-448-767.

Rocca al Mare Vabaõhumuuseum (Rocca al Mare Open-Air Museum), western end of town, Vabaõhumuuseumi tee 12, open daily in the summer 10am-8pm; admission into the buildings, Wed-Sun 10am-8pm; tel: (372)-2-559-176.

A H Tammsaare Memoriaalmuusem (A H Tammsaare Museum), east of centre, Koidula 12A, open Wed-Mon 11am-6pm; tel: (372)-2-427-208 and 426-300. The last home of the novelist, A H Tammsaare. Contains exhibits of his books, letters, manuscripts, etc.

Tarbekunstimuusem (Museum of Applied Art), Lai tänav 17, open Wed-Sun, 11am-6pm; tel: (372)-2-445-989. 20th century craftsmen's products, handsomely exhibited in a 17th century warehouse.

Teatri-ja Muusikamuuseum (Museum of Theatre and Music), in the Old Town

Müürivahe 12, open Wed-Mon 10am-6pm; tel: (372)-2-442-884. A collection of manuscripts, books, documents and musical instruments, started in 1924. The entrance to the museum is in the Old Town Wall.

Tervishoiumuuseum (The Health Museum), Lai tänav 28/30, open Tues-Sat 11am-5pm; tel: (372)-2-601-602 or 601-708.

Tuletõrjemuuseum (Fire Fighting Museum), in Old Town, Vana-Viru 14, open Tues-Sat, noon-6pm; tel: (372)-2-444-251.

Opticians

Optical-Boutique Store, Endla 12.
Optika, Tartu mnt 45.
Prillid, Pärnu mnt 72.
Tallinna Optika, Tartu mnt 6.

Parks and Monuments

Most of the parks are concentrated around the Old Town. Formerly, moats, bastions and war ruins existed in their place. The favourite ones for strolls and relaxation are *Harjumägi* (Harju Hill), *Hirvepark* (Deer Park), *Tornide väljak* (Field of Towers), *Rannavärava Mägi* (Coast Gate Hill).

At Toompea, at the site of a former Swedish bastion, is *Lindamäe Park* (Linda's Hill). Here is the statue of the mourning Linda, widow of Kalev, the mythical founder of the Estonian nation.

Tammsaare Park, located between Estonia Theatre and Concert Hall and Viru Hotel, contains a monument to the country's greatest novelist, A H Tammsaare, sculptured by Jaak Soans.

At *Tõnismägi*, across the street from *Kaarli Kirik* (St Charles's Church), stands a monument erected during the Soviet occupation in memory of the Red Army soldiers that fell in the 1944 battle to capture Tallinn. This monument was preceded by a wooden one immediately after the war that was destroyed in 1946 by a group of young Estonian patriots who received sentences from three to ten years from a military tribunal for their expression of resistance against Soviet occupation. Although for Estonians this monument is associated with a very painful period in their history, it very likely will be preserved as a visual reminder of that history.

The north side of *Niguliste Kirik* (St Nicholas' Church), on Harju tänav, has a monument to the beloved novelist and playwright, Eduard Vilde. The largest park in Tallinn is *Kadriorg*.

Philately

Estonian Philatelists Union, Toompuiestee 7; tel: (372)-2-453-741.

Tallinn Philatelists Society's exchange meetings take place in the hall of Mustamäe EEV, Tammsaare 135; open Wed 5pm-7pm and Sat 10am-1pm. Philately Shop, Roosikrantsi 16; open Tues-Sat; tel: (372)-2-445-434. Philately secondhand shop, Raekoja plats 16; open Tues-Fri; tel: (372)-2-443-058.

Post

Use the Central Post Office for posting of express mail, letters and parcels, and the purchase of postage stamps. Some post offices also sell postcards, guidebooks and stationery.

Central Post Office, Narva 1; across from Viru Hotel, open Mon-Sat 8am-8pm. For postal information call: 441-909.
DHL, courier service. Ravi 27; tel: (372)-2-446-798, fax: 445-769, telex: (372)-2-173-894 BTCSU: Rävala pst 6; tel: 454-489, fax: 454-488, telex: 173-917 DHL TL SU. You can send letters and parcels to 194 countries and vice versa.
Express Mail Service, Central Post Office, Counter 55, 1st floor; letters and parcels up to 20kg can be sent worldwide in 1-4 working days, depending on the destination. Tel/fax: (372)-2-442-137
Express System delivers door-to-door between Tallinn and Helsinki, Tallinn and Rīga within 24 hours. HRX AS, Mere pst 6-308, EE0001 Tallinn; tel: (372)-2-430-270, fax: 430-273.

Public conveniences

Most public and many private restrooms are not up to western standards. Some are very lowly indeed and are not recommended short of an emergency. Tallinn's best public restroom is at 9 Pikk Jalg. You must pay a small fee, but it's worth it. If in dire straights, these are passable: the ones in the department store *Kaubamaja*, first floor of the B building; Dunkri 5; Maneezi 1; Valli Street near Viru Gate.

Sport

Limited facilities are available at the time of writing. The complex at Piirita, on Regati puiestee, offers a swimming pool and a gym with facilities for weightlifting, wrestling and boxing.

Yachting: **Kalev Yacht Club**, Piirita tee 17. Tel: (372)-2-239-154, 239-028, fax: 239-028.
Yacht Charter: **Top Sail**, Regati Pst 1, at the Piirita Marina. Tel: (372)-2-237-055, fax: 237-044.
Squash: **Harjuoru** on Toompea. Open daily. Tel: (372)-2-631-3025.
Tennis, contact **Kalev Tennisclub**, at Herne 28. Tel: (372)-2-661-669 or 439-078.
Horse riding: **Niitvälja**, Keila vald, Harju maakond EE3053, west of Tallinn. Horses rented by the hour. Lessons available. Tel: (372)-2-742-656, fax: 771-602.
Golf: **Niitvälja Golf Course**, 30km west of Tallinn. Open daily. Tel: (372)-2-771-690, fax: 771-513.

Consult local publications for basketball, soccer, tennis and other games. Estonians are fond of sports and some activity goes on almost all the time.

Taxis

Estonian taxi drivers are the most honest in the Baltic states. Most invariably turn on the taxi meter without asking — most, but not all. Some are liable to cheat foreigners so be forewarned. It should cost 3 kroons per kilometre (4 kroons after 10.00pm). Insist on the taxi meter running. A trip from the airport to town should cost about 35 to 45 kroons.

There are state operated taxis and you can order one by dialling 603-044. Privately operated taxis can be ordered: E-TAKSO, tel: (372)-6-312-700; TULIKA, tel: (372)-2-442-500 or 603-044; ESRA, tel: (372)-2-631-2666 or 430-330; VIP, tel: (372)-6-399-399. VIP has new Mercedes cars, accepts credit cards and is the most expensive. You can also get a taxi at stands marked *Takso*. Locations include the Viru Hotel, the train station and next to the drama theatre.

Theatres and concert halls

Estonia Teater, Estonia puiestee 4; the national opera and ballet theatre, box office open Mon, Wed-Sat 1pm-7pm, Sun 11am-7pm, tel: (372)-2-449-040.

Estonia Kontserdisaal (Estonia Concert Hall) Estonia puiestee 4, box office open daily 1pm-7pm, tel: (372)-2-443-198, fax: 445-317.

Raekoda (Town Hall), Raekoja plats; chamber concerts and recitals, tel: (372)-2-440-819.

Mustpeade (Blackheads House), Pikk 26; concerts are given in the White Hall.

Travel agents

Baltic Tours, Aia 18, EE0001 Tallinn, tel: (372)-2-440-760, fax: (372)-6-313-287.

CDS Tours Ltd, Raekoja Plats 17, EE0090 Tallinn, tel: (372)-2-445-262, fax: 313-666.

Comtour Ltd, Kentmanni 13, EE0001 Tallinn, tel: (372)-2-666-942, fax: 441-955.

Concordia, Sakala 14, EE0001 Tallinn, tel: (372)-2-442-951, fax: 443-221.

Estonian Tours Ltd, Roosikrantsi 48, EE0106 Tallinn, tel/fax: (372)-2-442-034.

Eesti Puhkereisid (Estonian Holidays Ltd), Viru väljak 4, EE0100 Tallinn, tel: (372)-6-301-930.

Estair Ltd, Toompuiestee 35, EE0006 Tallinn, tel/fax (372)-2-490-679.

Hermann Travel, Pärnu mnt 10, tel: (372)-2-444-037, 440-500, fax: 440-290.

Mainor Meelis Ltd, Raua 39, EE0010 Tallinn, tel: (372)-2-424-808, fax: 421-829.

Multi-Matkad, Olevimägi 12, EE0101 Tallinn, tel: (372)-2-601-664, fax: 601-307.

Raeturist, Raekoja plats 18, EE0001 Tallinn, tel: (372)-2-444-333, (372)-2-173-264, fax: 441-100.

Tallinn Zoo, Paldiski mnt 145, tel: (372)-2-599-855. Trolley-buses 6, 7 & 8 from the centre.

Tallinntuur, Pikk 71, EE0001 Tallinn, tel: (372)-6-601-547, fax: 313-594.

Vikerling, Pikk 37, EE0101 Tallinn, tel/fax: (372)-6-311-226.

WRIS, Pääsukese tänav 1, EE0001 Tallinn, tel: (372)-2-441-364, fax: 426-251.

Part Three

Regional Guide

SITES AND SIGHTS IN THE REST OF ESTONIA

As is usually the case, the region's history leaves its footprints on the land. The indigenous peoples' settlements are today's archaeological projects and they can be found all over Estonia. Nothing remains above ground of the settlements that existed before the Crusaders came in the early 13th century except, sometimes, the mound. If one wishes to visit some of these sites, it is best to enquire at the area tourist office, the local travel bureau, or the hotel desk.

The imprint of history, starting from the 13th century, is visible to the traveller. The crusading Teutonic Knights established their presence by building stone castles throughout the territory, and today most castles remain as ruins throughout the countryside. The ones in larger urban centres are mentioned in this guidebook and can be more easily explored than those located in remote areas.

The story is somewhat different with places of worship. Evidence suggests that pagan worship centred around huge rocks bearing man-made markings, natural springs and groves. Such rocks exist to this day, as do the other natural phenomena. The introduction of Christianity in the 13th century brought construction of churches and today some still stand, albeit much transformed.

Cities, whether large or small, evolved as commercial centres generally around the fortifications at strategic locations. The vicissitudes of history have determined their present appearance and thus one can see strong contrasts in architecture between such communities as Viljandi, Pärnu, Narva and Tartu.

Away from the urban centres, out in the country, the centuries of rule by the Baltic-German barons are evidenced by the presence of imposing mansions. During independence between the two world wars many of them were converted into museums, schools, sanatoriums or libraries. During the Soviet occupation after World War II, neglect or desecration by collective farms was the fate for most of them. With the restored independence of the country have come plans to restore some of them for use as hotels and conference centres. One such effort can be seen already in the Otepää region, at the former manor house named Sangaste.

As already mentioned, the country is divided administratively into 15 counties (*maakond*). Tallinn belongs to **Harjumaa.** Also worth repeating is that if you are not on a group tour with a guide, but a free-wheeling visitor with this book in hand, the best way to see the country is in a private car, whether rented or your own. Refuelling is no longer a problem, the country is adequately dotted with filling stations. The roads are in good condition for the most part, although driving can be hazardous in the dark and during a rain storm. Obviously, a car is unnecessary in Tallinn. The distances between sites are short and one can get around well with public transportation.

What to see in the rest of the country is a matter of preference, but the other focal point is **Tartu**, located in **Tartumaa,** southern Estonia. You could consider driving from Tallinn to Tartu (about 2½ hours) and returning via the eastern part after dipping deeper into the south. That can be done in two or three days. If you have more time, consider a return from Tartu via the western route and taking in one or more of the islands. That can be done in three or more days, depending on the number of stops and how long you want to spend at each. If you have a week or more, you can tour the whole country by either combining the two halves, or creating your own itinerary from information that follows.

When you go on your tour of Estonia's southern region on the way to Tartu, your itinerary should have a stop at **Pilistvere**, in Viljandimaa, which is located a short distance north of the main road between **Võhma** and **Põltsamaa**. Although a rather typical small town, it became the focus of Estonia's freedom movement on All Saints' Day 1988, when Estonians from every corner of the country came to place a rock at a cross erected in memory of the innocents deported to Siberia during Stalin's terror in the 1940s. Lying in the heart of the country, the mound looks like a huge grave today with each rock representing a victim. There is not a family in Estonia that was not touched by Moscow's genocidal plans. On many of the rocks is inscribed a name, sometimes a date also appears. Rarely was a date of death known, because most of the victims perished without any record and are buried in unmarked graves in remote Siberia. The memorial is located next to the town's cemetery and the grounds have been designed into a small park.

The church in Pilistvere is worth a visit. It is distinct from others of the same period in Estonia for its rosette window. It was constructed (at the very latest) in the early 14th century.

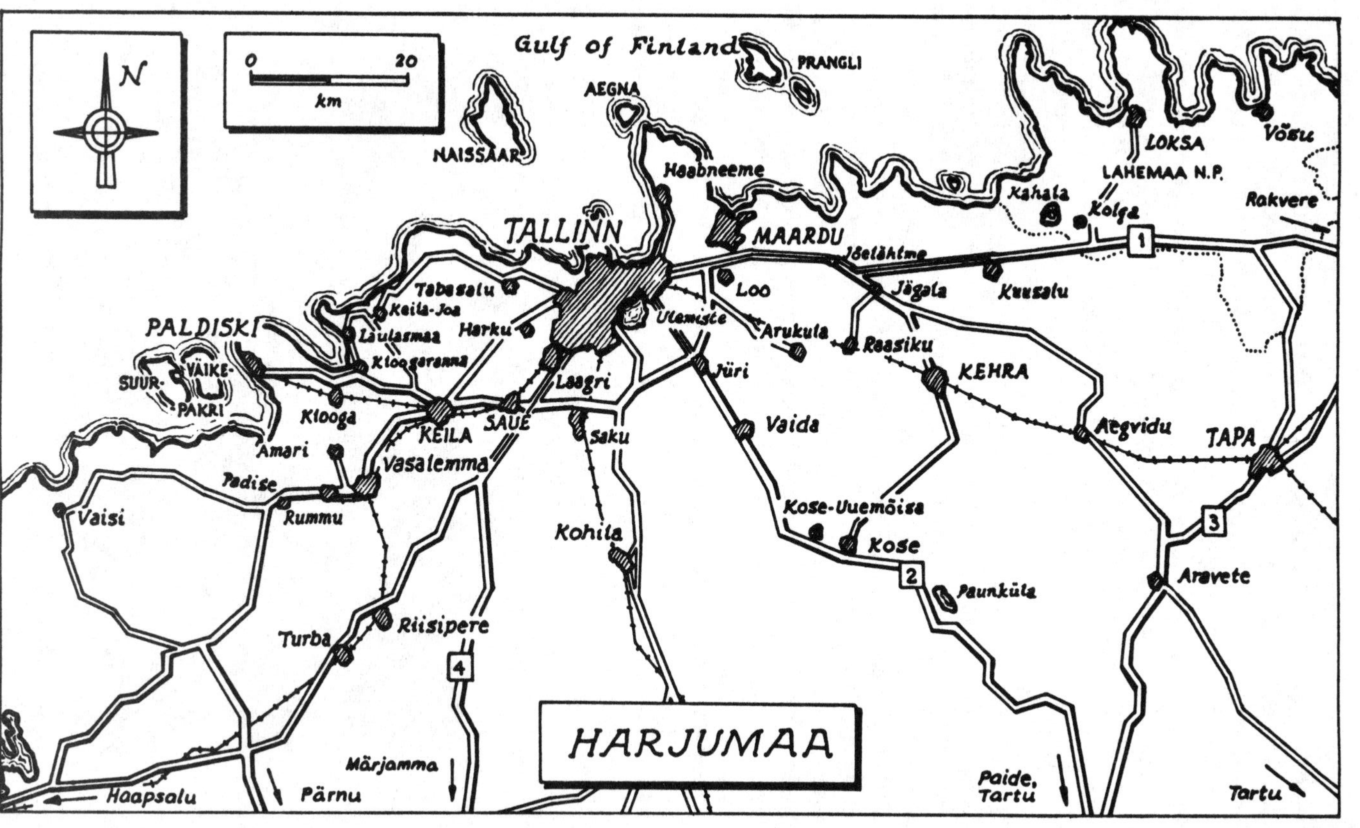
N
0
20
km
Gulf of Finland
PRANGLI
AEGNA
NAISSAAR
Haabneeme
TALLINN
MAARDU
LOKSA
Võsu
LAHEMAA N.P.
Kahala
Kolga
Rakvere
1
Jõelähtme
Loo
Jägala
Kuusalu
Tabasalu
Keila-Joa
PALDISKI
Harku
Ulemiste
Arukula
Laulasmaa
Raasiku
Kloogaranna
KEHRA
VÄIKE-
SUUR-
PAKRI
Jüri
Laagri
Klooga
KEILA
SAUE
Saku
Vaida
Aegvidu
TAPA
Amari
Vasalemma
Padise
Vaisi
Rummu
Kose-Uuemõisa
Kohila
Kose
3
2
Aravete
Paunküla
Riisipere
Turba
4
HARJUMAA
Märjamma
Haapsalu
Pärnu
Paide,
Tartu
Tartu

Chapter Five

Harjumaa

TO THE EAST

The northern county (*maakond*) surrounding Tallinn is known as Harjumaa. With an area of 4,147km^2 and a population of 128,250, excluding Tallinn, it is Estonia's most populated district. It offers the visitor with limited time an opportunity to see some of Estonia's natural beauty and history within a short distance from Tallinn. In the east, the district offers the beautiful vistas of Estonia's first national park, Lahemaa. To the west is a beautiful coastal highway leading to the wooded peninsula of Lohusalu, the waterfalls at Keila-Joa, and the formerly secret Soviet naval base at Paldiski.

To visit eastern Harjumaa take Tallinn's main road, Narva maantee, east from the Viru Hotel past Kadriog Park and then bear right up the hill. You are now on the old highway to St Petersburg. At first you will pass the huge residential district of **Lasnamäe,** built by Moscow from the mid 1970s to the late 1980s to house the many recent settlers sent by Moscow and those who had lived in sub-standard housing, such as the many wooden houses without hot water or baths which one can still see today in Tallinn's districts of Kopli or Lilleküla. Moscow planned to build housing for 160,000 people, most of them from outside Tallinn. The overall plan was to eventually build housing for 250,000 from Lasnamäe to Muuga, the huge Soviet-built port east of Tallinn. The additional thousands of inhabitants were to have come from various non-Baltic parts of the former USSR. Basically an eyesore, Lasnamäe has long been regarded by Estonians with derision and, one could say, it has caused Tallinners to wonder whether it wasn't time to tell the mythical old man of Ülemiste that the construction of the city was finished so that the lake waters would wash Lasnamäe away. Today, throughout the district, small bars, haircutters and food stores have opened, thus improving life for its residents who are half-an-hour by bus from the centre of Tallinn. As you enter the district you will see several old vacant stone buildings and aircraft hangars on your right: this was Estonia's first passenger and military airport.

Travelling eastward, you will traverse **Maardu.** This suburb is filled with Soviet-style industrial management buildings built to accommodate phosphorite mining just within the city limits of Tallinn. In the late 1980s Moscow planned to expand and intensify the mining. It was this proposal that became the spark which mobilized Estonians in 1987-88 to protest and form the Popular Front. This area also contains prehistoric settlements and ancient cultural/religious sites. Future plans include clean-up of the ecological disaster caused by phosphorite mining. The emphasis is now on recreation. Lake Maardu is also in this area.

Narva maantee follows the cliffs which rise above the Gulf of Finland. To your left are magnificent views of Tallinn, Piirita and the gulf waters. Twelve kilometres later one sees the sign announcing the end of Tallinn. You may wish to take the scenic tour by secondary roads north of the main Tallinn-Narva highway, the M1.

In the Rebala-Jõelahtme area, along this road, is the 25km² Rebala heritage reserve containing about 300 tumuli and sacrificial stones. Near the roadmaster's house is an ancient burial place dating back to 800 BC which consists of 36 tumuli. This whole area has had Estonian settlements for the last 4,000 years.

Another 12 kilometres brings you to the village of **Rebala**, from which the city of Tallinn and the surrounding region derived the names 'Reval' and 'Rävala'. Further on, one reaches **Jõelahtme**. Its church was erected in the 1300s as a fortress, and the beautiful stone bridge dates from the 19th century. A post-house, dating from the early 19th century served as a stopping point for the carriages from Tallinn to Narva and St Petersburg. Eastwards, the old highway crosses the Jägala river and the 8m high **Jägala waterfall,** the highest in Estonia. You can eat in Jõelahtme, at **KULD KUKK**, Lagedi tee, tel: 372-2-420-773.

A few kilometres later you'll come to the village of **Valkla.** At Valkla, 30km from Tallinn, the fledgling Estonian army finally stopped the advance of the Bolshevik Red Army in January 1919, and began an offensive which eventually drove Soviet forces out of Estonia two months later. They were not to return until 1940. Three kilometres south of Valkla one joins the main Tallinn-Narva highway. Travelling east a short distance you'll see signs for **Kolga** village, just north of the highway. At this point you have entered the **Lahemaa National Park.**

Kolga has two hotels:

KOLGA HOTEL, Kuusalu Parish, tel: 372-2-777-477. 17 double rooms with shower and WC, 34 beds in an old Swedish manor. Sauna, restaurant, bar, parking lot. Recommended.

TRAWELL HOTEL, Andineeme tee, Kuusalu, tel: 372-2-772-591.

Lahemaa National Park

A visit to this reserve, established in 1971 (which was the first nature preserve in the former Soviet Union) is a unique experience. Situated on the Gulf of Finland, 40km east of Tallinn, it is a 1,119km^2 park of beauty and unique natural landscapes, as well as recreational areas and villages. Although there are several reserves which are off-limits to the public (amounting to about 8% of the territory, which has been set aside for scientific research), ample areas are open to the tourist. Whether you are interested in history, geography, cultural anthropology, or you just want to enjoy Estonia's natural beauty, you will be delighted by Lahemaa.

The Baltic Sea has carved four peninsulas into the coast line and has created today's dunes, beach barriers and terraces. The pine dominated forests are broken up by numerous rivers, which are spawning grounds for trout and salmon. As the rivers flow through terraced limestone, they form picturesque waterfalls and rapids. The southernmost of the park's 14 lakes were formed by retreating glaciers, while the younger coastal lakes were once sea bays. Several underground brooks and springs are also situated within the park.

Lahemaa has a wealth of huge boulders: the *Tammispea* is the highest at almost 8m, while the *Majakivi* has the largest volume (580m^3). Stone fields — the most notable ones are found on the Kasmu Peninsula — cover large areas of the park. Sandstone and limestone outcrops are also visible throughout the area.

The park's flora consist of more than 800 species of higher plants, with over 30 of them classified as rare. Fauna are equally well represented with some 37 mammal, 213 bird and 24 fish species. Lynx, brown bear and European mink are common in Lahemaa Park, as are the black stork, crane and mute swan.

The cultural heritage in the park is as rich and varied as the natural. Hundreds of stone covered mounds — the remnants of ancient settlements — can be found at **Kahala, Palmse** and **Vihula**.

Vihula has a manor museum, one of the largest and best preserved in Estonia, beside an artificial lake, Vesiveski. Here you will find a furnished manor house along with water, wind- and saw-mills, barns, stables and sheds — 31 buildings in all, tel: 51-832, 92-637. For something more ornate, visit the **Sagadi Manor** 6km west of Vihula. Built in rococo style, the estate comes from the Baroque era and is one of Estonia's fanciest. Today it houses a Forestry Museum, tel: 98-642, 43-077, as well as a restaurant and shop. North of Sagadi is **Võsu** on the coast, a larger town with two hotels. It's considered Northern Estonia's most popular resort town. At the turn of the century Russian aristocracy and intellectuals from Moscow and St Petersburg flocked to Võsu for a summer holiday.

There are two hotels:
RANNALIIV HOTEL, Aia 5, Võsu, tel: (372)-32-99-456. 11 rooms, 25 beds. Single, double, and quad rooms with shower and WC. Sauna, indoor pool and fitness room. Sea — 400m. Fishing, sailing, tennis, bar, café.
VÕSU HOTEL, Mere 21, Võsu, tel: (372)-32-99-391, 99-297, fax: 99-197. Soviet-era building. Reservations. 75 rooms, 150 beds, double rooms with shower and WC. Sauna. On seaside. Tennis, bar.

You can eat at either the **NEPTUN**, Laine 12, Võsu, tel: (372)-32-99-233 or the **VÕSU GRILLBAR**, tel: (372)-32-99-300.

Tours
2-day tours of Lahemaa National Park, Loksa, Palmse, Sagadi, and Ilumäe manors are organized by Viru Tuur Ltd, Liimi 1, Tallinn, tel: (372)-2-580-002, fax: 526-211.

The Estonian Holidays office in Hotel Viru in Tallinn can arrange tours. They make good arrangements for local guides and meals. Viru Hotel: (372)-2-630-1311.

Car Service
25km east of Lahemaa National Park, Rakvere (Western Viru county), tel: 372-32-38-507 or 41-775.

The seaside villages of **Altja, Naturi, Kasmu**, and **Virve** evoke images of their seafaring past. Altja is a popular village and visitors enjoy the Altja Inn. Throughout the countryside you will come upon *mõisad* (former Baltic barons' manors). Many have been restored, and if they are not being used as schools or hospitals, they are open for tours. The most notable and well preserved of these is the *Palmse mõis*. A walk around the manor house itself, as well as the surrounding buildings, will provide you with a glimpse of how the German barons lived. All of the buildings, including greenhouses, farm structures, and guesthouses are open to the public.

Lahemaa National Park has a wide range of nature walks of varying lengths and degree of difficulty. Camping, open fires and fishing are allowed only by permission of the park directorate. For detailed information on the park, contact the Lahemaa Tourist Centre in Viitna, tel: 202-128.

The Park's headquarters are in **Palmse**, the old baronial property of the von Pahlen family. The manor was constructed by the Cistercians in the 17th century and was sold to the Estonian government in 1923 after Estonia's agricultural reforms nationalized the von Pahlen's land, thus making the operation of the estate financially impossible. The furnishings of the manor are not the property of the former residents, but do reflect the time when the manor was a dwelling. Much of the house was destroyed by the Russians in 1944. Surrounding the manor are stables, coach house, distillery, hothouse, bathhouse and a conservatory. The

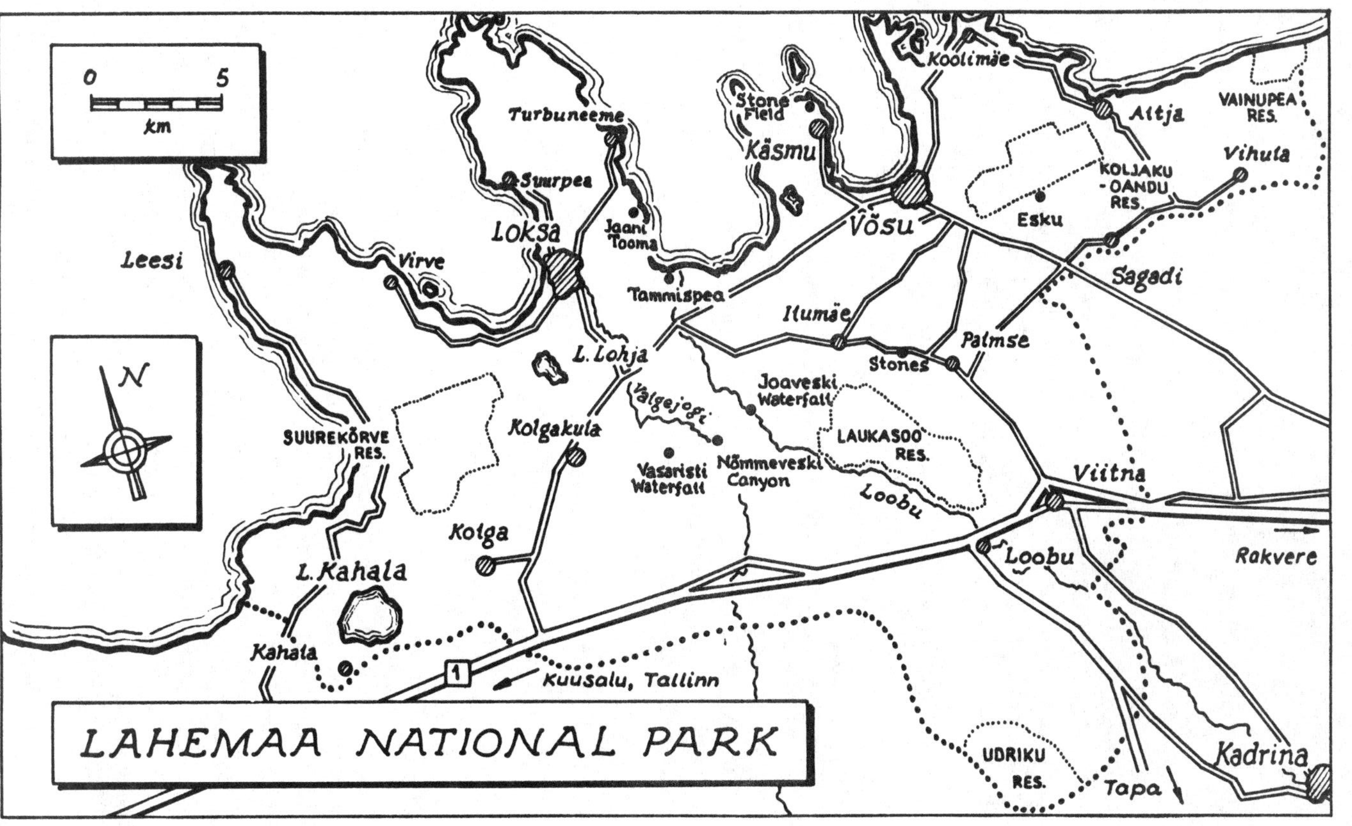
0 5
km
N
Turbuneeme
Suurpea
Loksa
Leesi
Virve
Jaani Tooma
Tammispea
Stone Field
Käsmu
Võsu
Koolimäe
Altja
Vainupea Res.
Vihula
Koljaku -Oandu Res.
Esku
Sagadi
Ilumäe
Palmse
Stones
L. Lohja
Joaveski Waterfall
Laukasoo Res.
Valgejõgi
Suurekõrve Res.
Kolgaküla
Vasaristi Waterfall
Nõmmeveski Canyon
Loobu
Viitna
Kolga
Loobu
Rakvere
L. Kahala
Kahala
1
Kuusalu, Tallinn
LAHEMAA NATIONAL PARK
Udriku Res.
Tapa
Kadrina

large apple orchard has some rare trees. The fish pond dates back to 1286 when some nuns from Tallinn received land on which they decided to build such a pond. You can visit the manor from Wednesday to Sunday. Just north of Palmse is the village of **Ilumäe** with a chapel from the 1700s where the von Pahlen family is buried.

Towards **Loksa** the road crosses the rapid waterfalls of Joaveski of the Loobu River. Loksa is an unremarkable town where the primary industry, a naval repair facility, has closed, but you can eat there at **PÕHJARANNIK**, Tallinna mnt 46, tel: 372-2-775-175.

A perfect place to enjoy the end of the day before heading back to Tallinn is the restored stage-house of **VIITNA INN**, 70km from Tallinn on the main highway to Narva at **Viitna**, just south of Palmse. The original wooden building burned down in the 1980s, but has been rebuilt with dining room, bar, sauna and discotheque.

Viitna

Where to stay

VIITNA MOTEL, Viitna, tel: 372-32-45-659. Lahemaa National Park Visitors' Centre. 95 beds. Sauna.

SÕSTRA MOTEL, Viitna, tel: 372-32-34-137.

KADAKA MOTEL, Viitna, tel: 372-32-49-419. 1km east of the Võsu crossroads. 20 beds in small cabins. One cabin sleeps 2 people. Sauna. Hot food available. Fast food kiosk open 24 hours.

Where to eat

VIITNA STAGE HOUSE, Tallinn-Narva highway, tel: 372-32-43-543. Hrs: 10am-2am. A magnificent reconstruction of an old St Petersburg staging house.

LAHEMAA NATIONAL PARK VISITORS CENTRE, tel: (372)-32-45-659, 93-651, fax: 45-759.

TO THE WEST

Western Harjumaa is distinguished by the beauty of its coastline, strewn with great boulders and bordered by steep, white limestone cliffs (which can be extremely dangerous near the edge due to the constant erosion below by the sea). Leave Tallinn by Paldiski maantee. This becomes the A205. A short distance from the centre of town there stood, until 1991, a sign warning motorists that only authorized Soviet personnel were permitted further, ostensibly to keep the hordes of Finnish, American and Estonian spies from detecting what the former Soviet Union was doing at the closed port city of Paldiski, 40km to the west.

At the fork in the road at the Tallinn district of **Õismäe**, bear right. The road will now wind along the top of the cliffs for 30km, offering spectacular views of the Gulf of Finland. At Rannamõisa cliff, you can see Tallinn to the east. Ten kilometres westwards is the village of **Keila-**

Joa, still dominated by the rusting remnants of a former Soviet radar and missile base. Park your car in the parking places along the road near the small Keila River and follow the paths next to the river to the Keila waterfall, the second highest in Estonia. Just opposite is the manor house of Count Benckendorff, which he received from Czar Alexander I after the defeat of Napoleon. It is surrounded by a park containing more than 80 species of trees and bushes. Unfortunately, the manor fell on hard times during World War II, and its subsequent use by the Red Army as an officers' club did not benefit its existence. Below it are many small waterfalls as the Keila River wanders to the sea.

The coastal road continues to the **Laulasmaa** and **Kloogaranna** vacation resorts. The beach is beautiful and the pine forests are full of summer cottages and resort centres. You will find places to eat and spend the night. At Laulasmaa is the 3km long Lohusalu Peninsula with a fishing village and harbour. The **Educational and Resort Centre** of the Chancellery of the Riigikogu, where many meetings are held, is located here. It offers full board, indoor swimming, saunas. Tel: 372-2-718-240.

Where to stay

LAULASMAA HOLIDAY CENTRE, on the peninsula just before Lohusalu, tel: 372-2-715-521, fax: 718-474. 90 rooms, singles and doubles with shower and WC. 160 beds, sauna, dining room on the sea, car park. Open May-September.

At **Klooga**, nearby, was a concentration camp, the site of mass executions. On September 19 1944, 2,000 Jewish prisoners were murdered and their bodies burnt on open fires. A monument to the victims was dedicated by Estonia's Jewish community and President Lenhart Meri in 1994.

At the turn-off to Lohusalu Peninsula, the road south rejoins the Paldiski highway. On the west side of the highway, at this junction, about 7km west of Keila, is located Estonia's only golf course, the Niitvalja Golf Centre. Tel: 372-2-771-690, fax: 372-2-771-513. The Niitvälja Riding Centre is nearby.

Paldiski was originally built by Czar Peter I as a large Russian naval base. Of the original fortress, built by forced labour, five bastions remain. After the Red Army invaded Estonia in 1940, Paldiski became a Soviet naval port, and after World War II it was closed to all but the few remaining Estonian residents (most Estonians were evicted from their homes to make way for Soviet military personnel) and soldiers and sailors of the Red Army and Baltic Fleet. In 1993 it was re-opened to the public. The nuclear reactor base (installed secretly) was the last in the Baltics whose fate was unresolved. On July 30 1994, an agreement was signed in Moscow between Estonia and Russia, which called for the facility's dismantlement by Russia by September 30 1995.

Besides its historic military importance, Paldiski was the place where one of Estonia's most famous sculptors, Amandus Adamson, lived and worked. His house still stands. He was born not far from Paldiski. You will come across his works in many parts of Estonia, including the *Russalka* monument in Tallinn.

South of Paldiski, along the road from Keila to Rannaküla, is the charming village of **Padise**. Its monastery is the oldest building in Harjumaa and was built in the 13th century by monks of the Cistercian order. It was damaged by the peasants' revolt of 1343-1345 against their German lords. Rebuilt in the 1500s, the monastery was again devastated by the Livonian Wars of 1558-1581 between Ivan the Terrible and the Livonian Order, and again later in 1766 during another war involving Russia.

Near Tallinn, in the village of **Harku,** stands another manor where, during the Great Northern War in 1710, the Commander of Tallinn's Swedish forces surrendered to Russian forces.

Also worth mentioning is **Saku**, 20km south of Tallinn. You're bound to run into the name for Saku houses Estonia's largest brewery. It's been making beer since 1820. You'll find a pretty manor house and park in the town as well.

Where to stay

RUUNAVERE HOTEL (In Rapla county), Pärnu maantee, Märjamaa, tel: 372-48-771-167, fax: 771-268. Recommended. Recently opened in an old 19th century stage house. 17 double rooms, with shower and WC, SAT-TV, sauna, restaurant, bar, car park.

KERNU MOTEL, Kernu, tel: 372-2-214-914. Kernu is south of Keila, not far from where the Tallinn-Pärnu highway splits (one branch goes to Haapsalu). 7 rooms, some with shared shower and WC. 21 beds, sauna, bar, currency exchange, parking lot. Modern and comfortable.

Chapter Six

The Northeast

East of Harjumaa, on Estonia's north coast, lie the two districts of **Lääne-Virumaa,** western Virumaa, (population 79,800, capital Rakvere, area 3,464km^2), and **Ida-Virumaa**, eastern Virumaa, (population 222,030, capital Kohtla-Järve). The name Virumaa is a Finno-Ugric word meaning land of the Viru people. The Finns call Estonia *Viro* and Estonians *Virolaised.*

The region has an ancient history, dating to the first millennium after the end of the Ice Age. In the 1200s the Danes conquered Virumaa; in 1343 it passed to the Livonian Order. The Russian invasions of the Livonian Wars (1558-1581) and the Swedish-Russian Great Northern War (1700-1721) devastated the region's towns and villages. The building of the railway to Tallinn from St Petersburg hastened industrialization of the eastern part of Virumaa at **Narva** (where the great textile combine, Kreenholm, was founded in the 19th century) and at **Kohtla-Järve**.

During the closing months of World War II the region was again devastated by the forces of Nazi Germany and the USSR. Narva, in particular, suffered. Only three buildings remained standing.

In the post-war period the eastern part of Virumaa was exploited for its oil-shale resources and huge, ugly mountains of black residue rose hundreds of feet above the cities of Kohtla-Järve and Kiviõli. Uranium was mined at Sillamäe, and the Soviets closed the town to all but the local residents.

Today, the region west and south of Kiviõli is still largely rural and agricultural, while the region to the east is industrial. The northern coast would offer some beautiful vistas of the sea and limestone cliffs were it not for the terrible polluting clouds emanating from the cement plant at Kunda.

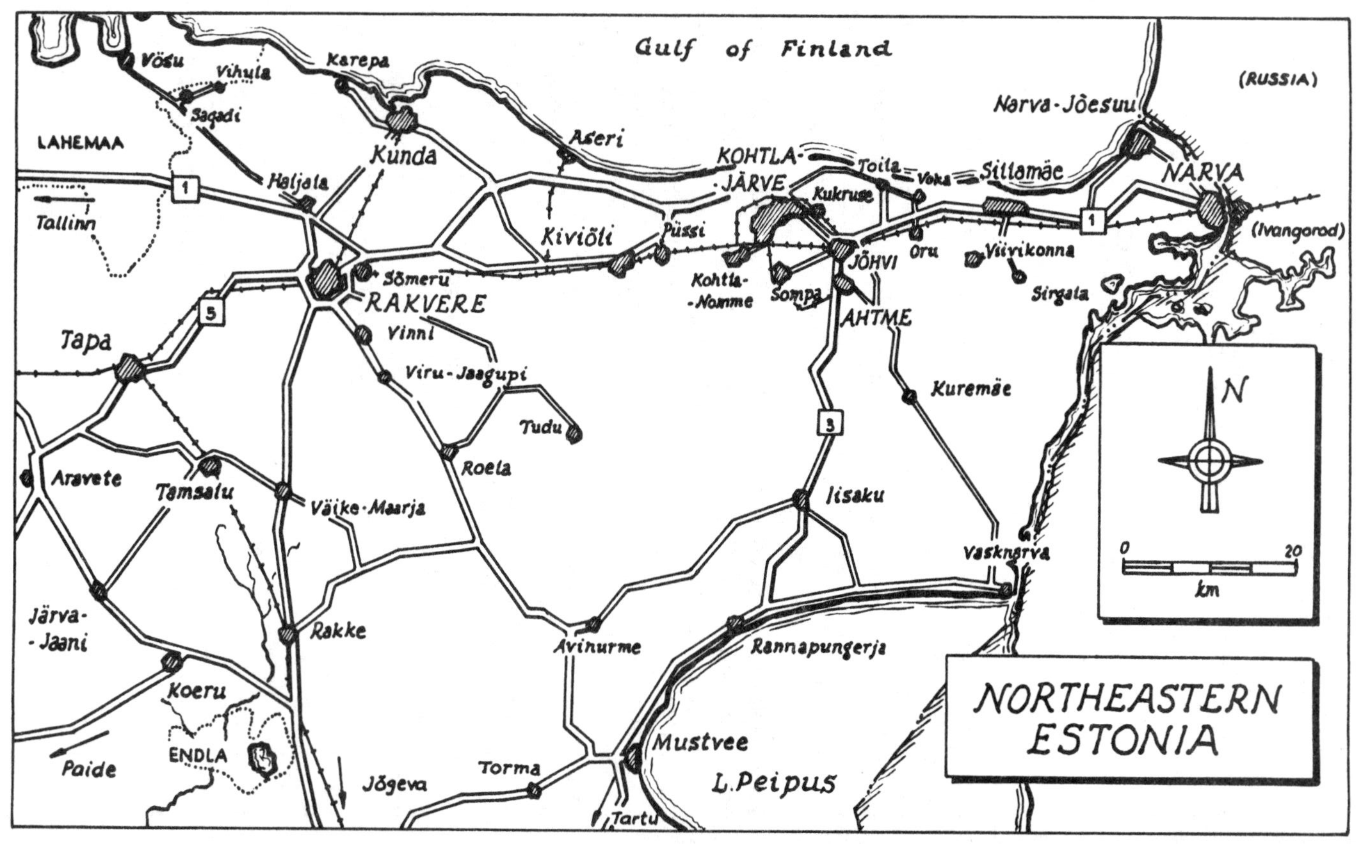
Gulf of Finland
(RUSSIA)
Narva-Jõesuu
NARVA
(Ivangorod)
Võsu
Vihula
Sagadi
Karepa
LAHEMAA
Kunda
Aseri
KOHTLA-
JÄRVE
Toila
Voka
Sillamäe
Haljala
Tallinn
Kiviõli
Püssi
Kukruse
JÕHVI
Oru
Viivikonna
Sirgala
Sõmeru
RAKVERE
Kohtla-
-Nõmme
Sompa
AHTME
Tapa
Vinni
Viru-Jaagupi
Kuremäe
Tudu
Roela
Aravete
Tamsalu
Väike-Maarja
Iisaku
Vasknarva
Järva-
-Jaani
Rakke
Avinurme
Rannapungerja
Koeru
NORTHEASTERN
ESTONIA
N
0
20
km
ENDLA
Paide
Jõgeva
Torma
Mustvee
L.Peipus
Tartu
1
3
5

Rakvere

Rakvere (population 19,900), is the capital of Lääne-Virumaa and lies 100km east of Tallinn on the Tallinn-Narva highway. It is an ancient town, first mentioned in 1252, and is an ideal city to visit for a day either by bus, car or train (two hours from Tallinn, 12 EEK one-way by bus or train).

Tourist information: Turuplats 2, tel: (372)-32-45-656. On the edge of the city centre, at Vallimägi on your right as you enter from the west, loom the ruins of a massive castle originally built by the Danes in the 13th century. It is on the site of the ancient Estonian stronghold, Tarvanpää. Expanded by the Swedes, it was destroyed at the end of the 1500s. The castle has been turned into an open-air concert hall, tel: (372)-32-44-369, and is the setting for summer cultural events: dancing, singing, instrumental music, theatre performances and rock concerts.

Below the castle is a monument to doctor/author Friedrich Kreutzwald, who lived for some years in Rakvere. He, along with F R Faehlmann, compiled the national epic, *Kalevipoeg*. Rakvere is also the home town of the renowned contemporary composer, Arvo Pärt. On the other side of Vallimägi is Pikk Street, which you can reach by proceeding along Tallinna maantee. Here you'll find an old windmill on your right, and on your left a reconstructed 15th century church with a three-tier gallery, organ and 16th century pulpit. House number 50 is the **Rakvere Citizen Museum**, tel: (372)-32-44-248, which illustrates the life of the town's citizens throughout the centuries.

Returning to Tallinna maantee and turning toward the town, you will find the **Rakvere Heritage Museum**, tel: (372)-32-44-369 at No. 3, the **Hotel Wesenbergh** at No. 25, and the **Restaurant Nord** at No. 68.

Off Tallinna maantee goes Posti Street which takes you to **Turuplats** (Market Square), where the town's tourist office, the Tsentrum Bar, market hall and bus station are located. Across Tallinna street is the **Rakvere Theatre** and at the foot of Pikk Street the former **Law Courts** which now house the **Local Museum.**

Where to stay

WESENBERGH HOTEL, Tallinna 25, tel: (372)-32-43-420; 42-720, fax: 44-209. 15 rooms, 40 beds. Single and double rooms with shower, WC, TV and phone (also SAT-TV and video channel). Five deluxe rooms with sauna. Tennis, secretarial services, car rental, restaurant, bar, café, car park.

Where to eat

BAR CAROLE, Kuke 1, tel: (372)-32-43-722.

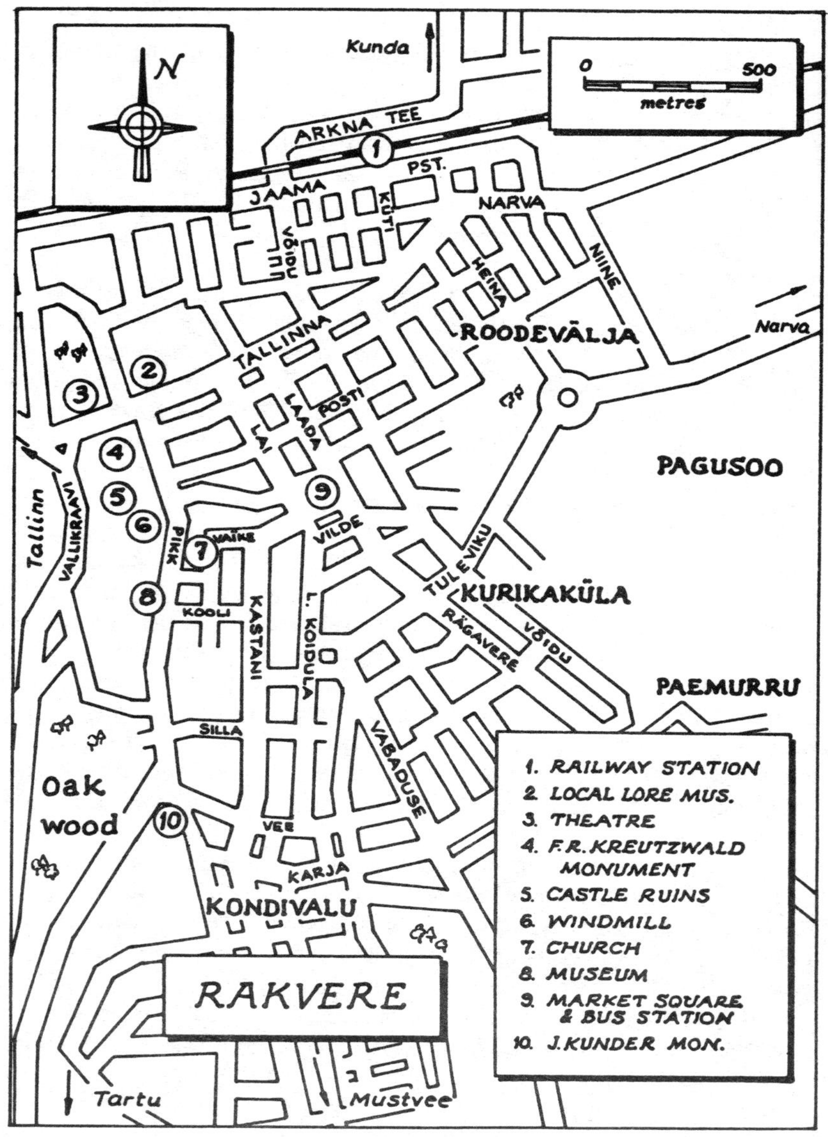

KUPU, Ragavere tee 35, tel: (372)-32-41-504.
RESTAURANT NORD, Tallinna 68, tel: (372)-32-44-464.
TSENTRUM BAR, Turuplats, tel: (372)-32-42-717.

You can have your car serviced in Rakvere. HAT, Tallinna 28, tel: (372)-32-43-206.

North of Rakvere, one can take the road to the beautiful manor village of **Sagadi.** The main building dates from 1749 and was based on a design by Rastrelli, but the manor was already mentioned in documents dated 1469. It is one of the most outstanding manors in Estonia with rococo decorations. Today it houses the **Estonian Forestry Museum,** tel: (372)-32-98-642.

Just east of Sagadi is the charming village of **Vihula**. Here the road travels to the coast, offering fine views of the Gulf of Finland as it winds eastward. At **Toolse,** just beyond **Karepa**, is a magnificent ruined castle, whose building commenced in 1471 to defend the coast from pirates.

From Toolse you will soon find yourself in **Kunda**, the site of a notorious cement plant which whitens the surrounding territory with its emissions. Recently privatized, the new owners (Greek, American, Finnish and Swiss) plan to add the necessary pollution control equipment. Kunda has a restaurant, the **VIRU**, Mai 1, 8, tel: (372)-32-51-620.

To the southeast of Rakvere is the well-restored Ragavere manor, built in the 1780s in neo-classical style. During the Soviet period it was restored by a collective farm. The manor's furnishings and museum are worth a visit, tel: (372)-32-473-12. West of Ragavere manor is the manor and park of **Mudriku.** Baron General Kaulbers erected a monument behind it to commemorate Russia's defeat of Napoleon.

Just south of here is the small village of **Viru-Jaagupi**, with a 15th century Gothic church. The Baltic baron and explorer, Baron F P Wrangel, is buried in the graveyard.

The Narva highway, or Route M11, reaches the coast of the Gulf of Finland at the village of **Korkküla**, east of Rakvere. A splendid view can be had of the sea and the limestone cliffs stretching eastwards. A great white stone cross stands by the road. It was placed there in 1590 in memory of Russian boyar Vassily Rosladin.

East of Rakvere, the next big town is **Kiviõli.** The name means 'oil-shale', and mining started here at the beginning of the 1920s. The settlement's present population is around 10,000. Kiviõli has the distinction of having Estonia's highest ash hill — about 115m. To the east, the next large town is **Kohtla-Järve** and it too owes its existence to oil-shale mines. The Estonian Oil-Shale Company (1922-1940) was founded by the state to develop the potential of the region's oil-shale resources. The Company built its own refineries and housing at Kohtla-Järva for its employees. In 1939, the oil-shale produced amounted to 1.7 million tons from which 179,000 tons of shale oil and 22 thousand tons of petrol were produced. By 1958, this figure had reached 8.9 million tons. The **Oil Shale Museum** on Järveküla tee 13, tel: 44-701, provides an interesting history of mining in the region. Kohtla-Järve's population is about 78,000, mostly Russians. It is the fourth largest city in Estonia.

Where to stay

REEDA GUEST HOUSE, Mõisa tee 27, tel: (372)-33-43-733, 43-265. Two rooms, five beds. Shower, WC, phone, TV, fridge, minibar and kitchen in the house. Car park and garage.
KOHTLA-JÄRVE GUEST HOUSE, Narva mnt 42, tel: (372)-33-44-434.

Where to eat

TURIST, Kesk Alee 12, tel: (372)-33-44-153.
RESTAURANT NORD, Pohjaalee 5, tel: (372)-33-44-655.

Other

Car Service:
Service Station, Järveküla tee 34a, tel: (372)-33-49-572.
Motor Department, Ehitajate 122, tel: (372)-33-47-804.

Although Kohtla-Järve has little of interest, to the north of the city lies the seaside village of **Toila** (population 1,000). There one can visit the site of the former **Toila Castle**, built at the end of the last century by the St Petersburg millionaire G Jelissejev. Surrounding the former castle, which was destroyed in World War II, lies a park of 105ha, which holds more than 270 different botanical objects. During the first independence period, the Castle served as the summer residence of Estonian President Konstantin Päts.

East of Kohtla-Järve is the town of **Jõhvi** (population 15,600). Its most historic monument is the 16th century church. En route to Jõhvi, at **Kukruse**, is the **Toll's Manor** which has a very large collection of coins, seals, and historical documents. And at the Kukruse windmill is an interesting display of rare rocks.

Where to stay in Jõhvi

NELE BOARDING HOUSE, Kaare 11, tel: (372)-33-22-084. 20 rooms, 37 beds. Single, double, triple and quad. WC. Shared shower. Four deluxe rooms. Café.
PÄÄSUKE HOTEL, Põllu 10, tel: (372)-33-21-285, 22-268. 13 rooms, 20 beds. Single, double and triple rooms. Four deluxe rooms with shower/bath, WC, TV and phone. Shower and WC on each floor. Sauna, indoor pool, fireplace, café, parking lot, Mastercard.

Where to eat

FOONIKS, Rakvere 12, tel: (372)-33-22-770. Very good food. Slow service.
VALGE HOBU TRAHTER, Edise, tel: (372)-33-22-742. A beautiful restaurant in a restored manor from the 18th century. On the main highway to Tallinn, outside of town.
AHTME, Tolstoi 19, tel: (372)-33-33-233.

Other

Car Service: AMV Service Station, centre of town, tel: (372)-33-26-596.

If you take the road south from Jõhvi to Vasknarva, you can visit one of the most popular tourist destinations in Ida-Virumaa, the **Puhtitsa Orthodox Convent** in the village of **Kuremäe**. It was established in 1891 and about 150 nuns run the place, which consists of many auxiliary buildings, a large park and gate towers. The Convent provides accommodation for guests and tours are given of the convent church, the museum and other buildings. Twenty-five kilometres south-east of Kuremae is the town of **Vasknarva**, on the shores of Europe's largest fresh water lake, **Lake Peipus.**

Fifteen kilometres east of Jõhvi lies the formerly closed town of **Sillamäe** (population 21,000, almost entirely Russian), built after World War II as a uranium mining centre. It offers one of the finest examples of 'Stalinist-classical' architecture in Eastern Europe — everything from the buildings to the street lamps and park benches look as if they were taken from a faded Soviet photo of the early 1950s.

Where to stay

MOTEL EDI, at Rannapungerja, on the northern shore Lake Peipus, tel: 93-654. 25 double rooms, sauna, bar, SAT-TV. Rental of bikes and boats. Open all year.

RETRO GUEST HOUSE, Kirovi 23, tel: (372)-49-17-343. Boarding house with 21 rooms, 40 beds. Single and double rooms. One deluxe room with shower, WC, TV and fridge. WC and shower on each floor. Café.

Other

Car Service: Tallinna mnt 19, tel: (372)-49-733-77.

Near Sillamäe, to the east, are the **Sinimäed** (Blue Hills), where desperate fighting between Germans, Estonians and Soviet forces lasted from the spring of 1944 until late August, resulting in the deaths of tens of thousands of soldiers.

Narva

Narva (population 83,000) lies just east. The city's name is derived from the word used by the Veps, Finno-Ugric people, for 'waterfall' or 'rapids'. Finno-Ugric people lived here from the Stone Age onwards. The city received its town charter from the King of Denmark in the early 1300s. This historic city with a natural harbour was formerly a Hanseatic League trading post.

Its **Castle** was built by the Danes in the 13th

century as a protective fortress against Russia. After the Estonian uprising of 1343, the Castle was sold to the Livonian Order who built the great tower called **Pikk Hermann**. In 1492, Ivan the Terrible began construction of the Russian fortress, Ivangorod, across the river. Four years later the Swedes destroyed it but Ivan again rebuilt the fort. The oldest part of Ivan's Castle is located on the edge of the Narva River — a courtyard with double walls and strong towers. Inside were two churches and the house in which the Czar lived. The Swedes later built a great wall around the castle on the western side of the Narva River after they captured the city in 1581, and in 1700 Swedish King Charles XII defeated the armies of Czar Peter I on its walls at the beginning of the Northern War. The **Castle Museum** located on Sankt-Peterburi mnt 2, tel: (372)-35-33-201, offers a fine view of Narva's history and the Castle's importance through the centuries as a guard on the border between East and West. In the gate tower is located a restaurant, *Rondeel,* Tel: (372)-35-33-244. From the Castle's tower you can view Ivan's fortress and the Koidula promenade beyond the bridge crossing the river. The promenade lies on top of nine huge bastions built at great cost by Sweden to protect her eastern empire — the bastions bear names such as *Wrangel, Victoria, Gloria* and *Triumph.* Beneath them are a maze of underground passages with stalactites hanging from the roof.

British traders became interested in Narva in 1566, since they hoped to obtain a monopoly on trade between Narva and Russia from Czar Ivan. In 1566 the English Parliament granted the Company of Merchant Venturers a monopoly on British trade with Russia through both Narva and Archangel. It was a dangerous period for merchants, and the Baltic Sea was rife with pirates. One English trader, William Barrow, captured six Polish pirate vessels and some 90 pirates; they were handed over to the Narva authorities who hanged them all.

British trade plans were ended when Sweden captured Narva in 1584 and British merchants relocated to Archangel. In 1630 most of Narva burned in a great fire and the city was later rebuilt in Baroque style. In the years after 1683 several British merchants lived in Narva, William Kettlewell, Henry Brown, Alexander Gilbert and Thomas Loftus. Kettlewell's house originally stood at Viru tänav 6 and his ships carried furs and timber from Narva to the West. In 1695, he built two ships, the *Vapu* and the *Narva.*

Peter I also loved Narva. At Rüütli tänav (Knight's Street) N° 20, he entertained his soldiers, courtiers and favourites. Later, he gave the palace to Duke Menshikoff as a present. The Czar particularly enjoyed walking the streets of Narva and chatting with local merchants. Although the palace is gone, one can imagine its appearance based on a description written in the 1930s:

'The house in any case, is fascinating, quite apart from its owner. The hall is full of ancient cannon, the tattered banners of the Great Guilds of Narva hang side by side with flags captured on many a battlefield. A beautiful set of carved settees and chairs originally in the Town Hall, and much armour and furnishings are early seventeenth century. The rooms above are baroque, with gilt chairs, the pale blue satin of which is still fresh and delicate. There are mirrors and clocks also, and some good pieces of furniture in walnut and tulipwood. From the ante-room which leads out of the large drawingroom where a quaint old clock as tall as a man stands and where the ghost (of Peter I) is said to linger longest, a little balcony gives on the street.'

On the Narva River, to the north of the Castle, is the **Victoria Bastion**, surrounded by **Pimeaed** (Dark Garden) offering a fine view across the river. Before the Soviet invasion of 1940, Jaanilinn was also part of Estonia. Estonia refuses to recognize its occupation by the Russian Federation and has requested its return, to no avail.

In the middle of January 1944, the Red Army launched a major offensive against the German army positioned between St Petersburg and Narva. Weakened by shortages, cold and terrible battle casualties, the German lines gave way. On January 20, the first retreating soldiers crossed over Narva's bridges. Determined to hold Estonia so as to secure their lines to the south and to keep Finland in the war, Hitler ordered General Model to hold Narva at all costs. All 20,000 civilians were evacuated on January 30 after soldiers placed signs on the walls of Narva's houses warning of the coming battle. On January 31, the Soviet Air Force bombed the city, causing severe damage. Fierce battles lasted until July 1944 when the Germans retreated to the Sinimäed. Tragically, the magnificent city had been reduced to ruin and only three houses survived. Meanwhile, German forces had executed thousands in trenches at the forest near Popovka and in trenches near the 'Red Barracks'.

Soviet reconstruction of Narva paid no heed to its ancient architecture, and instead focused on textile plants and hydro-electric power. As a consequence, by 1990 Narva became one of Europe's most polluted towns, with four big power stations annually burning more than 20 million tons of oil-shale, emitting about 380,000 tons of sulphur dioxide and 200,000 tons of toxic ash. A trip to Narva and Kohtla-Järve oil-shale mining region gives a better understanding of the Marxist marvels of Moscow's command economy than a thousand words can give. Estonians were denied the right to return to Narva, and a mostly Russian population was brought in to man the newly-created Soviet industries. Today, of Narva's 83,000 residents, less than 5,000 are Estonian. Estonia's insistence on using the Estonian language for official purposes has created hardship for the city's Russian-speakers, since there is

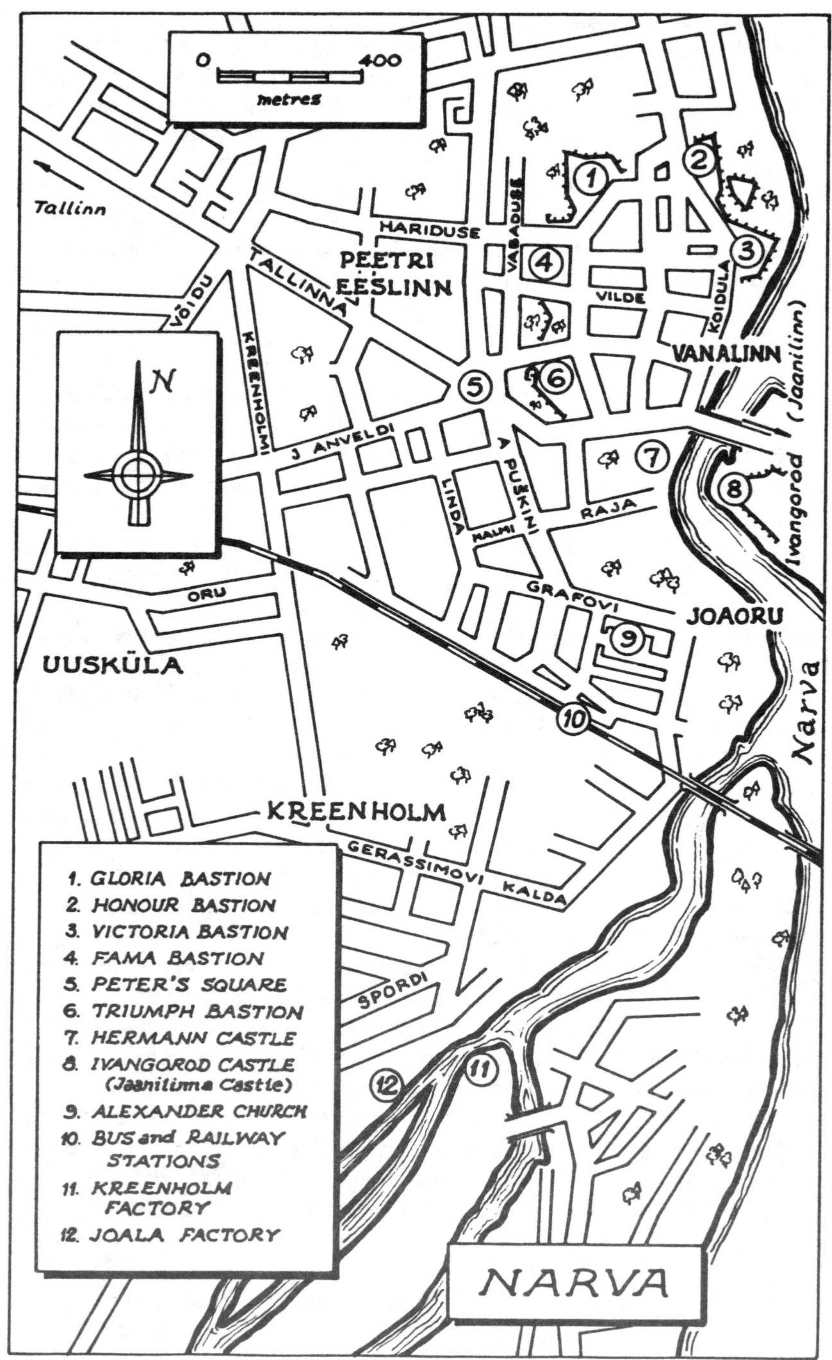

0 400
metres
Tallinn
HARIDUSE
VABADUSE
PEETRI
EESLINN
TALLINNA
VÕIDU
KREENHOLMI
VILDE
KOIDULA
VANALINN
(Jaanilinn)
Ivangorod
J ANVELDI
A PUŠKINI
LINDA
HALMI
RAJA
ORU
GRAFOVI
JOAORU
UUSKÜLA
Narva
KREENHOLM
GERASSIMOVI KALDA
SPORDI
1. GLORIA BASTION
2. HONOUR BASTION
3. VICTORIA BASTION
4. FAMA BASTION
5. PETER'S SQUARE
6. TRIUMPH BASTION
7. HERMANN CASTLE
8. IVANGOROD CASTLE (Jaanilinna Castle)
9. ALEXANDER CHURCH
10. BUS and RAILWAY STATIONS
11. KREENHOLM FACTORY
12. JOALA FACTORY
NARVA

virtually no practical opportunity to speak Estonian in what remains a Russian city.

In the centre of Narva is the beautiful **Town Hall**, originally built in 1674. It was the work of a master builder from Lübeck, Georg Teuffel. Ten years later, a Dutch sculptor, Millich, finished the facade with flat pillars and a beautiful sculptured door in the centre graced by a bronze group. The wrought iron staircase leading to the main entry is particularly well-composed. Near the railway station, on Tombi street, is the **Aleksandri Kirik** (Alexander Church), built between 1881-1884 by a Baltic-German architect, Otto Pius Hippicus. Hippicus also designed the Tallinn Kaarli Church and the Sangaste Manor as well as several buildings in Azerbaijan and St Petersburg. To the south stands the entrance to one of Europe's largest textile centres, the **Kreenholm Manufactory**, founded in 1857 by Ludwig Knoop (1821-1894), a Russian manufacturer but a German by nationality. The Russian Czar made him a baron after he gained control of many of Russia's cotton manufacturing plants. The Kreenholm factory began with two buildings. In the next 35 years a spinning factory, the Joala factory and the Georgi factory were added. After Knoop died, his sons Andreas and Theodor ran the plant until the Bolshevik Revolution of 1917 in Russia and the coming of Soviet power in 1940 to Estonia. With 12,000 workers at its peak, Kreenholm supplied much of the former Soviet Union and eastern Europe with finished textiles. In 1905, Kreenholm was a centre of revolutionary activity against Czar Nicholas II, and during the first independence period Narva workers were among Estonia's most active Communists. In December 1994, the huge plant was sold to Sweden's textile giant, Boreas AB. The Swedish concern agreed to invest millions of dollars in the company, retain 50% of its employees, and assume payment obligations with respect to Kreenholm's debts.

Where to stay

HOTEL LAAGNA, 12km west of Narva, 800 metres from the Tallinn-Narva highway. Tel: (372)-35-22-655, fax: 24-175. Built in 1994. 25 double rooms all with TV and bath, three luxury rooms. Finnish and Russian saunas. Restaurant and bar. Recommended.

HOTEL NARVA, Pushkini 6, tel: (372)-35-22-700, 31-552. Soviet-style building just south of the castle. 90 rooms, 150 beds. Single and double rooms. Shower and WC on each floor. Eight deluxe rooms with shower and bath/WC, telephone and refrigerator. Hairdresser/barber, café. Railway station 500m.

VANALINNA HOTEL, Koidula 6, tel: (372)-35-22-486. 15 rooms, 30 beds. Single 350 EEK, double 500 EEK. Just north of the castle. It is more attractive than the *Narva*. Singles, doubles and triples. One deluxe room with fireplace. All rooms with shower/WC. Some with TV. Sauna, two bars.

Where to eat

CAFÉ ANNA-MARI, Lavretsovi 6, tel: (372)-35-22-655. Opened in 1994. Restaurant in the centre of Narva. Food is well-prepared. Service accommodating and pleasant. Recommended.
BALTIKA, Pushkini 10, tel: (372)-35-31-531.
JOALA, Kreenholmi 6, tel: (372)-35-33-563.
REGATT, Anveldi 26, tel: (372)-35-40-155.
RONDEEL, St Petersburg 2, tel: (372)-35-33-244.

Churches

Voskresensky Cathedral, Bastrakovi 4. Orthodox.
Baptist Congregation, Jõe 42.
Methodist and Adventist Congregations, Fedjuninski 4.

Other

Bus and Railway station, Vaksali 2, tel: (372)-35-31-595 (bus); tel: 31-454 (railway).
Travel agents: PROBA, Noukogude 6, tel: (372)-35-22-655, fax: 24-175. VIRU TUUR, Peetri plats 3, tel: (372)-35-22-012.
Car Service: Neste, Tallinn mnt 55a, tel: (372)-35-41-608.

North of Narva there is a pretty road hugging the banks of the Narva River to the seaside resort of **Narva-Jõesuu**, frequented in the 19th century by wealthy holiday makers from Tallinn and St Petersburg. Though factory chimneys dull the atmosphere, the town offers some quaint early 20th century homes and a lovely beach lined by pine forests.

Where to stay

HOTEL ARCADIA, Linda 15a, tel: (372)-35-73-161, fax: 24-260. Six rooms, 10 beds. Single and double rooms with shower, WC, fridge and TV. Solarium. Café, bar, dining room, car park. Recommended.

The following 'health resorts' are actually Soviet-era 'sanatoriums'.

MERERANNA HEALTH RESORT, Aia 17, tel: (372)-35-73-981.
NOORUS HEALTH RESORT, Koidula 19, tel: (372)-35-73-311.
KAJAKAS HEALTH RESORT, Vabaduse 72, tel: (372)-35-71-251, 73-661.
PÕHJARANNIK HEALTH RESORT, Vabaduse 75, tel: (372)-35-71-181.
LIIVARAND HEALTH RESORT, Koidula 21, tel: (372)-35-74-391.
OOKEAN HEALTH RESORT, Raja 10, tel: (372)-35-70-131.
NARVA-JÕESUU HEALTH RESORT, Aia 3, tel: (372)-35-70-051, 70-931 for reservations, fax: 31-535. Huge modern sanatorium with 273 beds; single, double and triple rooms. Three deluxe rooms, some with WC, shower, telephone, TV (also SAT-TV) and fridge. Others use shower and WC on each floor. Sauna and indoor pool. Fireplace room for conferences. Video equipment. Gulf of Finland 200m away. Bar and dining room.

Chapter Seven

Central Estonia

The three counties of **Järvamaa** (capital Paide, area 2,620km^2, pop 43,800), **Jõgevamaa** (capital Jõgeva, area 2604km^2, pop 42,650), and **Viljandimaa** (capital Viljandi, area 3,589km^2, pop 65,030) lie in central Estonia, between Tallinn and Tartu.

Leaving Tallinn on the Narva Road, take the turn to Aegviidu, just after Maardu, and head south. South of Aegviidu you cross into Järvamaa. At the village of **Jäneda** (just southeast of Aegviidu) is one of Estonia's most beautiful baronial castles, now housing an agicultural school.

Paide Castle ruins

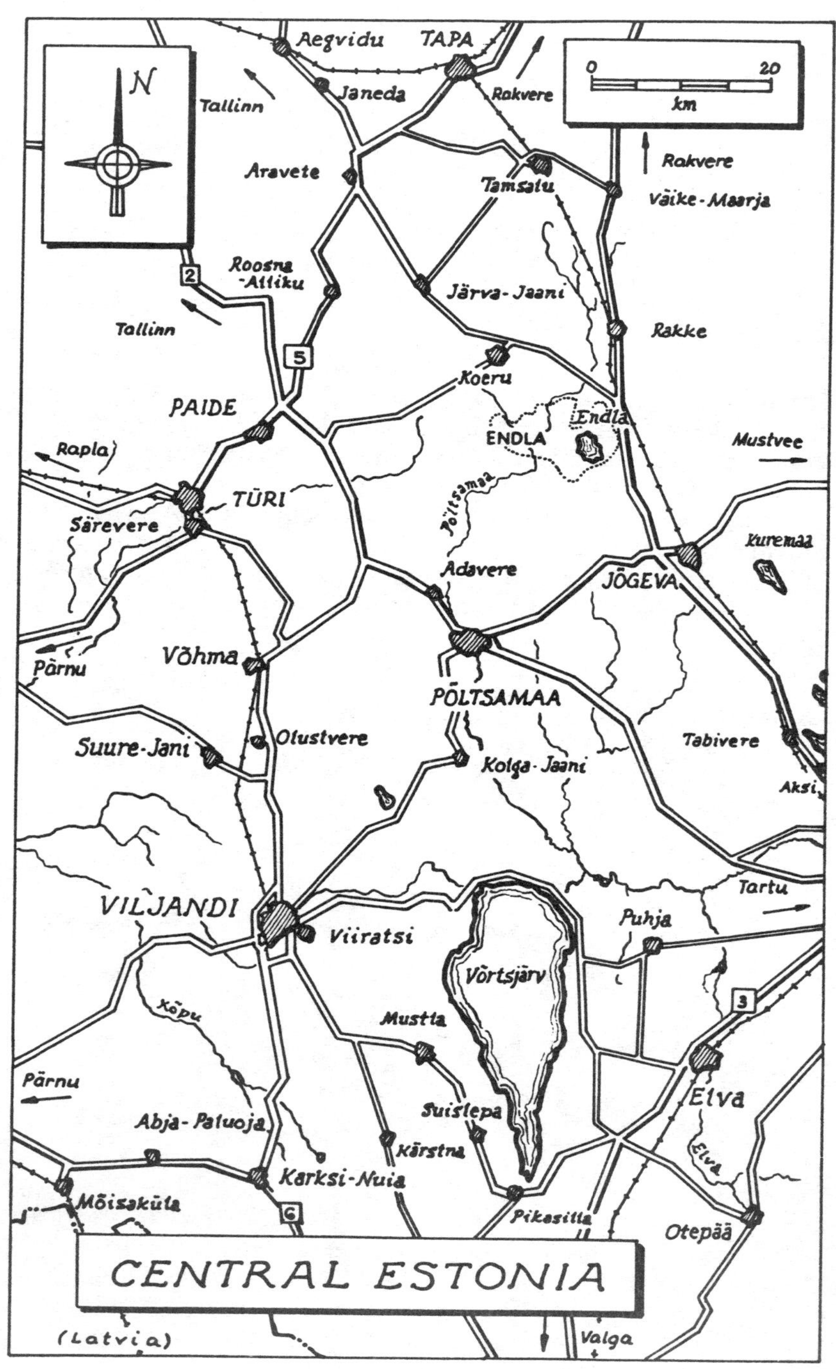

N
0
20
km
Aegvidu
TAPA
Janeda
Tallinn
Rakvere
Rakvere
Aravete
Tamsalu
Väike-Maarja
2
Roosna -Alliku
Järva-Jaani
Tallinn
Rakke
5
Koeru
PAIDE
Endla
ENDLA
Mustvee
Rapla
Põltsamaa
TÜRI
Särevere
Kuremaa
Adavere
JÕGEVA
Võhma
Pärnu
PÕLTSAMAA
Olustvere
Tabivere
Suure-Jaani
Kolga-Jaani
Aksi
Tartu
VILJANDI
Puhja
Viiratsi
Võrtsjärv
Kõpu
3
Mustla
Pärnu
Elva
Suislepa
Abja-Paluoja
Elva
Kärstna
Karksi-Nuia
Mõisaküla
Pikasilla
6
Otepää
CENTRAL ESTONIA
(Latvia)
Valga

Where to stay

NELIJÄRVE, Holiday Centre. (Located in Aegviidu Parish, just north of Jäneda in Harju County.) Tel: (372)-2-442-812. Resort on a lake — 68 rooms, 120 beds. Double and triple rooms with WC and shower. TV in hall. Sauna. Restaurant, bar.

Museum

A H Tammsaare Museum, Vargamäe, Albu, tel: (372)-38-37-756. Located near the Ambla River in Albu, a few kilometres south of Jäneda.

South of Jäneda are three more German barons' manors: in **Käravete, Aravere** and **Roosna-Alliku.** The towns are several kilometres apart. The manor house at Roosna-Alliku was built some 200 years ago and was part of a Soviet collective farm until recently.

Paide

The capital of Järvamaa is Paide (pop 11,200), first designated a town in 1291. The primary object of historical interest is the ruin of the 13th century limestone **Castle of the German Order**, whose main tower, Pikk Hermann, has recently been restored. There's a fine view of the town from the top, which is open year round. Nearby, just off Tallinna Street, is the **Orthodox Church**. Beside it, on Tallinna, are stores and dwelling houses from the 18th century. Paide is also the birthplace of the internationally known composer Arvo Pärt.

At the corners of Tallinna and Pärnu streets is the **Püha Risti Kirik** (Holy Cross Church). Note its spire. Instead of gracing the front of the church as is standard, it rises from the side wall. Its stained glass windows show Paide's coat-of-arms. Beside it stands the Town Hall along with the town's main square. The **Regional History Museum** is located just off Lai Street at Lembitu 5, tel: (372)-38-413-30.

Five kilometres north of Paide lies part of the **Viraksaare bog road**, a 3km stretch of an ancient pine and birchwood road leading to an island in the bogs. Built in the 16th century during times of war, it was buried under peat and considered a major archaeological find.

Where to stay

HOTEL PAIDE, Parkali 18, tel: (372)-38-41-464. 15 rooms, 40 beds. Double, triple and quad rooms with shower and WC. 50-seat conference room. Pool, tennis, restaurant, bar, car park. Türi railway station — 13km. Modern, attractive exterior.

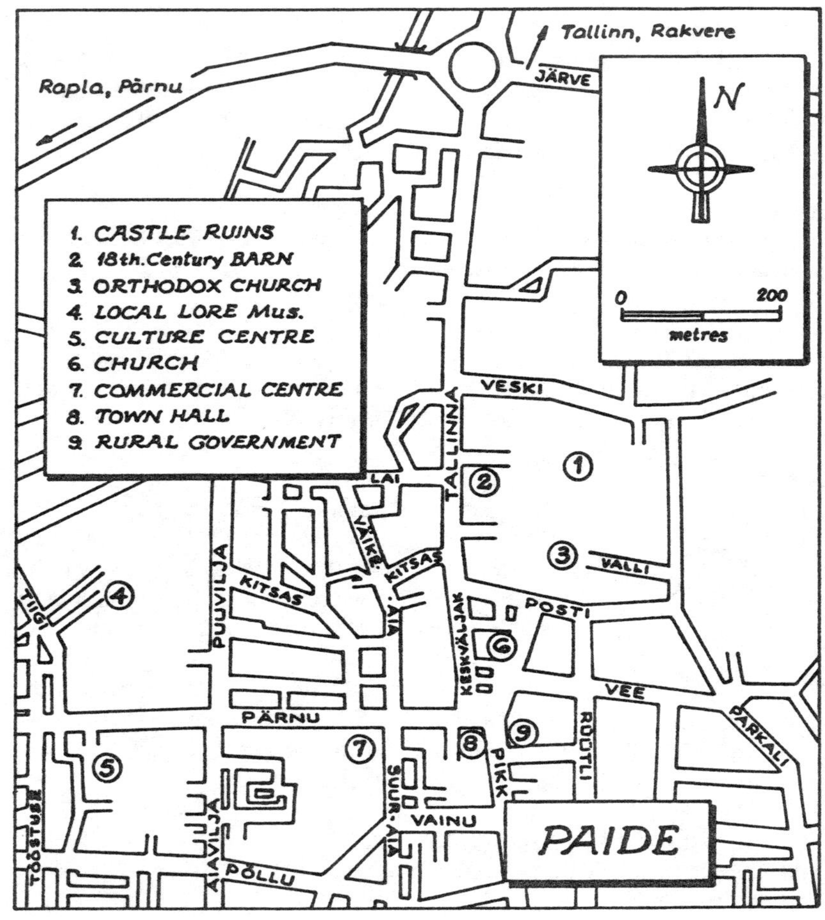

HOTEL TORU, Pikk 42a, tel: (372)-38-21-385, fax: 41-884. Nine rooms, 15 beds, two apartments of three rooms with lounge, bathroom, WC, fridge and TV. Breakfast. Modern, attractive exterior.

VALLI HOTEL, Parkali 18, tel: (372)-(38)-41-866, 21-836 for reservations, fax: 21-170. Seven rooms, 20 beds. Single, double, triple rooms. All with WC, TV, phone, fridge and mini-bar. Shower on each floor. Sauna, 20-seat conference centre, restaurant, bar, tennis court, car park.

PAIDE GUEST HOUSE, Telliskivi 8. Tel: (372)-38-21-227. Small, basic facility.

Where to eat

PAIDE Restaurant, Keskväljak, tel: (372)-38-41-330.

KAVAL-ANTS (beerhouse), Aia 20, tel: (372)-38-21-168.

CAFÉ SKAT, Pärnu mnt 116, tel: 41-425. Food, videos, 24-hour shop.

BASTION CELLAR (café), Vallimägi, tel: 41-258.
ALVA BAR, Vabaduse 29, tel: 43-262.

Museum

Paide Regional Museum, Lembitu 5, tel: (372)-38-41-330.

Car Service

Telliskivi 17, tel: (372)-38-41-869.
Assotraus Ltd, Pikk 42, tel: (372)-38-41-875.
Tööstuse 36, tel: (372)-38-41-730.

Where to stay in Türi (a few kilometres southwest of Paide)

MATEKO HOTEL, Kalevi 11, tel: (372)-38-78-579. Eight rooms, 20 beds. Single, double and triple rooms. Shower and WC on each floor, car park. Railway station 3km.
TERVIS HOTEL, Tallinna 60, tel: (372)-38-70-187. Six rooms, 20 beds. Double and quad rooms. Shower, WC and fridge on each floor. Sauna, indoor pool and fitness room. Tennis court, car park. Railway station 1.5km.
TÜRI GUEST HOUSE, Jaama 7, tel: (372)-38-78-262. Seven rooms, 18 beds. Single, double and triple rooms with washing facilities and WC. TV, phone and fridge on the same floor. Sauna. Railway station 100m.
TÜRI INN, Eight rooms, 14 beds. Double rooms with shower/bath. WC on the same floor. TV in foyer (SAT-TV). Café. Railway 1km.

Where to eat

KANARBIK, Kalev 7, tel: (372)-38-70-153.

Five kilometres southwest of Paide lies Väätsa. Its guest house *Vana Tall* is in what used to be the town's manor's horse stables. Tel: 92-301. Southeast of Paide is the village of **Koigi** whose beautiful manor house was built by the Grunewalt family. South of Koigi the road diverges. Take the western spur and you'll soon reach the border of Viljandimaa and you'll pass through the town of **Võhma,** where you can eat at either **KALEVA**, Tallinna 26, tel: (372)-43-233-95 or **VÕHMA**, Spadi 2, tel: (372)-43-233-85.

Upon leaving Võhma, take the road leading to **Suure-Jaani.** In the town centre stands a statue of the great Estonian warrior **Lembitu,** who led the Estonians of Viljandimaa in a final unsuccessful war to destroy the power of the German Knights of the Sword. In 1217, a short 16 years after Bishop Albert of Bremen landed in Rīga to start the Crusade against the Baltic peoples of Livonia, Lembitu was killed in battle and Estonia was to become the victim of foreign predators for the next seven centuries. Suure Jaani has a restaurant: **LEHOLA**, Pärnu 11, tel: (372)-43-712-83.

Viljandi

East of Suure-Jaani is the village of **Olustvere**. A sign notes the location of the site of Lembitu's fortress (*linnus*) of **Lohavere.** From Olustvere rejoin Route A204, the main Tallinn road, for the 18km journey to **Viljandi** (pop. 23,500), a rather typical Estonian small town. In popular lore, Viljandi is the capital of Mulgimaa, meaning 'the land of mulks'. What is a *mulk*? *Mulk* is the appellation given to natives of this region and it implies prosperity. The soil in southern Estonia is the most fertile in the country and farmers in that region have historically been more prosperous than in the rest of the country. As a consequence, their personality tended to be proud and boastful.

Viljandi, too, is an ancient settlement. In the 13th century the Teutonic Knights subdued the native people and built a citadel on the hill near the romantic lake that has inspired songs. Outside the fortress's walls a town grew, but no buildings remain from that period. Even the citadel and the buildings inside became ruins in the early 17th century during one of the many wars that have swept over Viljandi. The citadel's ruins are part of a park now in which you will find a suspension footbridge, built in 1931 over the 'River of Sorrow', a deep ravine in which serfs were drowned. There is a fine view from the citadel.

Many of the buildings in the old part of town date from the 18th and 19th centuries. An exception is **Jaani Kirik** (St John's Church), which was built in the 14th-15th centuries and was recently restored after years of neglect under the Soviets. **Pauluse Kirik** (St Paul's Church), built in 1863-66, overlooks Valuoja valley. On the other side of the stream in the valley is the **Ugala Theatre** built in 1980. Behind the theatre is the **Forest Cemetery** in which was completed, in 1993, the restoration of the memorial to the men who died in the War of Independence. Also in 1993, the German government restored a memorial field in which are buried their men who died in World War II in the area. The local **history museum** is located in an 18th century chemist's shop at Laidoneri plats 12 (Laidoner Square); open Thur-Mon 10am-5pm, tel: (372)-43-52-663.

Where to stay

VILJANDI HOTEL, Tartu tänav 11; tel: (372)-43-53-852. Built in the 1930s. Not recommended at the time of publication. Often dirty and poorly kept.

VILJANDI TRAINING AND SPORTS CENTRE, Ranna pst 6; can accommodate 80 guests, tel: (372)-43-54-770 or 54-870 for reservations.

MANNIMÄE HOTEL, Riia mnt 38, tel: 372-43-57-785. 32 rooms, 56 beds. Single and double rooms. All with shower and WC. Restaurant. Railway 2km.

SAMMULI MOTEL, Sammuli Street, about 5km out. On Lake Viljandi. Tel: (372)-43-57-785, 52-815 for reservations, fax: 53-104. 10 rooms, 32 beds. Double, triple and quad rooms. Shower and WC on each floor. Four summer cabins for triple occupancy. Sauna and two indoor pools, parking lot. Open May-September. Railway station 6km.

HESTIA TOURISM FARM, Ramsi (just 10km south of Viljandi). Farm with seven rooms and 16 beds. Double and triple rooms with shower, TV, WC. Sauna and fitness room, bar, dining room, car park. Bus stop 1km.

KIVI FARM at Ramsi, 5km south of Viljandi; tel: (372)-43-91-457. Single 70 EEK, double 150 EEK. Hospitable hosts offer a guest house of six bedrooms, lounge, dining room, shower and sauna at bargain prices.

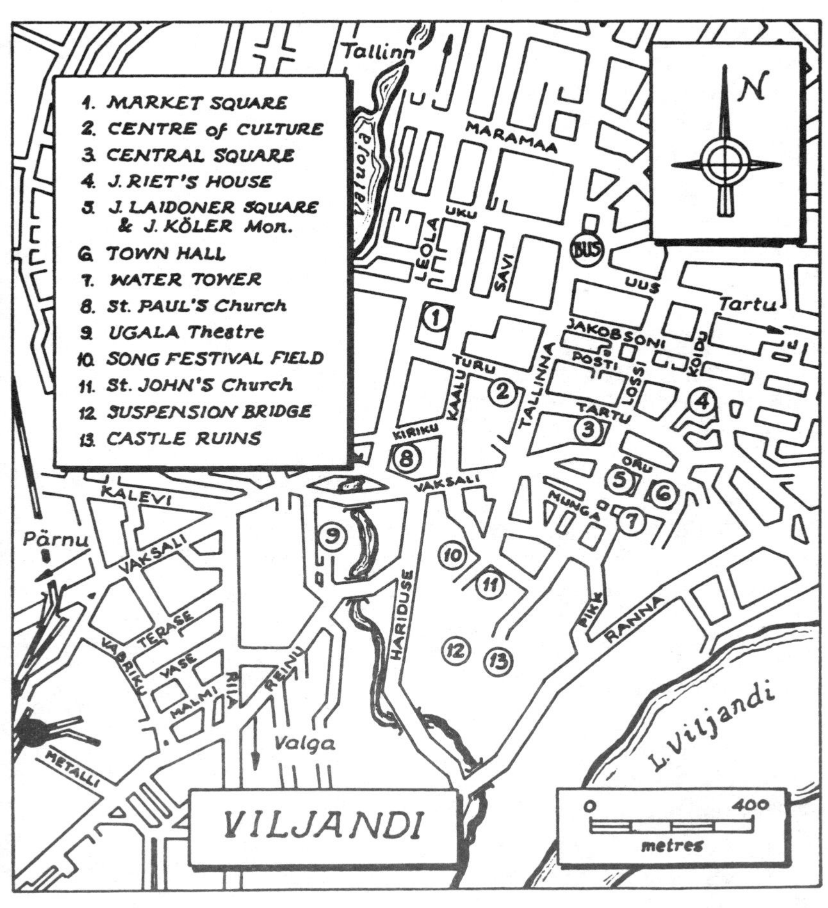

Camping
VILJANDI CAMPING, Tallinna 6 in Holstre-Nõmme. 10km southeast of Viljandi. Tel: (372)-43-29-777, 54-418 for reservations. Double and triple occupancy summer cabins. 70 beds. Shower. WC and sauna in separate buildings. On a lake, fishing, bar, summer café. Open May-Sept. Viljandi railway station 12km.

Where to eat
IVA, Kauba 11, tel: 52-493. Near Castle Hill. Dining hall and bar.
VILJANDI HOTEL, Tartu 11, tel: (372)-43-547-95.
VILJANDI CAFÉ, Lossi 31, tel: (372)-43-54-424.
VIKERKAAR, Roo 5, tel: (372)-43-529-09.

Cafés
DRAAKON, Tartu 34.
MENU VILJANDI, Jakobsoni 11.
MULGI KELDER, Tartu 5.
POSTI TRAHTER, Posti 18.
KOIT, Turu 6.

Museums
Viljandi Museum, Laidoneri plats 12, tel: (372)-43-52-663, 53-316. Closed Mon-Tues.

Car service
Viljandi, Tallinna mnt 99a, tel: (372)-43-55-500.
Abja, Auto-Motor, Posti 6, tel: (372)-43-52-628, 61-163.
Suure-Jaani, Oja 2, tel: (372)-43-71-186.

Churches
Pauluse Kirik (St Paul's), Kiriku 5. Evangelical-Lutheran.
Jaani Kirik (St John's), Tasuja pst. Evangelical-Lutheran.
Adventist and Baptist congregations, Uku 11a.

Post
Post Office, Tallinna 11.

Public transportation
Bus Station, Ilmarise 1, tel: (372)-43-53-980.
Railway Station, Metalli 1, tel: (372)-43-53-825.

Travel agents
Viljandi Reisid (Viljandi Travels), Tallinna tänav 6, tel: (372)-43-54-418, fax: 52-720.

Some 25km east of Viljandi lies the beautiful **Võrtsjärv**, the second largest lake in Estonia. Probably because of its opaque water the lake was once called *Virtsjärv* ('virts' meaning liquid manure). Today it is Estonia's largest inland lake — 270km^2. It has an average depth of 2.8m with two deep spots, each 6m deep. This present lake site emerged about 1,200 to 1,300 years ago during the last Ice Age. About 8,000 years ago the lake in this area was huge, reaching up to Põltsamaa in the north and Elva in the east.

Today's lake has few peninsulas, five islands and about 20 inflowing rivers which supply Vörtsjärv with water, the largest being Väike-Emajogi. Since the lake isn't very deep its waters warm and cool rapidly. The lake is home to a large number of flora — about 81 species. Thirty-six different fish have been caught from its waters. There probably were many more in the last century. Today Vörtjärv remains important as a fishing ground, resort and water reserve.

If you want to go to Tartu from Viljandi, the main road running north of Võrtsjärv is the one to take. At Võrtsjärv you can look for a road that goes to the lake (narrow country paths) and take a refreshing dip. Võrtsjärv also provides the country with eel — a delicacy.

South of Viljandi you can take a beautiful drive on a circular route by heading to **Mustla**. Continue to **Suislepa** and then towards **Kärstna** and drive through the rolling hills until you reach Kärstna. A beautiful old manor stands on the hill. This town is just 75km north of Valmiera, Latvia. In this area you can see the fabled lush *Mulginaa.*

From Kärstna, drive on to **Karksi-Nuia**. An ancient Estonian fortress stood here, which later served as a stronghold for the Livonian Order. Karksi-Nuia is the birthplace of the well-known Estonian playwright, August Kitzberg.

Põltsamaa

To the west, on Route A208, is the town of **Abja Paluoja.** You can return north from Karksi-Nuia to Viljandi. From Viljandi you can journey on to Jõgevamaa via Route A204 north to **Põltsamaa** (pop 5,300), a charming old city on the river of the same name. The heart of the city is the ruin of the **Castle of the Livonian Order**. During the Livonian Wars (1558-1581), Ivan the Terrible invaded Livonia and captured Põltsamaa. Duke Magnus of Denmark, who had purchased Estland from his brother, the King of Denmark, and had concluded an alliance with Russia against the German Order, was briefly installed as 'King of Livonia' in Põltsamaa with Russian support.

In the late 1700s the German, Woldeman von Lauw, turned Põltsamaa into an early industrial centre, building a glass factory, metal industries and porcelain works. A vast Palace was also built on the site of the old Order fortress. The Palace and its surrounding park were so beautiful that Catherine II of Russia journeyed to Põltsamaa to be entertained by

Lauw. Lauw also started a hospital in Põltsamaa, naming Peter Wilde to manage it. Wilde started a printing shop, and between 1766 and 1780 16 books in German, Latvian and Estonian were printed here, including the first Latvian periodical *Latviešu Ārste* (Latvian Doctor). On Veski Street, near the centre of Põltsamaa, is a manor house and a monument to those who gave their lives in the War of Independence, 1918-1920.

Where to stay

HOTEL PARGI, Pargi 1, Põltsamaa, tel: (372)-37-51-679. Five rooms, 15 beds. Shower and WC on each floor, car park. Bus stop 1km.

Where to eat

BAR KURVI, Lossi 5a, tel: (372)-37-51-780.
PÕLTSAMAA GRILL BAR, tel: (372)-37-51-366.
RESTAURANT KONVENT, Lossi 1, tel: (372)-37-51-390, 51-681.
TABIVERE WINDMILL CAFÉ, tel: (372)-37-36-302.

Northeast of Põltsamaa is **Jõgeva**, and 20km further on is the **Endla Nature Reserve** (82km^2), an area of marshlands, hills and springs. You can get guided tours of this area. Tel: 46-429.

Where to stay in Jõgeva

HOTEL VIRTUS, Aia 40, tel: (372)-37-21-319. Also known as a sports centre. Has a weight-training room.
JÕGEVA GUEST HOUSE, Jaama 4, tel: 21-454. (Near railway station.)

Where to eat

BLACKJACK, Aia 3, tel: 22-995.
BAR CARMEN, Pargi 5, tel: 23-506.
BAR SIMARO, Suur 5, tel: 23-565.
PIZZERIA, Puiestee 38.
CAFÉ KASTANI, Tallinna mnt 1.
CAFÉ KABLIK, Suur 24, tel: 21-890.
BEERHOUSE VALGA, Suur 15a, tel: 31-291.

Other

Car service, Jõgeva, tel: (372)-37-21-278.

Just north of Põltsamaa is **Adavere.** Along the Tallinn-Tartu road is an old windmill which now houses one of the best restaurants in the country, tel: (372)-37-57-311, 57-351. Offers breakfast from 7am to 11am. Great for dinner, traditional Estonian food. Its hall has a fireplace. Live music on weekends. Recommended.

South of Põltsamaa is **Puurmani,** where a magnificent palace was built

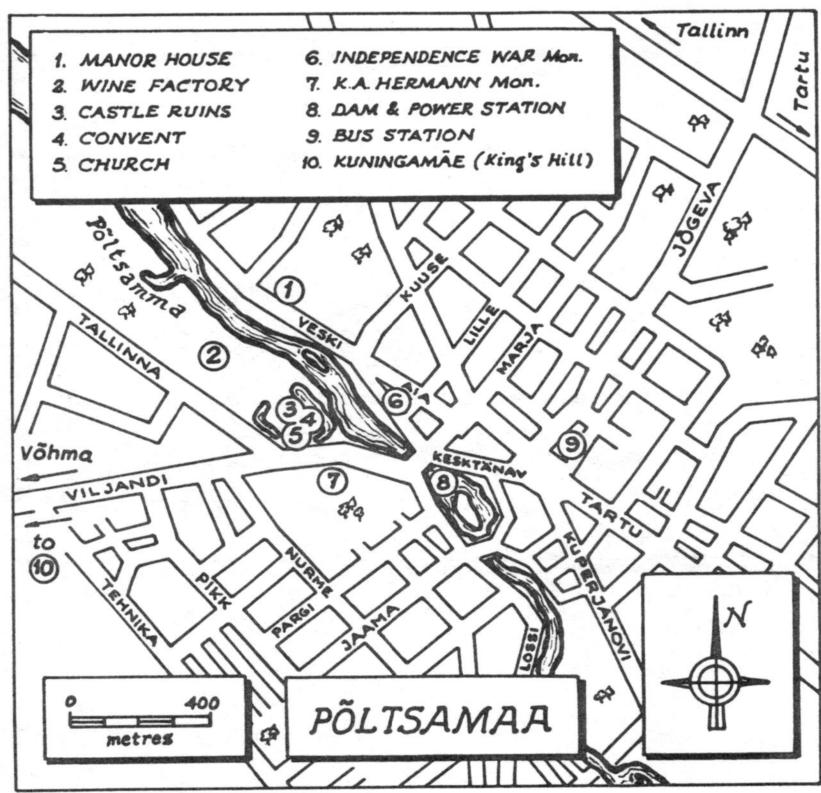

in the 19th century by Count Mannteuffel. With 42 rooms, central heating, parlours, game rooms and a beautiful park with rare species of trees and plants, the manor is well worth a visit.

Forty kilometres south of Puurmani lies Tartu. However, an interesting side trip to take would be **Tabivere** and **Aksi** on legendary **Saadjärv** (Lake Saad), 7km^2. Some boulders on its shores figure in the Estonian epic, *Kalevipoeg*. Turn left and take the road to Tõrve and there, take the road southeast to Tabivere. Head for Aksi, a town on the southwestern shore of Saadjärv that has remained the same for a century with its church (the first one was built in the 15th century), former vicarage, and park surrounding them. The famous Estonian linguist, O W Masing, worked here as a clergyman from 1815-1832.

AKSI HOLIDAY CENTRE, Tabivere, tel: (372)-37-36-318. 13 rooms, 28 beds. All rooms with shower, WC and TV. Sauna, café, tennis courts, car park. Railway station 3km.

Chapter Eight

Tartu

Tartu (population 115,000) is an ancient city, known over time by different names: *Tarbatu, Jurjev, Dorpat*. Archaeological finds show that the area around present-day Tartu has been inhabited since the fifth century. First mentioned as a settlement in 1030, it became the seat of the Tartu bishopric in 1224, and was granted city rights in 1248. Situated along the east-west waterway linking southern Estonia with the Russian hinterland, Tartu was an important trade centre by the mid-16th century, and was the second largest city in Estonia. By the mid-1800s, during Estonia's national awakening, Tartu had become the cultural centre of Estonia. In 1900 the city's population had grown to 40,000.

The medieval town was nestled between *Toompea* (Cathedral Hill) and *Emajõgi*, Estonia's longest river. These natural barriers, however, did not provide sufficient protection from enemies. Historical records show that Tartu has been burned to the ground 55 times. Only two buildings, both in ruins, date back to the Middle Ages: the 13th century Saints Peter and Paul Cathedral (*Toomkirik*) on Toompea, and, at the foot of the hill, the 14th century St John's Church, which has very singular terra cotta miniature sculptures on the outside as well as inside. The rest of Tartu is built in Classical and Baroque styles.

Since the establishment of the university in 1632 it has been known as a university town, and also as the 'Athens of the North'. One of the oldest in Europe, the university was established by King Gustavus II Adolphus of Sweden as *Academia Gustaviana* on the basis of the great Swedish University at Uppsala. The Northern War (1700-21) between Sweden and Russia brought unbearable hardship to Estonia's native population — destruction, famine and plague. The entire population was deported to Russian in 1708 and the city burned. The university was closed for 100 years, re-opening under the Czar's *ukase* in 1802. The

Rakvere
Tallinn
Emajõgi
Narva
Räpina
see City Centre
Map, page
NURME
PUIESTEE
STAADIONI
LIIVA
NARVA
JAAMA
RAATUSE
PIKK
FORTUUNA
F TUGLASE
FR KREUTZWALDI
LAULUPEO
JAKOBI
TAARA
NÄITUSE
K.E. v. BAERI
VAKSALI
ILMATSALU
J KUPERJANOVI
TIIGI
VANEMUISE
KASTANI
RIIA
VÕRU
KALEVI
AIDA
TURU
VILJANDI
N. LUNINI
L. PUUSEPA
Viljandi
RAVILA
VÄIKE-KAAR
KESK-KAAR
RAJA
Valga
KABELI
AARDLA
Võru
Põlva
TARTU
N
0
600
metres
1
2
3
4
5
6
7
8
9
10
11
12
13
14
15
16
17
18
19
20
21
22
23
24

six-columned, neo-classical main building is a legacy of that revival period. *Toomkirik* became part of the university campus.

German served as the language of instruction. A lectureship in the Estonian language was established in 1803 and it provided a stimulus for linguistic research. Very gradually, the number of Estonians attending the university increased. By the end of the 19th century, over 100 were enrolled. Toward the end of that century, the university was subjected to Russification. On December 1 1919, after independence was declared, Estonian became the official university language. Today, 7,500 students are enrolled, of which 6,800 are undergraduates, 500 masters and 200 in other post-graduate programmes. There are ten faculties — Physical Education, Law, Medicine, Economics and Business Administration, Social Sciences, Theology, Physics and Chemistry, Biology and Geography, Mathematics and Philosophy.

In 1992, Swedish King Carl XVI Gustaf rededicated a statue of Gustavus II Adolphus behind the main building of the university. The

1. RAADI CEMETERIES
2. St. PETER'S CHURCH
3. UNIVERSITY STADIUM
4. UNIVERSITY SPORTS COMPLEX
5. St. GEORGE'S CHURCH
6. CINEMA
7. ESTONIAN AGRICULTURAL UNIVERSITY
8. SONG FESTIVAL FIELD
9. SPORTS CENTRE
10. CATHOLIC CHURCH
11. CITY MUSEUM
12. MUSEUM
13. NEW ANATOMICAL THEATRE
14. & 15. MUSEUMS
16. ART MUSEUM
17. UNIVERSITY LIBRARY
18. MARKET HALL
19. RAILWAY STATION
20. St. PAUL'S CHURCH
21. MUSEUMS
22. FR KREUTZWALD MUSEUM
23. ART GALLERY
24. CINEMA

TARTU – Key to Map

original statue had been destroyed by the Soviets after they occupied Estonia in 1940.

The Library of the University, the largest in the former Soviet Union after the former Lenin Library in Moscow, is housed in a soviet era building at 1 Struve Street and is open from Monday to Friday, 8am-9pm, and weekends from 10am-6pm. Unfortunately, its walls have already developed cracks.

The park surrounding *Toomkirik* is an area for pleasant strolls revealing monuments to the biologist Karl Ernst von Baer; the university library's first director JKS Morgenstern; War of 1812 field marshall MA Barclay de Tolly, whose home was in Tartu. *Inglisild* (Angel's bridge) is another noted attraction in the park. It was built in memory of the university's first rector, GF Parrot, appointed by the Czar in 1802. From *Inglisild* one can get a view of the town below. Not far from **Inglisild** is *Kuradisild* (Devil's Bridge), named after the German professor Mannteuffel (*Teufel* means devil in German).

Monuments dedicated to literary figures who made significant contributions to the national awakening are located around the city. Among the most moving is that erected in 1983 to Kristjan-Jaak Peterson (1801-1822), showing him with a book in one hand and a walking stick in the other. He walked back and forth between Rīga, where his parents lived, and Tartu to attend the university. In his short lifetime (he died of tuberculosis at the age of 21) he was the first poet to write in Estonian.

The centre of Tartu is the old part and contains a few baroque buildings among structures of mostly classical style, rebuilt after the town burned in 1774. The two best known buildings are *Raekoda* (Town Hall) and the university's main building. *Raekoda*, designed by Tartu architect JHB Walter, is an early Classical building of the late 18th century. The present building is already the third at that location. Tartu University's main building, originally built in the early 19th century, is the second landmark in the city. It suffered heavy damage during World War II and the present building is a post-war restoration. North of the University, on Jaani Street, stand the ruins of *St John's Church*, destroyed by Soviet bombers in March, 1944. The church is being rebuilt. Nearby, at 20 Ülikooli Street stands a memorial stone on the site of the first Estonian printing house (1631). On Vanemuise 19 the *Estonian Writers' Union* is renovating a fine Classicist building which formerly housed the Tartu KGB headquarters. Next door, the building at Vanemuise 21 formerly housed the German Gestapo.

For Estonians, Tartu is considered the spiritual capital of the country. Here national awakening stirred early, the first civic organizations were formed, the first Estonian language newspaper was published, the national epic, *Kalevipoeg*, was issued, and the first song festival was held. Valued educational institutions are located in Tartu, and on February 2 1920, the Tartu Peace Treaty was signed, in the building at

Tõnissoni 1, with the newly established Bolshevik regime in Russia, which recognized Estonia as an independent nation and renounced 'for all times' any Soviet claims on Estonia's territory. The Soviet regime did not keep its word. Less than a generation later, Tartu, and all three Baltic countries were occupied by the Red Army, and the war that raged in Europe once again inflicted destruction on the city. Post-war occupation made this old university town a closed city due to the large military base on its outskirts. It's only in the last few years that Tartu has been open to foreign visitors again. Since the restoration of independence, educators want to restore the university to its former status as the seat of higher learning in the country.

Being a university town, Tartu has the look of youth to it. On its streets are students with their colourful caps, traditional fraternity life has been restored, and many of the customs and festivities associated with academia can be periodically observed in the city. It is also home to the Estonian Agricultural Academy. The southern region of Estonia is dominated by agriculture and the service the academy provides to its development is vital.

Where to stay

HOTEL KANTRI, Riia pst; tel: (372)-7-240-715. 22 rooms. 390-1,300 kroon. Opened in 1994. Nice country-style motel on the Rīga highway. Offers currency exchange, saunas, solarium, souvenir shop and caters to business needs.

HOTEL MAI, Tuglase 13; tel: (372)-27-61-780, fax: 31-481. 24 rooms, 54 beds. Converted apartment building with triple or double bed suites with shower, WC, TV and fridge. Restaurant and bar. 15 minute walk from the centre, railway 1km.

PARK, Vallikraavi 23; tel: (372)-27-31-745/33-663, fax: 34-382. 20 rooms, 31 beds. 140-800 kroons. Seven rooms with shower, bath and WC. Sauna, conference facilities, café, bar, casino, car park. Reasonably priced, basic, clean hotel at a convenient location.

PRO STUDIORUM, Tuglase 13; tel: (372)-27-61-853, 61-386, fax: 31-481, telex 173209PTBSU. Converted apartment building with triple or double bed suites, restaurant, bar, 15 minute walk from the centre, car park.

RÄNDUR, Vasara 25; tel: (372)-27-75-691. 20 rooms, 37 beds. 100 EEK and up. Small hotel. Single and double rooms. WC and TV, shower on each floor, café, car park. Railway 4km.

REMARK, Tähe 94; tel: (372)-27-77-720, fax: 76-911. 350 EEK and up. Small hotel, four rooms all with shower, seven beds, WC, phone, radio. SAT-TV, sauna, café, car park. Railway 1km.

SALIMO, Kopli 1; tel: (372)-27-70-888, fax: 77-768. Small hotel, 20 rooms, 56 beds. Doubles have shower, WC. TV and radio in lounge, café, car park. Distant from centre. Railway 4km.

SEPA, Sepa 26; tel: (372)-27-72-494. Small hotel, distant from centre.

TÄHTVERE SPORDIKLUBI, Laulupeo 19; tel: (372)-27-61-708. 14 rooms. 83 kroon and up. Café, sauna. Small hotel, singles and doubles with WC, shower, TV and fridge. Tennis court, fitness room and sauna, car park. Convenient location.

TARIM, Rahu 8; tel: (372)-27-71-594.

TARTU, Soola 3; tel: (372)-27-33-041. 214 beds in 131 rooms (230 kroon and up) all with WC, radio and some with TV. Shower on each floor. Car park. A gloomy state-owned hotel from the Soviet period, next to the bus station. Cheap.

TARU, Rebase 9; tel: (372)-27-73-700, fax: 74-095, telex 173104TARU. 72 rooms, 116 beds. Expensive. All rooms with shower, WC and TV. Car park. Run by the Finest Hotel group. Good restaurant, bar, sauna, business services, all major credit cards accepted. Far from centre; not recommended if you are on foot. Industrial surroundings.

YOUTH HOSTEL, enquire 'Estonian Youth Hostels', Liivalaia 2, EE0001 Tallinn, tel/fax: (372)-2-441-096 or 445-853. In the city centre; 1-2-3 bedded rooms, price EEK 100-280, includes bed linen and breakfast.

Where to eat

ANNE, Anne tn 36; tel: (372)-7-436-307. A seafood restaurant opened in 1994. Modern decor, good service.

ARLI, Vanemuise 26. One of the best in town.

BISTRO TAVERNA, Raekoja plats 20; tel: (372)-27-31-222. Italian dishes and ambience.

CAFÉ CENTRAL, Raekoja plats 3; tel: (372)-7-441-297. Hrs: noon-2am. The best in Tartu. Great food and service. Adjacent to Town Square. Also has a small disco and nice bar.

CENTRAL, Küüni 1. New art-deco style cellar restaurant with several rooms, bar, disco and reasonably good food.

THE FOX AT TARU HOTEL, Rebase 9; excellent food but service needs improvement; tel: (372)-27-73-700.

KASEKE, Tähe 19; tel: (372)-27-70-386. 125 seats in two rooms.

KAUNAS, Narva mnt 2; tel: (372)-27-34-600. Across the river from downtown. Great disco for young people and students in the evening. Several bars.

PÜSSIROHUKELDER, Lossi 28; tel: (372)-27-34-231. Located in a vast underground Czarist gunpowder magazine. Good food and service. Live music, dancing, show. Go and take a look, even if you don't plan to eat here.

TARVAS, Riia 2; tel: (372)-27-32-253. Good food, disco. In an ugly shopping hall.

Cafés and bars

CITY HALL CAFÉ, Raekoja plats. Entry to noon, Mon-Fri.

GILDI TRAHTER, Gildi 7. Also serves food; tel: (372)-27-31-895.

HUMAL ÕLLETARE, Rüütli 9. Entrance on Rüütli 5. Hrs: 11am-10pm. The main pursuit is beer as the name implies, although food is served. Interesting place to meet students and Tartu 'personalities'.

MAURUSE VEINIKELDER, Veski tn 35; tel: (372)-7-422-389. Hrs: Tues-Sat, 1pm-11pm. Wine bar in cellar.

RÜÜTLE BISTRO, Rüütli 2; tel: (372)-7-443-523. Hrs: 7.30am-midnight. Delicious food. Nice bar.

TARTU DIRECTORY

Car rental

TARBUS, Ringtee 14, EE2400; tel: 745-38, 752-50.

Churches

Pauluse kirik (St Paul's), Riia 27. Evangelical-Luteran.

Peetri kirik (St Peter's), Mrva mnt 104. Evangelical-Lutheran.

Uspenski kirik (Uspensky), Magasini 1. Orthodox.

Jüri kirik (St George's), Narva mnt 103. Orthodox.

Rooma Katoliigu kirik (Roman Catholic), Veski 3.

Adventist and Methodist Congregations at Alexander Nevsky Church, Sõbra 19a.

Baptist Congregations at Võru 18 and Tähe 66.

Galleries

ILLEGAARDI GALERII, Ülikooli 5. Additional feature — a pleasant bar. Run as a club.

JAANI JUURES, Lutsu 7. Gallery and shop.

KUNSTNIKE MAJA. Artists' Union Building.

KUU GALERII, Ülikooli 15.

RÜÜTLI GALERII, Rüütli 1.

SINIMANDRIA GALERII, Kompanii 2.

SEBRA GALERII, Jaani 20. Gallery and antique shop.

Library

Tartu University Library, Struve 1; tel: (372)-27-32-467.

Museums

EESTI RAHVAMUUSEUM (The Estonian National Museum), Veski 32; holds a rich collection of old farming tools, household utensils, folk costumes and ornaments. Open Wed-Sun 11am-6pm; tel: (372)-27-32-254.

FR KREUTZWALDI NIM KIRJANDUS MUUSEUM (FR Kreutzwald Literary Museum), Vanemuise 42; named for the 19th century great Estonian literary figure, the museum has a collection of manuscripts, publications, photographs, letters and phonographs. Open Mon-Fri 10am-4pm; tel: (372)-27-33-396.

KUNSTIMUUSEUM (Art Museum), Vallikraavi 14; 19th century Baltic-German artists' works and 20th century Estonian artists', a large part of them Tartu residents. Open Tues-Sun 11am-6pm; tel: (372)-27-35-521.

LINNAMUUSEUM (The City Museum), Oru 2; sizeable collection of archaeological relics and ancient coins are among its most prized items. Open Wed-Sun 11am-6pm, Mon 11am-5pm; tel: (372)-27-32-033.

PÕLLUMAJANDUSE MUUSEUM (Agricultural Museum), Ülenurme; 7km outside Tartu, in a former manor. Open Tues-Sat 10am-4pm; tel: (372)-27-12-396.

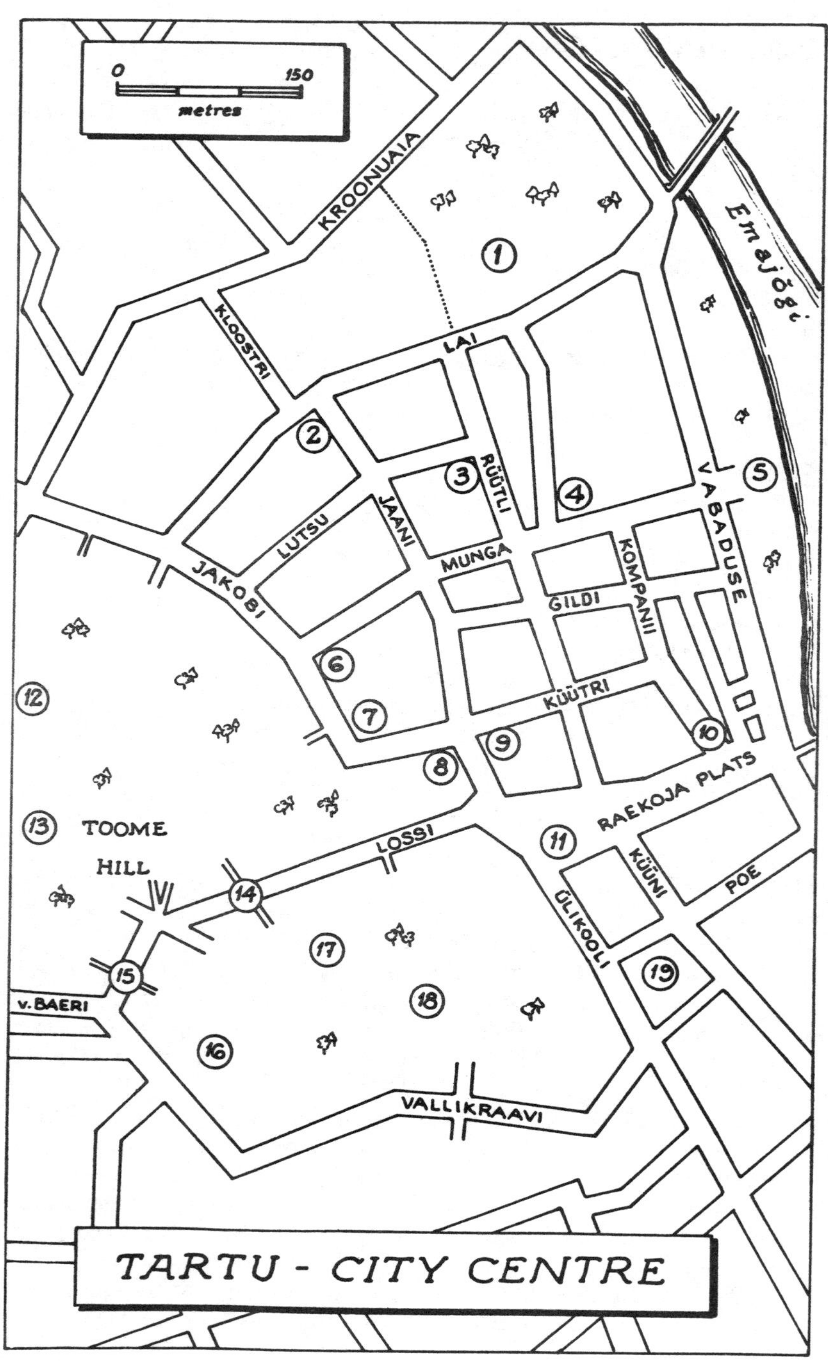
0
150
metres
KROONUAIA
KLOOSTRI
LAI
RÜÜTLI
JAANI
LUTSU
JAKOBI
MUNGA
GILDI
KOMPANII
VABADUSE
KÜÜTRI
RAEKOJA PLATS
LOSSI
TOOME
HILL
KÜÜNI
POE
ÜLIKOOLI
v. BAERI
VALLIKRAAVI
Emajõgi
1
2
3
4
5
6
7
8
9
10
11
12
13
14
15
16
17
18
19
TARTU - CITY CENTRE

SPORDI MUUSEUM (Sports Museum), Riia 27a; founded in 1967, it collects, studies, and displays materials on physical education and sports in Estonia. Open Wed-Sat 11am-7pm, Sun 10.00-3.30pm; tel: (372)-27-34-602.
TÄHETORN (Observatory), Toomemägi; built in 1810 and had a celebrated past, now displays history of astronomy in Tartu. Open Wed-Mon 11am-4pm; tel: (372-27-34-932.
TARTU ÜLIKOOLI AJALOO MUUSEUM (History of Museum of Tartu University), Toomemägi; opened on the 350th anniversary of the university, emphasis is on the history of science. Open Wed-Sun 11am-5pm; tel: (372)-27-32-635.

Police

Call 002, just as in the rest of Estonia. Headquarters: Kompanii 10; tel: 34-114.

Post

Post Office, Lai 29.

1. UNIVERSITY BOTANICAL GARDENS
2. OLDEST BUILDING IN TARTU (1546)
3. St. JOHN'S CHURCH
4. USPENSKY ORTHODOX CHURCH
5. FR KREUTZWALD MONUMENT
6. GUSTAVUS II ADOLPHUS MONUMENT
7. & 8. UNIVERSITY BUILDINGS
9. CINEMA
10. GALLERIES
11. TOWN HALL
12. HILL of KISSES
13. CATHEDRAL RUINS
14. ANGEL'S BRIDGE
15. DEVIL'S BRIDGE
16. OLD ANATOMICAL THEATRE
17. GUNPOWDER CELLAR
18. OBSERVATORY
19. BARCLAY de TOLLY SQUARE and Monument

Key to Map

TARTU CITY CENTRE

Public transport

Bus station, Turu 2; tel: 32-406.
Railway station, Vaksali 6; tel: 39-950.
Airport, Tõrvandi; tel: 32-445.
River harbour, Turu 2; tel: 33-234.

Taxi

Taxi station, Riia 20; tel: 33-867.

Telephone

The Tartu telephone exchange is being modernized as we go into print. Consult locally for the latest information.

Travel agents

Pro Studiorum, Tuglase 13, EE2400 Tartu; tel: (372)-27-61-853 or 61-386, fax: 31-481, telex: 173209.
Tartu Reisibüroo (Tartu Travel Bureau), Lai 35, EE2400 Tartu; tel: (372)-27-34-564 or 31-517.

THE NEXT EDITION

Events are moving fast in Estonia, and we plan to update this guide regularly. Readers play an important part in bringing changes or new information to our attention. All contributions will be acknowledged and the most helpful will receive a free copy of the next edition.

Chapter Nine

Southeastern and Southern Estonia

THE SOUTHEAST

Lake Peipus, Põlvamaa, Võrumaa, and Valgamaa

From Tartu you have a fine opportunity to visit the nearby shores of the fifth largest lake in Europe — Lake Peipus or **Peipsi Järv** — 3,555km^2. It consists of three separate parts. The northern lake is also known as Lake Peipsi or *Suurjärv* (Grand Lake), the largest and deepest of the three (2611km^2, deepest spot 12.9m with an average depth of 8.3m). The southern lake, or Lake Pihkva, is about 708km^2, its deepest spot is 5.3m and its average depth is 3.8m. The strait between the two is called Lake Lämmi (*Lämmijärv* — 'lämmi' meaning very warm). It is about 236km^2 with 2.5m average depth. The deepest spot is about 15.3m.

Lake Peipus has 29 islands making up an area of 25.8km^2. Interestingly, only about 1500km^2 of the lake's territory belongs to Estonia. Most of its northern coast has sandy beaches and nearby pine forests. The western coast is home to two large towns, Kallaste and Mustvee, along with several villages. Thirty inflowing rivers feed the lake; the largest is Suur-Emajõgi. The River Narva is the largest outflowing river.

Though a large lake, its flora is limited, but it is considered one of the best fishing spots in Europe containing 36 types of fish. During the 19th century fish resources decreased. The first fishing regulations introduced in Russia were at Lake Peipus. Today the lake provides 90-95% of Estonia's inland fishing production. In addition to its economic value, Lake Peipus is one of the most popular resorts in western Estonia and is a great tourist attraction. It is also considered an important future water reserve for Tallinn and northern Estonia.

Travel 56km due north from Tartu via Route A201 to the scenic town of **Mustvee**. It offers beautiful views of the lake and picturesque small wooden homes built by Russian and Estonian fishermen who have lived here for centuries. The road from Mustvee to Kallaste to the south hugs close to the shore and goes through a series of Russian villages — note how the houses are all on one street. The villages are also rather unique

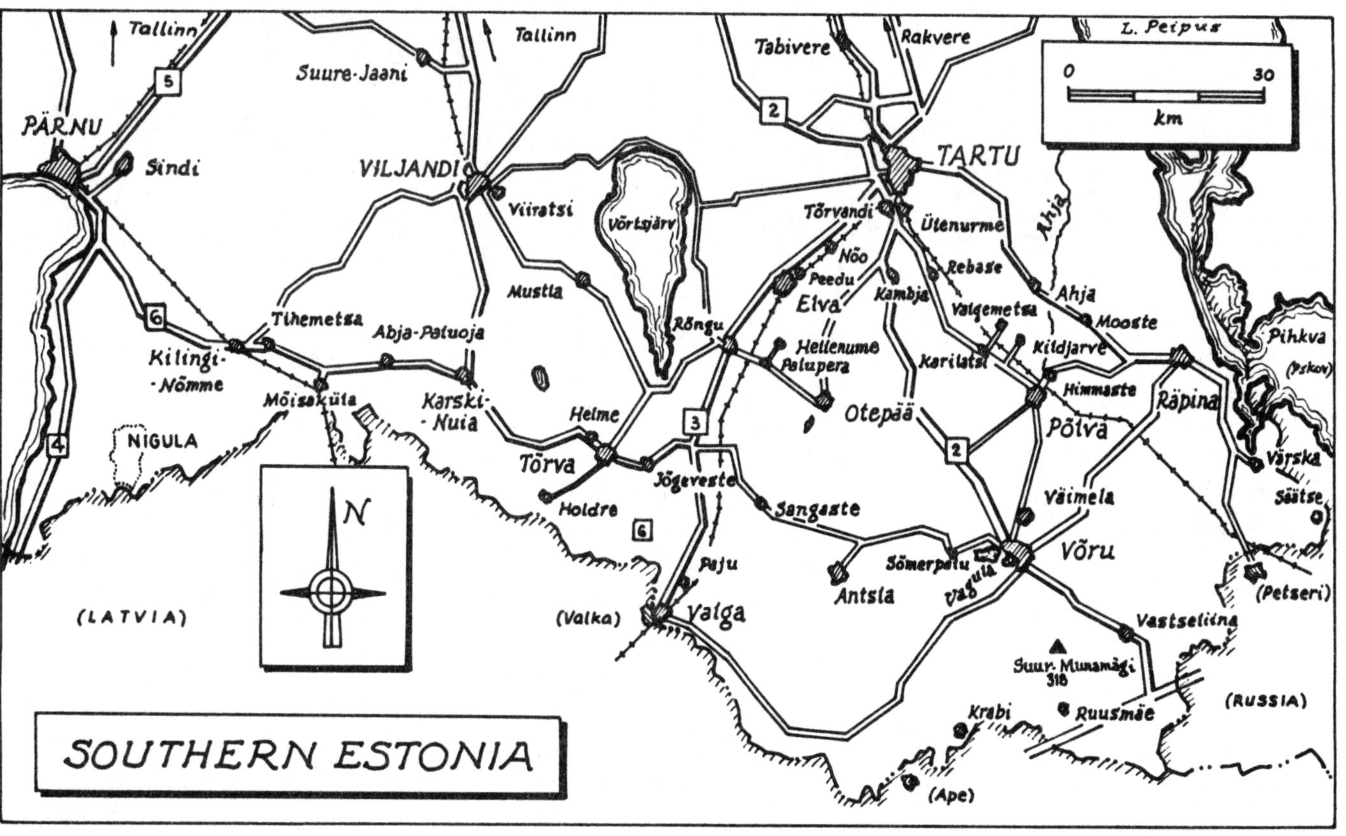
Tallinn
Tallinn
Suure-Jaani
Tabivere
Rakvere
L. Peipus
0
30
km
5
2
PÄRNU
Sindi
VILJANDI
TARTU
Viiratsi
Võrtsjärv
Tõrvandi
Ülenurme
Ahja
Nõo
Peedu
Rebase
Ahja
Mustla
Elva
Kambja
Valgemetsa
Mooste
6
Tihemetsa
Abja-Paluoja
Rõngu
Hellenurme
Palupera
Kildjärve
Pihkva
(Pskov)
Kilingi-Nõmme
Karilatsi
Himmaste
Mõisaküla
Karski-Nuia
Otepää
Räpina
Helme
3
Põlva
NIGULA
4
Tõrva
2
Värska
Jõgeveste
Sangaste
Väimela
Sätse
N
Holdre
6
Võru
Paju
Sõmerpalu
Vagula
Antsla
Vaabina
(Petseri)
(LATVIA)
(Valka)
Valga
Vastseliina
Suur. Munamägi 318
(RUSSIA)
Krabi
Ruusmäe
SOUTHERN ESTONIA
(Ape)

in that the houses are built along the water, the back gardens containing fields of onion and cucumber for sale on the roadside next to the fields. Why not stop and become acquainted with some local produce?

The town of **Kallaste,** a typical fishing village, is inhabited by Old Believers — those who refused to accept the reforms of the Orthodox liturgy and ceremony carried out by Peter I and his successors. Persecuted as supporters of a backward Russia, the Old Believers sought religious freedom on the edges of the Russian empire — often in Lithuania, Estonia and Latvia. Five kilometres north, at Ranna, is a small beach on the lake.

South of Kallaste is one of Estonia's most magnificent manors, in the village of **Alatskivi**. Built by the baron Ernst von Nocken in the style of a Scottish castle, beginning in 1870, it is surrounded by a fine park. Alatskivi is also the birthplace of one of Estonia's major poets, Juhan Liiv. What was once his bath house is now a museum. At the time of writing, there was no place to eat on the road from Mustvee to Alatskivi. At Alatskivi, on the main road through town, you will see, on the right, large farm buildings of field stone, and in one of them is located the modest but good restaurant *Talli Tare*. Alatskivi would be a good place to stop to have a meal and to walk around. Juhan Liiv is buried in the Alatskivi cemetery across the street from *Talli Tare*, not far from the main gate. Down the street, on the left, is the school with the bust of its most famous son in the schoolyard. To the right is the path to the former baron's manor house. It has been leased to a Finnish enterprise which will implement the necessary repairs.

Continuing southward to lower Lake Peipus, through the towns of **Koosa** and **Kavastu**, you reach **Võnnu,** southeast of Tartu. The town was first mentioned in 1341. Its church, one of the oldest in Estonia (built in 1236) contains a crypt for Baron von Nocken's son, killed in the 1812 Battle of Borodino fighting for the Czar against the forces of Napoleon.

Further on, the road reaches **Mehikoorma** on the lake. From here ferries leave for the little island of **Piirissaar** — the only Estonian island in the lake and a place of refuge for Estonians fleeing Russian army service in past centuries.

From Võnnu you can decide either to go in a southeasterly direction and visit **Räpina**, a city developed after 1734 when a paper mill was built, and its manor house which houses Estonia's largest horticultural school, or to head south to **Põlva** and **Taevaskoja**, and see some of the most picturesque country in the land.

If you go to Räpina, it's worth mentioning that the quaint Russian fishing village, **Võõpsu,** lies just east of it. Here, you are on the edge of **Pihkva Jarv** (Lake Pskov) — named for the historical Russian trading city and citadel of Pskov which is located just below the southern edge of the lake.

From Räpina you can continue southward and tour the Petseri district and the rest of Põlvamaa, Võrumaa and Valgamaa, or return to Tartu whence you can proceed westward.

Many visitors believe that Estonia's pristine and largely unspoiled counties of Põlvamaa, Võrumaa and Valgamaa are the most attractive tourist destinations in the country. One reason for the region's popularity is the fact that the landscape here is marked by rolling hills, graceful river valleys, deep lakes and magnificent forests which cross into neighbouring Russia and Latvia. The highest elevation in the three Baltic states, the hill **Suur Munamägi** (318m), is located just south of the city of Võru. Põlva county is one of the smallest in Estonia, but its picturesque hills are bisected by ancient rivers and countless pristine lakes. Southeastern Estonia is home to a small number of Finno-Ugric people related to the Estonians — the Setukesen or Setus. The reasons for the differences between Setus and the Estonian culture, language and traditions are due to the fact that in the early Middle Ages the Setus came under the control of the Russian principality of Pskov whereas the Estonians were largely subjected to German and Swedish or Polish-Lithuanian rule. As a result, the Setus developed cultural and linguistic aspects which demonstrate the influences of Slavic culture and language. Setus are largely Russian Orthodox in belief, and their wooden villages display building techniques and architectural styles very different from those one finds in Estonian communities.

In 1944 Stalin decreed the annexation of much of the Setu homeland and the Setu capital city, Petseri, to the Russian Federation. It was made part of the admininstrative region based in Pskov. The Republic of Estonia refuses to recognize the annexation, and the Estonian-Russian border, recently unilaterally marked by the Russians, is a source of conflict between the two countries.

From Tartu to Petseri

Leave Tartu heading southeast towards the town of **Räpina.** Halfway to Räpina is the village of **Ahja**. A river by the same name lies below it. The manor was built in 1740 and its greatest distinction is that the renowned Estonian writer and literary critic Friedebert Tuglas was born in one of the outbuildings. The Ahja river valley south of the village offers beautiful sandstone cliffs, the highest being Suur Taevaskoja — 24m high and 150m long. Boat trips on the river are a worthwhile excursion, with the most stunning scenery found between the villages of **Valgemetsa** and **Kiidjärve**. Kiidjärve is the site of one of the largest operating watermills in Europe (built in 1914, restored in 1991). The original machinery is still operating in the four-storey mill.

At nearby Taevaskoja, the Ahja rapids were stemmed by an hydro-electric power station, forming the artifical lake Saesaare. The power station houses the Ahja Wildlife Reserve Museum.

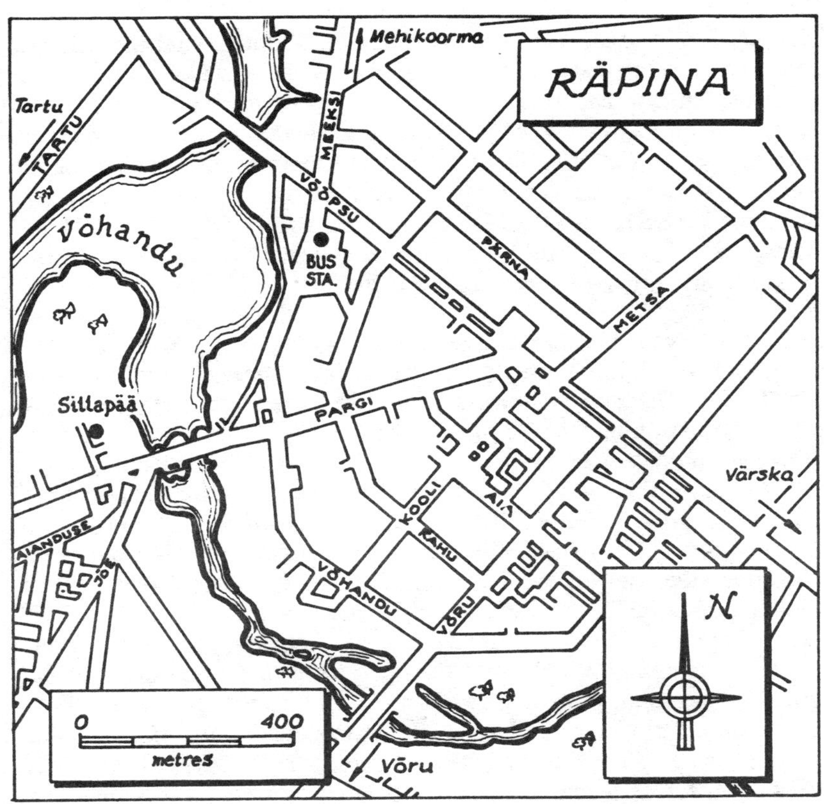

Nine kilometres east of Ahja is the village of **Mooste**, with a manor house of peculiar architecture built in the late 19th century. From Mooste, **Räpina** is a short distance. In 1734, a paper factory, one of Estonia's first industrial enterprises, was constructed at Räpina thus necessitating the kilometre-long lake on the edge of the town. Later, in 1842, a beautiful classical-style manor house, Sillapää, was built on the lake. Today the palace is home to the largest horticultural school in Estonia. Surrounding the manor is a fine park, containing over 300 different kinds of trees and shrubs.

Where to stay in Räpina

JUKU MINIHOTEL, Estakaadi 5; tel: (372)-30-61-937. Two rooms, four beds, shower, WC, phone, TV and sauna. Bicycle and windsurf rentals. On beautiful river bank. Breakfast. Recommended.

RÄPINA BOARDING HOUSE, Rahu 1; tel: (372)-30-61-444, 61-085. Five rooms, 18 beds. Shower and WC on each floor. Bar, car park and garage.

Continue southwards, You are now entering Võrumaa and the historic lands of the Setu people. South of Räpina is the town of **Värska**, the centre of Setu life and culture in Estonia. Every summer Värska holds a Setu singing festival. The fine Russian Orthodox church was built in 1904. Located on an inlet of Lake Pskov, Värska is also known for its fine mineral water that is bottled and sold throughout Estonia. You can stay at the **VARSKA SANATORIUM**, Varska; tel: (372)-30-64-693. 43 rooms, 86 beds. All rooms with WC and shower. Mineral water baths, massage, physiotherapy, restaurant and bar.

South of Värska is the so-called **Setu Sahara**, where sand dunes can rise up to 30m in height. At this point the de facto Russian border is very close by. It is distinctly marked as Russia does not want there to be any further discussion on its possible change.

Further on one comes to the tiny Setu village of **Säätse.** Here one can visit the **Setu Village Museum**. The Setu are Orthodox and speak a dialect of the Võru tongue. Their culture and customs, including songs and costume, differ from other parts of Estonia. Setu women wear distinctive silver jewellery. The Russian Orthodox church was built in 1801. The Russian border here is only metres away.

Access to the Russian-occupied city of **Petseri,** the Setu capital, requires a return to Värska and then a right turn for the drive to the border. A Russian visa is necessary for all travellers except those possessing a former Soviet Union passport or a passport of one of the member states of the Commonwealth of Independent States. Petseri is well-known for its magnificent **Russian Orthodox Cloister**, which was fortified to protect the monks from attacks by the German knights, Swedes, Lithuanians and Baltic tribes. The Cloister was founded in 1473 and its walls encircle eight churches, many of them dating from the 16th century, and a bell tower. The monastery flourished in the 16th century under the auspices of Abbot Cornelius, who was treacherously murdered by Ivan the Terrible. Later, repenting the crime, the Czar had the abbot's body returned to the monastery and laid to rest in a beautiful tomb. In the gold-domed Cathedral of the Dormition is the holy icon of the Most Pure Mother of God (1521) and the sacred relics of St Cornelius. Underneath the monastery are catacombs where monks and wealthy, private individuals are buried in holy ground.

Today the monastery is home to 60 orthodox monks who attend religious services in the morning and evening, serve the faithful in the Petseri region, and work in the monastery's fields. An icon restoration and icon painting centre are housed within the monastery as well. To visit the monastery, contact the Võru Farmers' Union Tourism Centre, Rainis Ruusamäe, Chairman at Liiva tn 11, Võru, EE-2710; tel: (372)-41-217-58, telefax: (372)-41-226-69.

You may return to Estonian territory by leaving Petseri and entering

Estonia just north of the village of **Vastseliina**. Here you can see the remains of one of the region's mightiest castles built in the 14th to 15th centuries and destroyed in the Great Northern War. The castle is situated on a strategic overlook above the small River Piusa. There's a fine walk along the banks of the Piusa for several kilometres north of the castle. Near the castle ruins is the oldest inn in the Baltics — **Piiri Inn**, where customers have been served since the 13th century. You might as well join them.

From Vastseliina take the back roads south to the village of **Ruusmäe**. The village has a fine manor built with a bell-tower and a local history museum. Just north of Ruusmäe is **Suur Munamägi** (Great Egg Hill). At 318m, it's the highest point in the three Baltic states. A small sandy path leads to the summit where an observation tower offers the visitor a magnificent panorama of the surrounding countryside, and the nearby **Vallamägi** (Valla hill, 297m). The view includes regions of the Russian and Latvian countryside as well.

This region of Estonia is known as the Haanja Heights and the surrounding hills are included in the Haanja Natural Preserve. The hills of the preserve are the source of many of Estonia's rivers. 18% of the Preserve is covered by wetlands and bogs — there are more than 16 lakes per 100km^2. The Preserve is also home to many storks. The birds' nests can be seen near the many farmhouses lining the roads from Ötepää to Võru.

The Võru Farmers' Union handbook notes that the use of tractors on farms in the Haanja Heights is difficult since steep inclines result in the higher elevations in local fields being dry and dusty while at the same time the lower portions of the same field are still wet and muddy.

Where to stay in the Suur Munamägi region

LIIVA FARM. Open May 1-Sept 1. Elle and Tasu Prangli offer their beautiful farm to visitors — one bedroom sleeps 2+, 215 EEK per guest. Reservations: (372)-2-683-410.

UTSALI FARM. Open all year. Ecological vegetable farm on lake. Margit and Akti Utsali offer two bedrooms, each of which sleeps four persons. 215 EEK per guest. Reservations: (372)-2-683-410.

KUUSEMÄE FARM. Open all year. 19th century. 1km from the Latvian border. 30km from Suur Munamägi. Tiina and Johannes Kalamees offer two bedrooms, sleeping four. 250 EEK per guest. Reservations: (372)-2-683-410.

MÄE FARM. Open all year. 10km to Suur Munamagi. Cattle, poultry and corn farm. Luule and Kalmer Kobak offer two bedrooms sleeping four persons at 200 EEK per guest. Reservations: (372)-2-683-410.

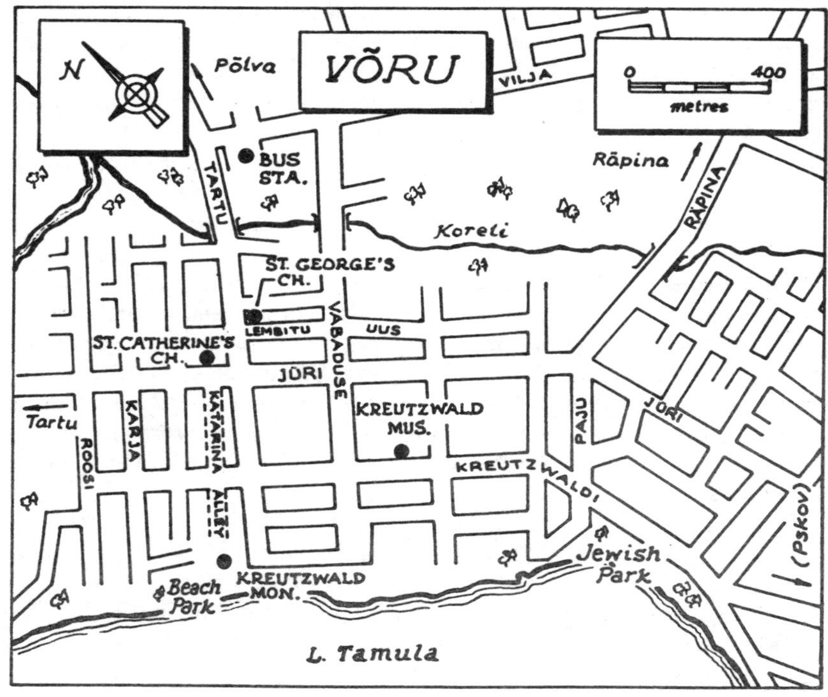

Võru

The road at the base of the hill leads to the capital of Võrumaa, the city of Võru (population 18,000). Here the people speak their own dialect. Võru's position on the border between East and West has long subjected the city and its people to war and destruction. Originally the region surrounding the city was known as Ugandi. In the 1200s, the German Order, the first foreign attackers, subdued those living in the area and placed them under the rule of the Diocese of Tartu. In the Livonian Wars (1558-1581), between the expansionist Russia of Ivan the Terrible and the Livonian Order, great destruction was visited on the region. The city of Võru was established in 1784 by Catherine II of Russia, and so is relatively young. The Lutheran church of St Katherine was built in 1793; the Russian Orthodox Church dates from the same period and houses many beautiful icons. Many of Võru's buildings are wooden.

The compiler of the great Estonian national epic *Kalevipoeg*, Friedrich Reinhold Kreutzwald, practiced medicine in Võru from 1833-1877, and you can visit the **Kreutzwald Museum**, Kreutzwaldi 31; tel: 22-798, dedicated to his life and work. The Estonian army's elite **Kuperjanov Regiment** is based in barracks on the edge of town. The surrounding area has lakes and beaches while inland you can go hiking and skiing.

Where to stay

HOTEL HERMES, Jüri 32a; tel: (372)-41-21-326. 11 rooms, 22 beds. All with shower, WC and TV. Two deluxe rooms. On lakeside. Fishing. Eurocard and Mastercard. Café, lobby bar, casino. Võru railway station 2.5km.

KUBIJA HOTEL, Männiku 43; tel: (372)-41-31-757, fax: 42-498. 70 rooms, 140 beds. Single, double, triple rooms with WC, shower, and radio. 13 summer cabins. On lake. Outdoor pool, restaurant and bar, car park and garage. Railway 2.5km.

MOTEL WALLA, Räpina mnt 15; tel: (372)-41-193-98. Nine rooms, restaurant, sauna. A pretty new motel on a hillside near Võru. Horse riding, hiking, downhill skiing, canoe trips offered according to the season.

VÕRU TOURIST CENTRE, Männiku tee 43; tel: 71-581, 31-757, fax: 42-498. By Lake Kubija. 4km from Võru centre. Rooms with shower, bathroom and balcony. Café and restaurant. Money exchange, car park, conference hall. Also offers cabins for camping — up to four people in one cabin. Nearby volleyball and tennis courts, and minigolf.

Farm stays

In the hamlet of Rannu, bed and breakfast can be booked through Võru Taluturismi Ühendus (the Võru Farm Association for Tourism), Liiva tn, Vöru; tel: (372)-41-217-58 or 41-226-69.

VIRVE RIDING FARM, Pikakannu Küla (a village), near Lasva; tel: 41-210-75, is a beautiful villa specialising in horse riding. 25 persons, tennis court, sauna. Phone in advance.

Where to eat

VÕRU RESTAURANT, Vabaduse 8, (Hrs: noon-midnight).

VÕHANDU RESTAURANT, Koidula 16a, (Hrs: Mon,Tues 7.30am-4pm; Wed-Fri 7.30am-midnight; Sat, Sun 10am-midnight).

CAFÉ KATARIINA, Katariina 4; tel: 42-490. Street (and presumably café) are named after Russia's Czarina Catherine II, official founder of Võru. Pizza available.

CAFÉ WORO, Jüri 11; tel: 21-053.

GRILL DÜNASTIA, Vabaduse 1; tel: 31-481. Open 24-hours. Fast food.

BAR KODOKONO, Petseri mnt 23; tel: 41-074. Hot food available.

Bars

Nightclub bar **METRO**, Vabaduse 5; tel: (372)-41-24-131.

Museums

FR Kreutzwald Museum, Kreutzwaldi 31; tel: (372)-41-22-798.

County Museum, Kreuzwaldi 16; tel: (372)-41-23-939. Exhibits on Võru date back to pre-history.

Travel agents

WORO TRAVEL AGENCY, Jüri 11; tel: (372) 41-21-053.

HERMES LTD, Juri 32; tel: (372)-41-21-326, fax: 21-326.

Service Stations

Rööpa 41.
Rapina mnt 10.
Antsla mnt 23 (repairs).

Others

Aircraft trips over southern Estonia, Võru Farmers' Travel Service, Liiva tn 11, Voru; tel: 41-217-58. From 1000 EEK per person per hour.
Antiques: KARMA, Jüri 17, Võru; tel: 217-78. Hrs: Mon-Fri 9:30am-6pm, Sat 9am-3pm. The largest choice of antiques, samovars, icons, furniture, coins and dishes in southern Estonia.

South of Võru,by some 20km, near the village of **Krabi,** is a magnificent landscape known as *Paganamaa* (Satan's land) located on the Latvian border. The area offers hikers pristine forests, many small lakes, a rolling panorama of hills, and camping. The **Kikkajärv** (Kikka Lake) on the Latvian border has a small island in its centre. Five kilometres west of Võru is the village of **Sõmerpalu** with a manor and a fine surrounding park. Another fine manor, built in the early 20th century, is located just north of Võru in the town of **Vaimela.** Vaimela has a boarding house; tel: (372)-41-74-286. 25 rooms, 50 beds. Single, double and quad rooms with shower, WC, TV and SAT-TV. On a lake. Dining room, car park. Credit cards accepted.

Põlva

From Vaimela proceed north some 20km to **Põlva**, (pop 7,000) the capital of Põlvamaa. The Church of the Virgin Mary was erected in the 13th century and rebuilt in 1645.

Where to stay

HOTEL PESA, Uus 5; tel: (372)-30-90-086, fax: 90-087. 32 rooms, 64 beds. Single 380 EEK, double 520 EEK, luxury 700 EEK. Includes breakfast. Extra bed 110 EEK. Opened in November 1991. All rooms with shower, WC, phone and TV (also SAT-TV). Indoor pool, sauna, solarium, conference facilities, restaurant, bar.

Where to eat

ÕLLERESTORAN, Kesk 10, (in the department store).

Travel agents

KAGUREOS, at the Serviti Health Centre, next to Hotel Pesa in Põlva; arranges local tours as well as tours to Petseri Monastery and to Latvia and Lithuania.

Service stations

JAAMA 70, 3km on the road to Rapina.
PIIRI 16, (repairs).
P-AUTO, Võru mnt 29; tel: 96-552.

Just north of Põlva is the small village of **Himmaste**, best known as the birthplace of the famous Estonian educator and clergyman, **Jakob Hurt** (1839-1907). Hurt was the founder of the Estonian National Museum in Tartu, and became a leader of the national awakening of the 19th century. Today there is a museum dedicated to him in Himmaste.

East of Põlva at **Karilatsi** is an interesting **Peasant Museum**; tel: (372)-30-99-213. Some 18km south of Tartu, at **Rebase**, turn to the left on the road leading to the village of **Kambja**. The village school, built in 1686, is one of the oldest in Estonia. The manor was built in the 1800s.

Return to Tartu via Route A202.

FROM TARTU TO VALGA

Whether you are interested in travelling by train or car to Latvia, or you simply enjoy the beauty of Estonia's rolling countryside, a visit to Valgamaa, or Valga county, is inspiring. Leave Tartu via Route A201. Some 20km south is the town of **Nõo**. It has a beautiful church built in 1683 with one of the first church organs in Estonia, dating from 1781. A monument in nearby Lemmatsi remembers the thousands who lost their lives here during World War II.

Elva

Some ten kilometres south of Nõo is **Elva** (pop 6,000). The town is not interesting in itself, but it is surrounded by a rich landscape of hills, forests and lakes, and is attractive to holidaymakers. In the middle of the town is *Artsi järv* (Artsi Lake). Estonia's second largest lake, Võrtsjärv, is only about 15km west of town.

Where to stay

WAIDE MOTEL, Elva; tel: (372)-27-57-119. 12 rooms, 40 beds. Twin 350 EEK. On Lake Verevi. Double and quad rooms with shower, WC, and TV. Sauna, bar, car park. Elva railway station 3km.
PUHKEBAAS ELVA and MOTEL VEREVI, 2km from Elva; tel: 56-582. Doubles, triples and quads with shared showers.
MOTELL VEHENDI, eastern shore of Võrtsjärv; tel: 54-556. Converted old farmhouse offering singles and doubles. Price includes breakfast. Can be booked at Taru Hotel in Tartu.

Where to eat

ABELI (restaurant and bar), Kesk 10; tel: (372)-27-56-349. Hrs: noon-midnight. Excellent food and service. Recommended.

South of Elva on Route A201 is the village of **Rõngu** with the remains of a 14th century fortress of the German Knights, a church from the same period (rebuilt in 1901), and a famous historical local tavern, *Kõverkõrts* (Crooked Inn) restored in 1989.

From Rõngu take the road eastward to the Estonian 'mountain' resort centre of **Otepää** (population 3,000). Halfway between Rõngu and Otepää, just north of the village of **Palupera**, is the village of **Hellenurme**. Here is the dilapidated manor of Alexander Theodor Middendorf (1815-1894), formerly the director of the Russian Academy of Sciences. Middendorf used the manor's grounds to implement many of his agricultural improvement schemes. Today the manor is an orphanage.

Otepää

Otepää, 150m above sea-level, is an ancient settlement known for its wonderful landscape and winter skiing. The town's name is derived from the word *Ott*, or bear, and the word *pea*, or head. Archaeological exploration reveals that at about 500 BC a fort already existed on the steep hill, **Linnamägi,** east of town. In 1224 Bishop Hermann of Tartu built a brick castle on that spot, and it was the residence of the Bishop of Livonia. Otepää's pretty 17th century church was preceded by a 1224 church on the same site. On May 23 1884 the Estonian Students' Society consecrated its new blue, black and white flag in this church. Thirty-eight years later the flag was adopted by the founders of the new Estonian republic as the national flag. **Pühajärv** (Sacred Lake), below the city, is a beautiful place for water sports. On the lake's shore is a monument dedicated by the Dalai Lama in 1992.

Among well-known visitors to Otepää have been Alexander Solzhenitsyn, Andrei Sakharov, Simone de Beauvoir, Jean-Paul Sartre and Urho Kekkonen, the former President of Finland.

The city is surrounded by the Otepää Upland Landscape Preservation Reserve covering more than 200km^2. The Upland's varied landscape includes rivers, lakes, forests and old farms. There is an average of one lake in each nine square kilometres of territory. The Reserve was established in 1957 and enlarged in 1979. Most of it is 100-175 metres high with 13 hills higher than 200m; the highest, 217m, is the hill *Kuutsemägi* at the ski resort of the same name. At the nearby hill Väike Munamägi (207m) one can find the source of the Estonian river, *Emajõgi* ('Mother River'), immortalized by the writer Lydia Koidula.

Otepää's Uplands receive much more snow than the rest of Estonia,

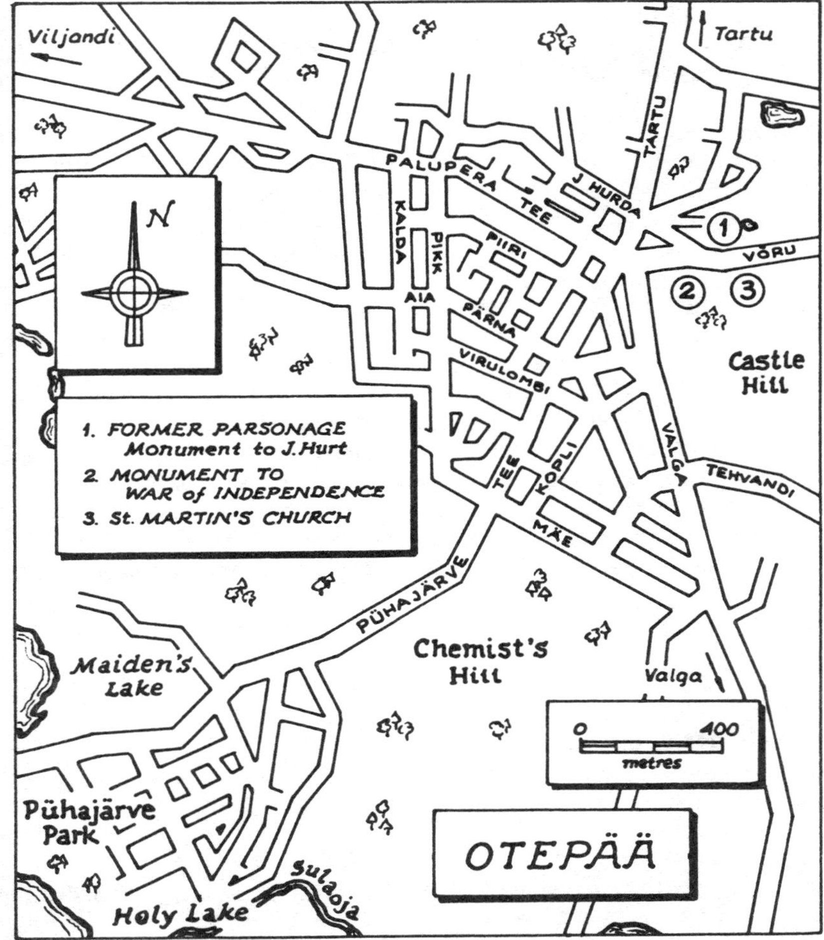

and the average 40cm snowfall usually lasts 110-115 days of each year. In summer, the Uplands remain cool, with an average temperature of 15°C. In the forests of birch, aspen, alder and spruce roam wild boar, elk, roe deer, hare and squirrels. The beaver, which has been extinct in the region, has now made a reappearance. Red fox, pine martens, skunks and weasel also inhabit the woods. The Reserve is home to more than 130 bird species, including the endangered black stork and spotted eagle. Some other birds you'll find are the wren, robin, warbler, and seven species of woodpecker. Owls dominate the skies at night.

One of the most famous trees in Estonia, the great Trepimäe Oak, 400 years old and 6.6m in diameter, can be found just outside Otepää on the side of Trepimäe Hill at Lake Pilkuse. The oak became a symbol for local peasants during the rebellion of 1841.

You can enjoy the Reserve by contacting its main office in Otepää at Kolga tee 28; tel: 55-876 or 55-108.

Where to stay

HOLY LTD HOTEL, Pühajärv, Valgamaa EE2513. Tel: (372)-42-55-103, 55-080, 55-051, fax: 61-206. Large and rather institutional. 95 beds, singles, doubles and triples with shower/bath, WC and TV. Sauna, solarium, shops, two bars, restaurant and playroom. Tennis court, riding, sports equipment rental. Near Pühajärv, fishing. Car park.

KOLGA-ORU HOTEL, near Pühajärv. Tel: (372)-42-55-213, fax: 61-202. Nine rooms. Twin 650 EEK, suite 950 EEK. Sauna, tennis court, fishing and sailing on lake. On Kolga Road, 3km from Otepää.

KUUTSEMÄE SKI CENTRE; tel: (372)-42-57-263. Bed and breakfast rooms for 2-4 people, 50 EEK per person. Slalom slopes, ski lifts.

MAHA HOTEL, 3km southwest of Pühajärv. Tel: (372)-42-54-003. Nine rooms, 32 beds, rustic and well kept lodge. Shared showers and toilets. Sauna. Tennis court, ball games, croquet, car park. 600m from ski lift.

OTEPÄÄ HOLIDAY HOME, Tamme pst 6, Otepää EE2513. Tel: (372)-2-531-942, 609-604 (booking). 23 beds, double, triple and quad rooms. Near lake. Car park.

OTEPÄÄ HOTEL; small, 1¼km south-east of town centre. Tel: (372)-42-55-431.

OTEPÄÄ SUUSAKLUBI (Ski Club of Otepää), Lipuväljak 13. Tel: (372)-42-55-264.

REAL HOTEL, Lipuväljak 22, Otepää EE2513. Tel: (372)-42-54-343, fax: 55-078. Two rooms with phone and TV, shower and WC on each floor. Equipped with secretarial service. Sauna, car park.

Youth Hostel

Hundisoo Hotel, Kastolatsi tee 3; tel: 55-238, 55-934. Double, triple and quad rooms with shower and WC on each floor. Sauna, shared kitchen, TV lounge. Car park. Railway station 10km; bus stop 1km.

Camping

Annimatsi, 4km outside Otepää. Tel: 55-317, 54-060 (booking), fax: 611-229. Double, triple and quad rooms and cabins. Sauna, bar, caravan sites. Car park.

Where to eat

PÜHAJÄRVE, at the edge of Püharjärv in Otepää. Tel: 55-217. 3km from centre. Hrs: 1pm-6pm, and 7pm until last client leaves. Delicious food, good service. Dancing in the evenings. Recommended.

Travel agents

Otepää Reisibüroo (Otepää Travel Agency), Lipuväljak 11. Tel: (372)-42-54-060, fax: 55-293.

Otepää Tourist Information, Lipuväljak 9. Tel: (372)-42-55-364, fax: 55-293.
Real Reisid, Lipuväljak 5. Tel: (372)-42-55-009, 54-042, fax: 55-293.

Other

Public transport between Tallinn and Otepää. Buses leave Tallinn for Otepää daily at 8.10am, 2.45pm, and 3.35pm, arriving at 1.05pm, 6.30pm and 8.40pm respectively.
Upland Preserve Administration, Kolga tee; tel: 55-108.

Sangaste

South of Otepää is the small village of **Sangaste** with perhaps the finest **manor** in the country. The manor's earlier incarnations stood on the spot as early as 1287 and belonged to the Bishops of Tartu. In 1873 the estate passed into the hands of Duke Frederick Magnus von Berg (1845-1938), a wealthy and well-known world traveller of the last century. Interested in agriculture, he grew, among other things, a type of rye called *sangaste*. The building of Sangaste Palace took nearly 60 years. After his death the state continued the work. Duke von Berg is buried in the grounds of the palace, which became a youth camp for the Soviet Communist 'Pioneer' movement until the end of the Soviet empire. Today, the palace serves as a hotel. The building is designed to follow the architecture of the famous Windsor Castle. The architect, Otto Hippicus, also designed **Kaarli Kirik** (St Charles Church) in Tallinn and the Alexander Church in Narva. Surrounding the castle is a beautiful park. A walk through the park is recommended. On a hill above the **Ema River** stands a chapel, first built in the 14th century. The present structure dates from 1742.

Where to stay

SANGASTE CASTLE HOTEL; tel: (372)-42-91-343, fax: 55-078. 22 rooms, 100 beds. Single, double, triple and quad rooms. Shower and WC on each floor. Sauna, solarium, swimming pool, restaurant, bar. Riding, fishing and boating. Car park. Railway 10km.

Valga

Twenty kilometres south of Sangaste are the city of **Valga** (pop 17,900) and the Latvian city of **Valka.** The two actually form one town which is divided by the national borders of Estonia and Latvia right in the middle of the town centre. Previously, Valga was a town right on the border of two ancient Estonian provinces, Ugandi and Sakala, so its split personality has a long history. It is now the administrative seat of Valga county.

Valga was first established as a fortress by the German Knights in the early 1200s in order to advance into Estonian lands from their base in Rīga. Later, however, the town, unlike its peers, had no true

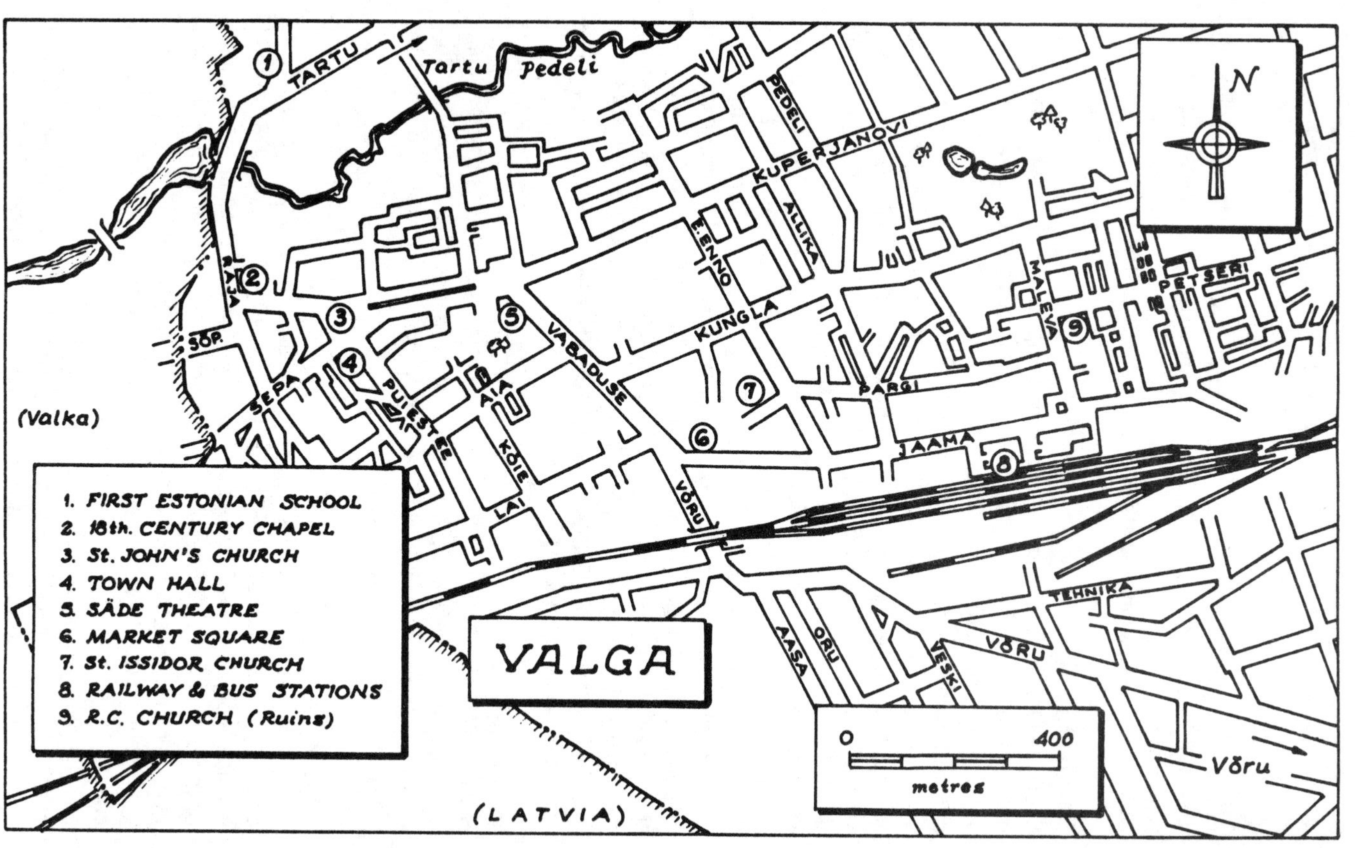
VALGA
N
0
400
metres
(LATVIA)
(Valka)
Tartu
Võru
TARTU
Pedeli
PEDELI
KUPERJANOVI
ALLIKA
E. ENNO
KUNGLA
VABADUSE
VÕRU
PARGI
JAAMA
MALEVA
PETSERI
TEHNIKA
VESKI
ORU
AASA
AIA
KÕIE
LAI
PUIESTEE
SEPA
RAJA
SÕP.
1. FIRST ESTONIAN SCHOOL
2. 18th. CENTURY CHAPEL
3. St. JOHN'S CHURCH
4. TOWN HALL
5. SÄDE THEATRE
6. MARKET SQUARE
7. St. ISSIDOR CHURCH
8. RAILWAY & BUS STATIONS
9. R.C. CHURCH (Ruins)

fortification, which made it perpetually vulnerable to attack. In 1560, the city came under the control of Russia after Ivan the Terrible defeated the German Knights at the climactic battle of Helme. Russian control ended after Lithuania and Poland defeated Russian forces, and in 1582 Valga passed to Poland-Lithuania. In 1584 the Polish king, Stefan Batory, granted Valga the rights of a town. Since its beginning, Valga developed as a market town, and the opening of the Rīga-Pskov railway in 1889 brought about the town's industrialization. Today the town has furniture, needlework, meat and grain industries.

Despite its history, Valga does not offer any particularly significant monuments. However, its charm lies in the city's overall architectural ensemble. **Jaani Kirik** (St John's Church) in the centre, was built in 1787 in early Classical style from a design by Christian Haberland. The **Town Hall** dates from 1865. The **Regional Museum** is also worth a visit.

Where to stay

HOTEL SÄDE (spark), Jaama pst 1; tel: (372)-42-41-650. 40 rooms. Sauna, swimming pool, restaurant, casino. Near the railroad station. Car park.
HOTEL METSISE (woodgrouse), Kuperjanovi 76; tel: (372)-42-40-975, 41-704. Rooms for 20. Café, sauna, car park. Beautiful modern hotel.

Where to eat

BAR MARET, Kesk 16; tel: (372)-42-42-647, fax: 55-078. Dancing in the evenings.
CAFÉ KOIDU, Vabaduse 2/4.

Just north of Valga is the village of **Paju** and a monument to Finnish volunteers who fought in the battle for Paju estate in Estonia's War of Independence. The manor was built in 1873. In the battle, the great Estonian war-hero, Julius Kuperjanov, together with 20% of the Estonian forces present, was mortally wounded fighting the Bolsheviks.

Travel from Valga to Tõrva. At Kalme, four kilometres southeast of Tõrva, turn right to the village of **Jõgeveste**, which offers the visitor the beautiful Mausoleum of the Field Marshal Barclay de Tolly, erected in 1812. Prince Michael Bogdanovitsch Barclay de Tolly is known as one of the greatest generals in military history for his conduct of Russia's successful campaign against Napoleon I of France, which eventually saw De Tolly march into Paris on March 31 1814 at the head of a vast Russian military parade.

Tõrva (population 3,700), which came into existence in 1875, is a beautiful little garden town on the Õhne river. The word *tõrv* in Estonian means tar, a commodity the town is known for. South of it, on a hill, are the remains of Castle Liinmägi, dating to the 13th century. Southwest of Tõrva, in the village of **Holdre**, is a manor built in 1910 in Jugendstil and now owned by the Valga auto base. Eight kilometres west of Holdre is the village of **Taagepera** with a fine manor built in 1912 surrounded by one of the largest parks in southern Estonia.

Just west of Tõrva, at **Helme**, is the site of the decisive battle for the Livonian Order in 1560. Beaten by the Russian army, the Order ceased to exist as a state; its lands were usurped by Poland-Lithuania and its last remaining master became a vassal of Poland with his ducal seat at Mittau (Jelgava), Latvia. In the slopes near the ruins of the Livonian Order's castle are located Estonia's largest and best known caves.

Chapter Ten

Western Estonia and the Islands

PÄRNU

Pärnu (population 55,000), a coastal town and Estonia's fifth largest city, is located at the upper reaches of the Gulf of Rīga, on the Baltic Sea. It is best known as a resort and health centre. Its beaches attract thousands of holidaymakers each summer and its health spas have offered cures since the 19th century. It is the administrative centre for Pärnu county (4,798km^2). Nearly one half of Pärnu county is covered by forests of pine, birch and fir, and the timber industry is an important employer. One quarter of the county is marsh and peat bogs. The Nigula Natural Reserve protects a notable bog and forest landscapes.

Although evidence of settlement goes back thousands of years, Pärnu did not take on the contours of a town until the 13th century. It originally started as two towns — 'Old Pärnu' built by Bishop Heinrich in 1251, and 'New Pärnu' built by the Knights of the Sword in 1257. Constant fighting between the episcopal forces and the knights led to destruction of 'Old Pärnu' and 'New Pärnu' went on to become a member of the Hanseatic League. Briefly, it even had the status of a Hanseatic League member. Today it is still engaged in commerce and industrial activity, principally in timber and building materials.

On the left bank of the river a castle of the Livonian Order was built as early as 1265. The remnants of the city's medieval fortifications can be seen in the **Red Tower** (15th century) and the **Tallinn Gate**, which dates from the 17th century. The **City Hall** at Uus 4 is built in the Classicist style, with a Jugendstil wing. The building dates from 1788. Nearby, on Rüütli, at the corner of Nikolai Street, is the **Elisabeth Church**, dating from 1747 and named after the Czar's daughter, Jelisaweta. At the corner of Uus and Vee streets stands the Orthodox **Ekatarina kirik**, named after Catherine II of Russia. At Kuninga Street

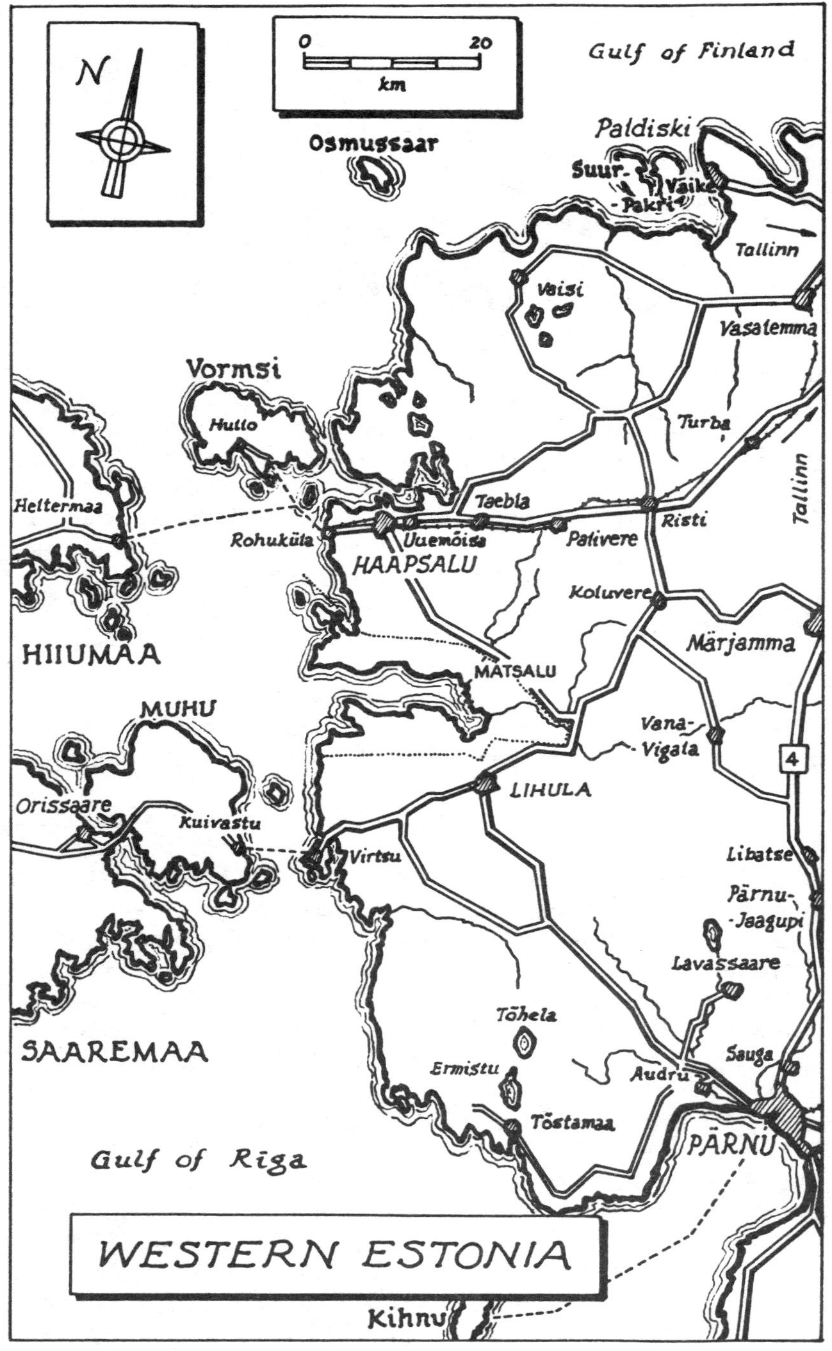

N
0
20
km
Gulf of Finland
Osmussaar
Paldiski
Suur-
Väike
-Pakri
Tallinn
Vaisi
Vasalemma
Vormsi
Hullo
Turba
Tallinn
Heltermaa
Taebla
Risti
Rohuküla
Uuemõisa
Palivere
HAAPSALU
Koluvere
HIIUMAA
Märjamma
MATSALU
MUHU
Vana-
-Vigala
4
LIHULA
Orissaare
Kuivastu
Virtsu
Libatse
Pärnu-
-Jaagupi
Lavassaare
Tõhela
SAAREMAA
Ermistu
Audru
Sauga
Tõstamaa
PÄRNU
Gulf of Riga
WESTERN ESTONIA
Kihnu

stands a second Russian Orthodox Church, the **Preobrazhenski Church.**

Toward the first half of the 19th century, the main recreation area was the old park, known as **Badesalon**, where townspeople relaxed by playing billiards and reading newspapers. They took their meals in the salon and danced to a live orchestra in the park. The city changed radically when, in 1837, several merchants got together to build an inn. Seeing no great economic opportunities in the existent leisure pastimes, they undertook the building of a full-scale spa modelled after the one in Rīga. By 1889, the city was in the resort business, promising rest and rehabilitation through restorative and pacifying mud baths.

Between 1850 and 1870 Pärnu became one of the largest export centres in Estonia. Grain from Estonia and Latvia was shipped to other nations, and the city's port handled four times the amount of traffic as Tallinn. The opening of the St Petersburg-Tallinn railway in 1870 changed this, and Pärnu's trade volume began to decline. Later, Rīga came to be the dominant Baltic export harbour for the Russian empire.

Shipbuilding activity in and around Pärnu developed rapidly in the 1860s with the nearby town of Häädemeste becoming the dominant port in the Gulf of Rīga. Between 1861 and 1916, 45,000 tons of sailing ships were constructed in Estonia — 72% in the ports on the Gulf of Rīga.

In 1860, Pārnu witnessed the maiden voyage of the first steamship under Estonian command, and by 1911 the city had ten coastal steamships regularly calling at its ports.

The last part of the 19th century also witnessed the opening in Pärnu of the largest pulp mill in Estonia. On February 23 1918 in Pärnu, the Estonian Rescue Committee of Konstantin Päts, Jüri Vilms an attorney, and Dr Konstantin Konik physician and later Tartu University professor, issued their *Manifesto to the Estonian People* in which they stated:

> 'Down the centuries, the people of Estonia have yearned to regain their independence. Generation after generation has nursed the hope that after the dark night of servitude and the violent rule of alien nations the time would come when in every home the torch will flash and flame at both ends... when Kalev will come home to make his children happy... In this fateful hour, the Estonian Diet, as the legitimate representative of the country and its people, having made its decision unanimously with the democratic political parties... has deemed it necessary to... (declare) Estonia an independent Republic.'

As a resort town it offers, in addition, the only professional theatre in Estonia, *Endla*, that operates in the summer. On the south bank is located the old town, with its charming downtown district, the theatre, the harbour, the sanatoriums and the famous beach. The town is so small that only a few hours of pleasant promenading are needed to introduce the sights. A short distance south is the small park in which stands the statue of Estonia's passionately patriotic poet of the national awakening period, Lydia Koidula. Her home, located on the north bank of the river, is a museum.

Pärnu is the host to the **Visual Anthropology Festival**, founded in 1987 by Lennart Meri, subsequently the first president of the Republic of Estonia after the restoration of independence in 1991. The festival is held annually in July. It has been sponsored by the Pärnu International Visual Anthropology Society since 1990, after the Society was founded by the internationally respected documentary film-maker, Mark Soosaar.

The festival serves as a forum for Eastern and Western scholars to discuss problems of cultural survival and integrity, and it awards prizes to the best films in different categories. The society awards a prize to the best native film-maker in memory of Andris Slapiņš, the famous Latvian cameraman and filmmaker murdered by Soviet troops in Rīga on January 20 1991, during the storming of the Interior Ministry.

Where to stay

AISA, Aisa 39, tel: (372)-44-43-186, fax: 45-932. Within walking distance of town centre. Has dining room, sauna, bar, souvenir shop, car park.

EMMI, Laine 2, tel: (372)-44-22-043, fax: 45-472. New small hotel by the seaside. All rooms with shower/bath, WC, phone and TV.

KAJAKAS, Seedri 2, tel: (372)-44-43-098, fax: 50-905. 42 rooms, shower and WC on each floor except for two rooms. Sauna, near beach, car park. Major credit cards accepted.

LEHARU, Sääse 7, tel: 44-45-874, fax: 44-40-064. 23 double rooms. (Single 210 EEK, double 310 EEK.) In the same building as Hotel Monate.

MONATE HOTEL, Sääse 7, 5th floor, tel: 44-41-472, fax: 44-43-092. 19 doubles, 4 singles (single 210 EEK, double 310 EEK). All rooms have showers and cable TV. Bar and sauna. Highly recommended for location, price and service. Price includes breakfast.

PÄRNU, Rüütli 44, tel: (372)-44-43-100, fax: 42-944. Singles 440 EEK, doubles 590 EEK. Centrally located, former Soviet-era plant now cleaned up and with lots of services. Major credit cards accepted. Good disco. 10 minutes to beach.

PÄRNU YACHTING CLUB, Lootsi 6, tel: (372)-44-41-948, fax: 42-950. Rooms with shower, WC and phone. Sauna, fitness room, café. On riverside, 1km to sea.

RANNA HOTEL, Ranna pst 5, tel: (372)-44-45-312, fax: 44-533. On the beach. Opened in 1994 after completely renovating 62 rooms. Singles May-Sept 945 EEK, doubles 1,180 EEK. Has a restaurant, bar, summer terrace, conference facilities. A Finest Hotel.

RUUNAWERE, on the Tallinn-Riia road (Pärnu mnt). A beautiful small restaurant and hotel, 47km from Tallinn.

STRAND, Tammsaare 27, tel: (372)-44-22-502, 24-243 (reservations), fax: 24-276. 60 rooms. A completely remodelled pre-war hotel on the beach. Now considered by many to be the best in Pärnu. Expensive. All rooms with

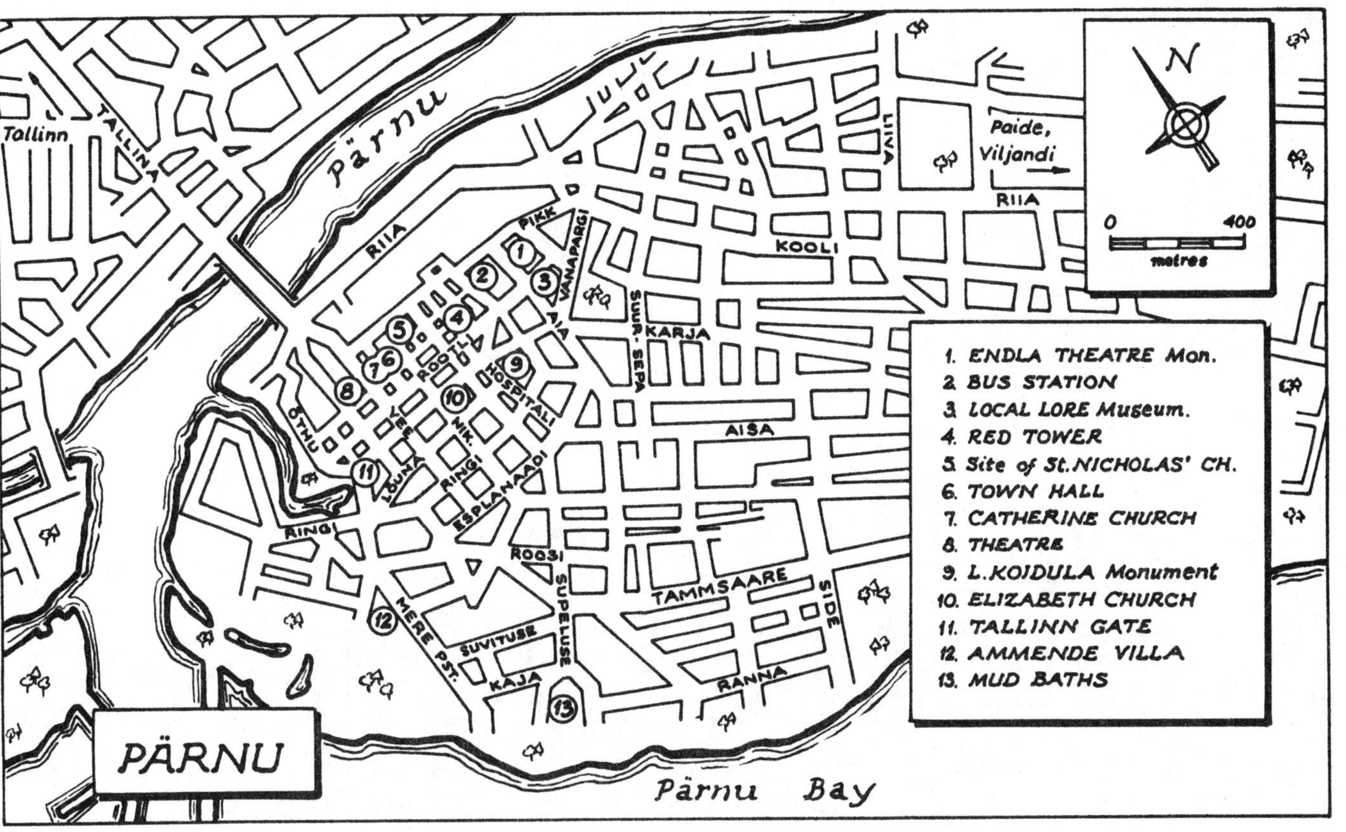
1. ENDLA THEATRE Mon.
2. BUS STATION
3. LOCAL LORE Museum.
4. RED TOWER
5. Site of St.NICHOLAS' CH.
6. TOWN HALL
7. CATHERINE CHURCH
8. THEATRE
9. L.KOIDULA Monument
10. ELIZABETH CHURCH
11. TALLINN GATE
12. AMMENDE VILLA
13. MUD BATHS
N
0
400
metres
Paide,
Viljandi
Tallinn
TALLINA
Pärnu
RIIA
LIIVA
RIIA
KOOLI
PIKK
VANAPARGI
AIA
SUUR-SEPA
KARJA
HOSPITALI
VEE
NIK.
ÕHTU
LOUNA
RINGI
ESPLANAADI
AISA
RINGI
ROOSI
SUPELUSE
TAMMSAARE
SIDE
MERE PST.
SUVITUSE
KAJA
RANNA
PÄRNU
Pärnu Bay

shower/bath, WC, phone and TV. Balconies with view of the sea. Sauna, indoor pool, meeting rooms, facilities for children. The only hotel in Estonia that has a parking garage for its guests' cars. Night club '4 Stars', restaurant 'El Mare'.
VALGA, Pärnu mnt 18, on the road to Latvia, 20km south of Pärnu; tel: (372)-44-98-265. 15 rooms. Double 440 EEK. Sauna, swimming pool, bar. Highly recommended.
VICTORIA, Kuninga 25, tel: (372)-44-43-412, fax: 43-415. Single 750 EEK, double 990 EEK, suite 1200 EEK. Located in the heart of Pärnu, has very attractive rooms, good restaurant, bar, sauna, and gift shop. Major credit cards accepted. Breakfast included. Highly recommended. A Best Western hotel.

Where to eat

BISTRO, Rüütli 45. Fast food, pasta, etc.
CROWN MARYA, Puhavaimu 8, tel: (372)-44-43-959. Bar and restaurant in a 1674 built house.
JAHISAAL CENTRAL (Hunters' Hall), Hospidali 6, tel: (372)-44-40-575, 40-707. Hrs: noon-1am. Game dishes, Holstein beer.
KADRI, Pühavaimu 15, tel: (372)-44-45-334. Spotless diner serving national food.
PÄRNU, Rüütli 44, tel: (372)-44-42-230. In the downtown hotel of the same name.
POSTIPOISS, Vee 12. In an old post office; tel: (372)-44-40-204. Good food. Pärnu beer.
RANNAHOONE, Ranna pst 3, tel: (372)-44-40-222. A large place on the beach with dancing.
RESTORAN RENDEZVOUS, Akadeemia 5, tel: (372)-44-40-468. A fine restaurant with a broad menu. Hrs: noon-midnight.
VICTORIA, Kuninga 25. Best restaurant in town.

Bars

BAAR SÕNAJALG, Kuninga 18. Entrance is at the rear of the building.
BAAR VIIKING, Ranna pst 7. Bar, casino, dancing.
BRISTOL, Rüütli 45, tel: (372)-44-44-800.
KOMANDANDI KELLER, Nikolai 8, tel: (372)-44-44-467.
ROOSI KELDER, Kuninga 18. Another of the abundant cellar bars.
SKY BAR, Ranna pst 3, tel: (372)-44-44-900.
TALLINNA VARAV, tel: (327)-44-45-073. Located in the *Tallinn Gate*, a remnant of the city's ancient fortification, near the intersection of Vana-Tallinn and Kuninga. One of the few bars not in a cellar.
TOMMI, Niidu 7, tel: (372)-44-44-277.
VIGOR CLUB, Riia mnt, near the bridge. River-front yacht club with three bars, a restaurant and a casino.

Museums

LINNAMUUSEUM (Town Museum), Rüütli 53; open Wed-Fri 11am-6pm, Sat-Sun 11am-5pm, tel: (372)-44-43-464.

LYDIA KOIDULA MEMORIAAL MUUSEUM (Lydia Koidula's House Museum), Jannseni 37; open Wed-Sun 10am-5pm, Sat 10am-4pm, tel: (372)-44-41-663.
PUNANE TORN (Red Tower), Hommiku 11; open Wed-Sun noon-5pm.

Churches
ELIISABETI KIRIK (St Elizabeth's), Nikolai 22. Evangelical-Lutheran.
KATARIINA KIRIK (St Katherine's), Vee 16. Orthodox.
BAPTIST CONGREGATION, Henno 3.
ADVENTIST AND METHODIST CONGREGATIONS, Karja 3.

Banks
PÄRNU KOMMERTSPANK, Rüütli 54.
PÄRNU MAAPANK, Rüütli 39.

Galleries
GRANIIT, Tallinna mnt 12. Sculptures, monuments, paintings. Tel: (372)-44-43-339.

Medical aid
Sillutuse 6.
Ravi 2.
Suur-Sepa 16.

Post
MAIN POST OFFICE, Akadeemia 7.

Mud baths
MUDARAVILA (Pärnu Mud baths), Ranna pst 1, tel: (372)-44-42-461. Curative mud treatments, mud baths, massage, curative baths for circulatory skeletal disorders, arthritis, neurosis.

Public transportation
Bus Station, Ringi 3; tel: (372)-44-41-554. Next to ticket office is a left-luggage office (*pakihoid*).
Railway Station, Tammiste; tel: (372)-44-40-733.
Airport, tel: (372)-44-40-752.

Car rental
TARVIS, Savi 3.

Handcrafts and gift shops
ARS, Ringi 4.
PÄRL, Supeluse 3; handmade sweaters and other pleasing gift items.
VALGE SALONG, Pikk 12.

Police headquarters
Pikk 18, tel: (372)-44-41-405.

Taxi
Taxi Station, tel: (372)-44-41-240.

Theatre and entertainment
ENDLA, Keskväljak 1, tel: (372)-44-42-480.
CHAPLIN CENTRE, Esplanaadi 10. Former Communist Party headquarters converted into a multi-space gallery, cinema and coffee shop. Charlie Chaplin theme throughout.

Tourist information
TOURISM DEVELOPMENT CENTRE, Supeluse 18b, Pärnu EE3600, tel: (372)-44-45-533 or 45-633, fax: 45-266 or 45-633.

Travel agents
Pärnu Reisibüroo (Pärnu Travel Bureau), Kuninga 32; tel: (372)-44-42-750 or 42-550.
Reiser Travel Agency, Rüütli 35; tel: (372)-44-44-500, fax: 44-885.

Yacht club
Tel: (372)-44-41-948, fax: 42-950.

Fuel
There's a new Shell station in town, the first in Estonia since World War II.

Around Pärnu
A fascinating daytrip from Pärnu is either a Kihnu or Ruhnu sojourn. Centuries ago, **Kihnu Island** (40km southwest of Pärnu) served as a penal colony for mainlanders. More recently, the islanders lived from fishing, seal hunting and, to a lesser extent, farming. Kihnu women still wear home-woven, colourful, striped skirts daily. The contemporary Western world with its advanced technology is still almost unknown on this flat, forest covered island of less than 600 people.

Ruhnu, smaller than Kihnu, is 100km southwest of Pärnu. Before World War II, Ruhnu had for centuries a Swedish population which fled in August 1944, in advance of the Red Army, leaving behind their homes, fields, animals and boats. The island's wooden church, built in 1644, is the oldest wooden building in Estonia.

Reiser Travel Bureau, Rüütli 35 in Pärnu, can arrange excursions for you to both islands.

South of Pärnu, towards the Latvian border, the principal attraction is 20km away at **Tahku**. Konstantin Päts, the Estonian president who was arrested and deported to Russia by the Soviets in 1940, was born here

and the monument to him was the first to be restored during the freedom struggle in the late 1980s. The landscape here offers lovely coastline, including Estonia's biggest dunes at **Rannametsa**.

HAAPSALU

Travelling northward from Pärnu along the coast on the main road, Haapsalu (pop 15,000) is the next reasonably-sized town on the coast of the Baltic Sea. It is an ancient settlement where an episcopal castle was built and completed in 1297 after a period of 150 years. Modified over centuries, it still stands and holds the legend of the White Lady in the window of the ancient cathedral in which regular worship services are still held. The White Lady, a lover who was walled up for the sin of entering the all-male castle, appears on an August night of a full moon in the cathedral window.

In the old town, around *Lossiplats* (Castle Square), the oldest building, **Jaani kirik** (St John's Church), dates from the 16th century. Others date from the 18th century: the apothecary, built in 1772; the late-baroque *Raekoda* (Town Hall), which currently houses the local museum, built in 1775; and the former court-house, built in 1787. Most of the wooden structures in the old town date from the 19th and 20th centuries, Haapsalu being almost totally destroyed in the Livonian Wars and its castle blown up in 1715 on the order of Peter I.

The city's real attraction is its restful atmosphere. Haapsalu became a health resort in the 19th century, when the first bath house and mud cure facility were built, due largely to the efforts of Dr Carl Abraham Hunnius, who investigated the curative muds in the bays around Haapsalu. Members of the Czar's court used to vacation here, as did Tchaikovsky. In his memory, the so-called Tchaikovsky Bench was erected in 1940. The unusually long covered platform at the railroad station was built to protect every eminent visitor stepping from the train against the slightest drop of rain.

During the Soviet occupation a military base was built on the edge of town and thus the city was closed to all visitors. Today, Haapsalu again welcomes foreign visitors. Although mud spas exist in Pärnu and Saaremaa, Haapsalu maintains that the mud from one of its bays is the best. With an energetic, new city government that promotes tourism, new hotels and pensions are entering the market. Check at the city's tourism office on Posti 34, tel: (372)-47-45-248, for the most suitable accommodations besides those listed below. Haapsalu can serve as a convenient base for visiting other places such as Noarootsi, Matsalu Nature Reserve, or the outer islands in the area.

Where to stay

BERGFELDT SPA, Suur-Liiva 15 A. A new mud-cure establishment, double rooms with shower and WC. Mud baths, laser treatment, herb baths, massage

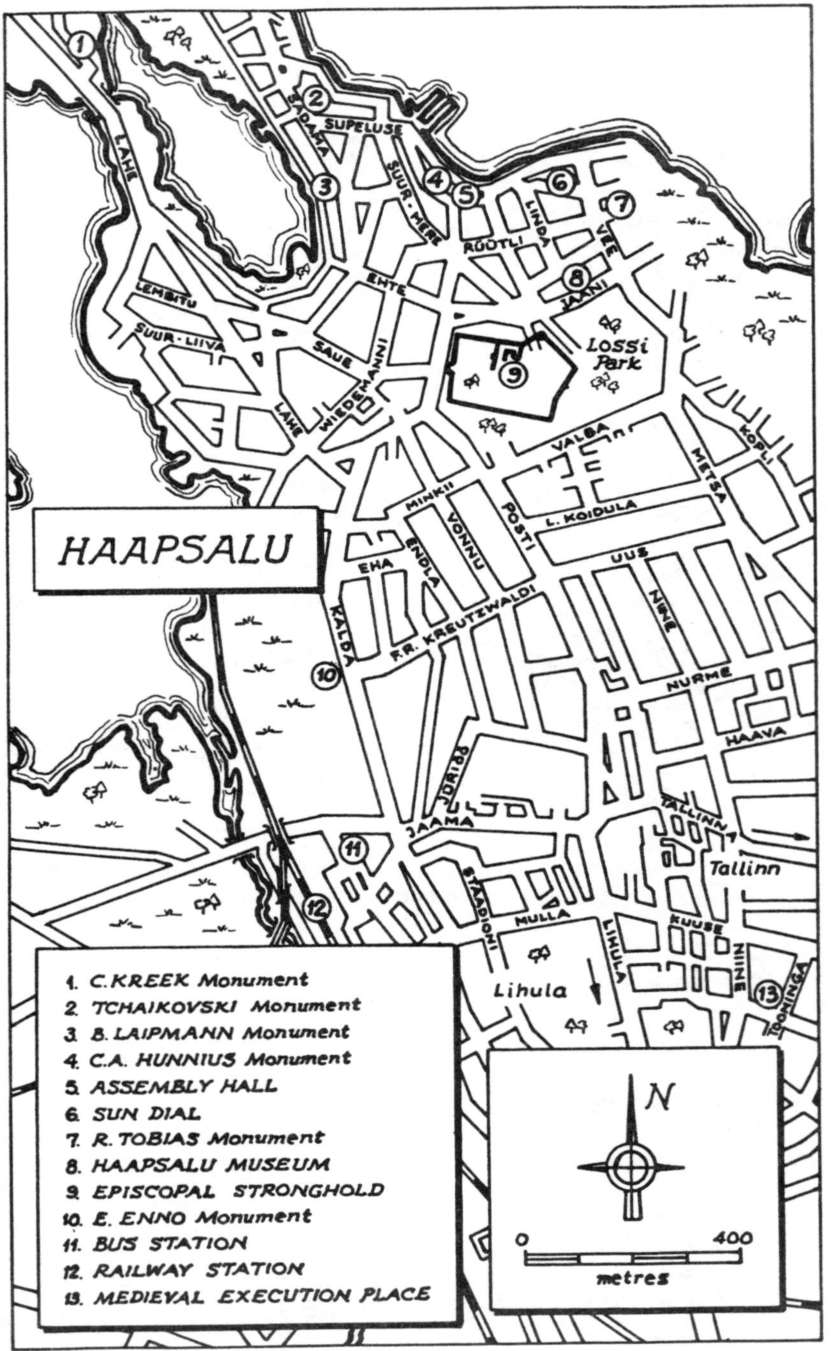
HAAPSALU
1. C.KREEK Monument
2. TCHAIKOVSKI Monument
3. B. LAIPMANN Monument
4. C.A. HUNNIUS Monument
5. ASSEMBLY HALL
6. SUN DIAL
7. R. TOBIAS Monument
8. HAAPSALU MUSEUM
9. EPISCOPAL STRONGHOLD
10. E. ENNO Monument
11. BUS STATION
12. RAILWAY STATION
13. MEDIEVAL EXECUTION PLACE
N
0
400
metres
LAHE
SADAMA
SUPELUSE
SUUR-MERE
RÜÜTLI
LINDA
VEE
JAANI
EHTE
LEMBITU
SUUR-LIIVA
SAUE
WIEDEMANNI
Lossi Park
VALBA
KOPLI
METSA
MINKII
VONNU
POSTI
L. KOIDULA
UUS
NIINE
EHA
ENDLA
KALDA
F.R. KREUTZWALDI
NURME
HAAVA
JAAMA
TALLINNA
Tallinn
STAADIONI
MULLA
LIHULA
KUUSE
Lihula
TOOMINGA

and special diets. On the sea. Tel: (372)-47-45-830, fax: 44-764.
HAAPSALU HOTEL, Posti 43. Single 420 EEK, twin 520 EEK, double 600 EEK. Very comfortable, reasonably priced, modern hotel in the centre of town. Restaurant, bar, conference hall, car park. Tel: (372)-47-44-847.
HOTELL LAINE, Sadama 9/11, beside Väike-viik Lake. Soviet-era sanatorium building transformed into hotel that has singles and doubles with private bath. Tel: (372)-42-45-639.
HAAPSALU JAHTKLUBI (Haapsalu Yacht Club), Holmi 5A. Pleasant wood-panelled rooms with shared bathrooms, bar and summer café. Tel: (372)-47-45-582, fax: 45-536.
PÄEVA PANSIONAAT, Lai 7. New, pleasant small hotel, double rooms with private bath; dining room, sauna, garage. Tel: (372)-47-45-244, fax: 45-484.
TAMMIKU HOTEL, Uuemõisa, Ehitajate tee 3A. Tel: (372)-47-56-773. 3km from centre. 24 rooms (double 350 EEK). Modern hotel, restaurant, sauna, bar, casino, tennis hall, swimming pool.

Camping
Kamping at Silma, east of Haapsalu, 12km off the Tallinn Road.

Where to eat
HAAPSALU HOTEL, Posti 43. Has a dining room as well as the *Monika Baar* which seems to be popular.
HOTEL LAINE, on Sadama, beside Väike-viik Lake. A large dining room on the second floor with a broad menu and live music.
ROOTSITURU KOHVIK, Karja 3, tel: (372)-47-45-058. The café at the 'Swedish market place'. Old style, near the castle. Has generous portions of good food.

Bars
AFRICA, in the Haapsalu Hotel. One of the best discos in Estonia. Patrons drive all the way from Tallinn to dance here. Disco open 9pm to 3am. Casino. Tel: (372)-47-45-291.
MERERIST, Tallinna mnt 1.
MONIKA at Haapsalu Hotell, Posti 43.
WESPO, Lihula mnt 10.

Banks
HAAPSALU HOIUPANK, Karja 4; open Mon-Fri 9am-1pm and 2pm-6pm, Sat 9am-1pm.
LEP HOIUPANK, Karja 17; open Mon-Fri 9am-5pm, Sat 9am-1pm.

Churches
JAANI KIRIK (St John's), Evangelical-Lutheran.
TOOMKIRIK (Cathedral), Evangelical-Lutheran.
ALEKSANDER NEVSKI KIRIK (Alexander Nevsky), Orthodox.

0
20
km
VORMSI
Haapsalu
Kärdla
Körgessaare
Hullo
Kõpu
Käina
Rohuküla
HIIUMAA
Heltermaa
Kassari
Emmaste
MUHU
Koguva
Liiva
Virtsu
SAAREMAA
Panga
Orissaare
Eemu
Kuivastu
Angla
Võhma
Poide
Veere
Mustjala
Lõõne
Pidula
Laimjala
Kaali
Valjala
Kihelkonna
Kõljala
Viki
Kärla
Kaarma
VILSANDI
VIIDUMÄE
Kuressaare
Salme
N
Torgu
Sääre
RUHNU
(Latvia)
WESTERN ISLANDS

Historic sites

MUUSEUM, Kooli 2; exhibits city's history, open Wed-Sun 11am-5pm.
TOOMKIRIK (Cathedral); open Sat-Sun noon-4pm, tel: (372)-47-45-456 or 44-862.

Post

POSTIMAJA (Post Office), Posti 1; open Mon-Fri 8am-12.30pm and 1pm-6pm, Sat 9am-4pm.

Public transport

RAUDTEEJAAM (Railway Station), Raudteejaama 1; tel: (372)-47-57-673. One of the finest stations in the Baltics, a legacy of the Russian Imperial Railway. Is being restored slowly.
BUSSIJAAM (Bus Station), Raudteejaama 1; tel: (372)-47-57-791.

Travel agents

WESTRA LTD, Posti 39, PO Box 67; tel: (372)-47-45-649, fax: 45-464.
LÄÄNEMAA REISID, Karja 2, tel: (372)-47-45-037.
HAAPSALU INTERNATIONAL TRAVEL SERVICES LTD, Kastani 12-5, tel/fax: (372)-47-56-667.

Books and maps

HELK, Karja 6.

Yacht club

Tel: (372)-44-45-582, fax: 45-536.

SAAREMAA

At 2,668km^2, Saaremaa is the largest of Estonia's 1,500 islands. Anchored in the Baltic Sea, it suggests summer getaways: charming fishing villages along the coastline, the occasional windmill, and tidy gardens around tidy cottages. The tranquil setting disguises its difficult past and the hard life the islanders have always endured, due to a combination of foreign invasions and poor soil for farming. Forty-thousand people live on the island.

The oldest archaeological sites on the island are the Stone Age settlements at Pihtla-Kõnnu, Naakamäe, Võhma. The inhabitants were hunters and fishermen. There is anthropological speculation that Saaremaa is *Ultima Thule,* the island discovered by Pytheas around 310 BC. In the 13th century, foreign invaders arrived. The episcopal castle in Kuressaare, and three Gothic-style churches, in Valjala, Kaarma and Poide, were constructed in the century thereafter.

Manor architecture is relatively modest, but quite individual in style. There are baroque mansions at Loona and Pidula. Classical style is represented at the Loona manor, and at Koljala and Laimjala. An eclectic ensemble, dating from the late 19th century, is at the Padaste manor.

The 20th century's two world wars did not spare Saaremaa. Particularly harsh was the second one. Saaremaa lost 25% of its population as a result of deportations by Moscow, war casualties and the flight to escape abroad. The last desperate battles fought between the German army and the Red army on Estonia's territory were fought on Saaremaa with heavy casualties. Memorials have been erected to note these happenings. At Jaagarahu's former harbour, located on the northwestern coast of the island, is a monument in memory of those islanders who were victims of the mass deportations of June 14 1941. At Tehumardi, at the entrance to Sõrve peninsula, is the island's most famous monument to fallen soldiers. In the vicinity are also several common graves. About 20km north of Tehumardi is the former Kogula airfield that was used for bombing raids on Berlin.

A singular phenomenon on the island, and indeed in the world, is the **Kaali** crater, dating from about the 8th century BC. It is the only easily accessible large meteorite crater. To the layman's eye it looks like a big bowl of split-pea soup. It's located 20km northeast of Kuressaare.

On the north coast are several picturesque, steep formations of limestone and dolomite base rock. The most noteworthy are at **Panga, Ninase** and **Pulli**. You'll find two large windmills at Ninase built to resemble a hardy folk-costumed couple. Makes for some interesting photo shots.

Fishing and farming are the occupations of the islanders. Nature preserves exist to protect the rich plant and bird species and the islanders themselves want to preserve their quiet way of life, their customs and traditions.

Bed and breakfast places, camping, cycling, excursions to outer islands, and wild boar hunting are available to visitors. Saaremaa can be easily reached from the mainland by the ferry that goes to Muhumaa, which is connected to Saaremaa by a causeway built in 1894-96. A direct ferry link with Sweden was established in 1993. A ship runs regularly between Veere harbour, on the northwest coast, and Stockholm. There's also passenger transport service by air between Saaremaa and the mainland.

Kuressaare

Kuressaare (pop 17,000) is Saaremaa's capital. The **Castle** is the only medieval fortress in the Baltic that has been preserved in its essential parts and it is the island's museum. It was built in the 14th century as the seat of the Bishop of Saare-Lääne. Later, under Swedish rule, the high walls surrounding the castle were built and a long tunnel connected the outer and inner wards. In the Great Hall one can see the initials of Queen Christina of Sweden on a window frame with the date 1645.

The highest of the castle towers, the 29m **Pikk Hermann** (Tall Hermann) houses the Saaremaa Museum with an exposition on the city's and island's history.

Below the castle lie extensive dungeons. Some 200 years ago the skeleton of a knight was discoverd here. He had been seated at a table with a jug and a piece of parchment before him. At the first touch he crumbled into dust. Sadly, his true story remains known only to God.

Among other historic buildings are the baroque **Raekoda** (Town Hall), built in 1670, and **Rüütelkonna hoone** (the Knights' House) built in the late 1700s. Near the Raekoda is a beautiful **Tuletõr jemaja** (firehouse), built in 1870 with a tower added in 1958. In the square near the town

Kuressaare Castle

RINGTEE
KALEVI
TEHNIKA
AIA
PIKK
KIHELKONNA
KADAKA
RISTIKU
J. SMUULI
VALLIMAA
HARIDUSE
Põduste
KOHTU
ROHU
TALLINNA
IDA
AIA
PIKK
ROOSTI
TORNI
PIHTLA TEE
KAUBA
KARJA
VAHTRA
PÄRNA
JAAMA
TRANSVAALI
KOIDU
KEVADE
UUS
PIKK
TALVE
AIA
LOSSI
VAHE
KAEVU
A. KITZBERGI
TÖÖ
KUNGLA
NOORUSE
TALVE
TUULE
ROOMASSAARE
KURESSAARE

hall is a monument designed by the sculptor Eric Adamson to commemorate those Estonian islanders who lost their lives in the Independence War. The town is also a resort, offering 'therapeutic treatment for common complaints'. The park around the castle moat was laid out in 1861 and some handsome turn-of-the-century wooden resort buildings are in and around it. The beautiful, ornate **Kurhaus** in the park was built in 1889 and its bandstand dates from 1920. Near the castle is a wall commemorating those killed by the Soviets in 1941. A monument to the victims of Nazi Germany is nearby on a small island.

Other notable buildings in the centre of Kuuresaare are the **Valkoda**, or weighing house, built in 1663 on Tallinna Street; a neighbouring **wooden house** (at the corner of Torni tn and Tallinna street) which was used as a post-station in the 18th century and a post office from 1889-1919; and the **Turuhoone** at Tallinna 5, a former cadets' school, built in 1740 and now a market hall.

Just north of the Turuhoone is **St Lawrence Church**, built in 1836. The **Russian Orthodox Church of St Nikolai**, built in 1790 is located between the Town Hall square and the castle.

Noteworthy also is the 17th century **House of the Governor of Livonia**, B von Compenhausen, at N° 19 Kommandandi Street, between Torni and Rootsi streets. Nearby is the Classical-style building of the former law courts, the **Kohtumaja** (late 1700s) at Tallinna 19.

Where to stay

GUESTHOUSE AGER, Kohtu 10. Tel: (372)-45-565-34.

KURESSAARE HAIGLA VÕÕRASTEMAJA (Guest House), Aia 25. Five rooms, 13 beds. No shower in rooms. Tel: (372)-45-59-783.

LOSSI (Castle Hotel), Lossi 27. Singles and doubles with shared baths. Singles 220 EEK, doubles 440 EEK. Tel: (372)-45-54-443, 56-859, fax: 56-084.

MARDI ÕÕMAJA, Vallimaa 5 A. A mid-sized hotel that has rooms with private bath and phone. Café, car rental, car park. Tel: (372)-45-57-436, 55-878, fax: 56-056.

PENSION PANGA, Tallinna 27. Nine rooms, 21 beds. Double, triple and quad rooms. Shower, toilet, and TV on each floor. Sauna. Tel: (372)-45-55-323.

REPO PENSION, Vallimaa 1 A. Small hotel. Rooms with shared shower, bath and WC. Sauna, bar, car park. Tel: (372)-45-55-111, fax: 55-552.

STAADIONI HOTEL, Staadioni 1. Singles, doubles, triples with shower/bath and WC. Sauna, café, car park. Tel/fax: (372)-45-55-202.

TARSA PENSION, Kauba 12. Small facility, rooms with shared shower, WC, phone. Accepts Diners Club, Mastercard. Tel: (372)-45-55-194.

THEODOR HOTEL, Kauba 8. Double rooms with shower, WC, phone and TV. Sauna, restaurant, bar, currency exchange. Tel: (372)-45-54-309.

TOLLI HOTEL, Tolli 4. Six double rooms with shower, WC and TV. Bar, car park. Tel: (372)-45-59-672.

Out of town
MÄNNIKÄBI, about 15km west of Kuressaare, at Mändjala. 34 beds in double rooms with WC and shower; restaurant and sauna. Tel: (372)-45-55-680, 75-106, fax: 57-341.
MEREKIVI HOTEL, 3km east of town. 25 beds. Rooms with private bath. Restaurant, bar. Tel: (372)-45-57-761.
TAHULA MOTELL, in the eastern suburb. Three single rooms, 10 double rooms. Sauna. Singles 290 EEK, twins 490 EEK. A new, pleasant, clean lodging with a good restaurant and bar. 6km from centre. Tel: (372)-45-57-410 and 57-490.

Camping
MÄNDJALA, 10km southwest from Kuressaare, located on the coast. Single, double and family cabins. Open June, July, August. Tel: (372)-45-75-193, 55-079, fax: 54-035. Operated by the Saaremaa Reisibüroo.

Where to eat
GRILBAR, Tallinna tänav 2.
KURESSAARE, Raekoja 1; open daily from noon to midnight. Tel: (372)-45-55-136.
KUURSAAL, in the park. Probably the best in town. Tel: (372)-45-59-250.
KOHVIK, Vallimaa, north of Keskväljak. Clean and spacious.
TOLLAKUR, Lossi 12. Tel: (372)-45-56-925.
TUULIK, Pärnu 19. Tel: (327)-45-54-858. Restaurant and casino. Expensive.

Museums
SAAREMAA MUUSEUM (Saaremaa Museum), Lossihoov 3; open Wed-Sun 11am-5.30pm, tel: (372)-45-56-307.
KURESSAARE KUNSTI GALERII (Kuressaare's Art Gallery), Pargi 5; open Wed-Sun 11am-5.30pm, tel: (372)-45-59-671.

Chemist/Pharmacist
APTEEK, Lossi 1; open Mon-Fri 8am-8pm, Sat-Sun 9am-5pm.

Churches
LURENTSIUSE KIRIK (St Lawrence's), Tallinna 13. Evangelical-Lutheran.
NIKOLAI KIRIK (St Nicholas'), Lossi 8. Orthodox.
BAPTIST, METHODIST AND ADVENTIST CONGREGATIONS, Karja 1.

Shopping
Shops are located mostly around Keskväljak and on Lossi Street. Native products are textiles, juniper-wood utensils and souvenirs.

Antiques
ANTIIK, 6 Kitsas tn.
HOLOSTOVI ANTIQUES, Turu tn 1. Hrs. 9am-5pm daily. Coins, medals, icons, glass, books, porcelain.

Handicrafts:
UKUARU, Lossi tn 9.
UKU, Turu tn 1.

Art:
HANSA, Tallinna tn 9.
KELDRISALONG, Vallimaa tn 4.
DJANA, Vallimaa tn 4.

Post

POSTIMAJA (Post Office), Torni 1.

Public transport

Bus Station, Pihtla tee 25; tel: (372)-45-57-380. It has a luggage room. BE SURE TO BUY YOUR TICKET IN ADVANCE as spaces are limited!

Buses to Kuressaare from Tallinn

Depart Tallin	Arrive Kuressaare	Depart Kuressaare	Arrive Tallin
7.40am	12.10pm	5.55am	10.30am
11.00am	3.30pm	7.30am	11.45am
2.50pm	7.00pm	10.30am	3.10pm
4.15pm	8.30pm	2.20pm	6.50pm
5.40pm	10.00pm	5.40pm	10.10pm

Airport, Roomassaare 1; tel: (372)-45-54-099.
Taxi: Tel: 54-939.

Car rentals:
MAKER, Tallinna 30, tel: 53-149.
MARDI, Tallinna 4, tel: 54-875.
METRA/RENT-A-CAR, Aia tn 25, tel: 59-363.
STEADY, Vallimaa 5A, tel: 55-878.
THULE, Pargi 2, tel: 59-690.

Car Repair: Kalevi tn 2, Roomassaare tee 6.

Service stations

KURESSAARE SERVICE STATION, Kalev 2. Tel: (372)-45-57-478.

Bicycle rental:
ERGO CYCLING, Kihelkonna tee 2, tel: 57-587.
MARDI, Tallinna 4, tel: 54-875.
STEADY, Vallimaa tn 54, tel: 55-878.

Telephone and telegraph

POSTIMAJA, Torni 1.

Tourist information centre

MARDI LTD, Tallinna 4. Centrally located in town. Tel: (372)-45-54-349, fax: 57-448, telex: 173111 saare su.

Travel agents

COMPLEX LTD, Kitsas 3; can arrange for B&B in town. Tel: (372)-45-54-349, fax: 57-448, telex: 173111 saare su.

MARDI LTD, Tallinna 4; also serves as Tourist Info Centre. Tel: (372)-45-54-875, fax: 56-241, telex: 173111 saare su.

SAAREMAA REISIBÜROO (Saaremaa Travel Bureau), Pihtla tee 2; can arrange camping at Mandjala. Tel: (372)-45-55-079, fax: 57-448.

THULE, Pargi 1; tel: (372)-45-57-470, 59-686, fax: 54-104.

WRIS, Tallinna tn. 9; tel: (372)-45-55-299.

In order to visit **Saaremaa**, and **Muhumaa**, which is attached to it by a causeway, you have to travel south from Haapsalu to **Virtsu.** At Virtsu harbour there is a ferry connection with these two islands. En route you will go through the small town of **Lihula**, an ancient settlement of archaeological interest. Near Lihula is the **Matsalu Nature Reserve** and bird museum, housed in the Haeska manor at Penijoe. The 486km^2 reserve is comprised of Matsalu Bay, the islands, coasts, wetlands, and the mouth of the Kasari River. The reserve also includes vast reed beds, coastal pastures and hay meadows. Around 350,000 water birds stop here on migratory flights. This includes circa 40,000 swans during peak migration periods. Nesting areas exist for hundreds of pairs of grelag geese, many mute swan and bittern. Altogether, over 100 species nest here, a major European bird sanctuary.

Guided boat trips to the reserve can be taken from the reserve centre. Advance reservations are advisable: Matsalu Riiklik Looduskaitseala, Lihula EE3170, tel/fax: (372)-47-78-413.

The rest of Saaremaa

Kaarma, a village 12km north of Kuressaare, has significant deposits of dolomite, the valuable building material often called ‘Saaremaa marble’. St Peter’s church was built in the 13th century and rebuilt in 1407. The village was an Estonian stronghold in the 12th-13th centuries. This is the birthplace of Oskar Kallas (1868-1946), a folklorist, founder of the Estonian National Museum, and Estonian ambassador to Helsinki, London, and The Hague. A memorial stone commemorates his achievements.

Kihelkonna is the centre for western Saaremaa. It is the third largest town on the island. It served as an Estonian stronghold in the 11th-12th centuries. St Michael's Church was built in 1270 and its tower in 1870. The town's school was established in 1695. The cemetery has a 1934 monument to those victims of the Estonian War of Independence.

At **Viki**, 3km east of Kihelkonna, is the **Mihkli Talumuuseum** (Mihkli Farm Museum), which is an old farm put to use as a museum showing farm and household implements over the generations.

Just south of Kihelkonna is the village of **Lümanda** with an 1870 Orthodox Church. Nearby is the picturesque village of **Leedri** with unusual high stone walls surrounding many of its homes. South of Leedri is the settlement of **Pilguse.** Here you'll find the former manor of the Bellingshausen family. It was home to the explorer FG Bellingshausen who was born at Lahetaguse manor in 1778. Built in baroque style in the late 18th century, it later served as the home of JW von Luce from 1793-1805. It is now a hospital.

North of Kihelkonna the road leads to the settlement of **Undva** on the **Tagamõisa Peninsula**. The region is perfect for hiking — the peninsula has a landscape which boasts beaches, steep cliffs, coastal lakes and botanical preserves.

At **Mustjala**, on the northern coast, you'll find an Orthodox Church (1873) and St Anna's Lutheran Church (1843). North of Mustjala is the island's highest cliff — **Panga Pank**, 22m high and 2.5km long. Ancient Estonians used the cliff as a place of sacrificial offerings. A lighthouse is located there today.

Travelling eastward from Panga cliff one passes through **Metsküla**, with a fine Orthodox Church (1914). North of here is the **Pammana Nina,** the northernmost part of Saaremaa island. At **Angla** you'll find the famous Saaremaa field of windmills, five remain of a former 21. Truly, this place is one of the most scenic in Estonia and the windmills are a photographer's delight.

At nearby **Karja** you'll find the Church of St Catherine (13th century), considered to be one of the finest architectural monuments in Estonia. East of Karja is **Orissaaare** (pop 1,200), the second largest town in Saaremaa; it dominates the eastern part of the island. It owes its growth to the building of the causeway to Muhumaa. The ruins of the 16th century Teutonic **Maasilinna Castle** lie north of town.

Seven kilometres to the south stands the 13th century Põide Church of St Mary, the biggest in Saaremaa. It is under restoration, having suffered neglect and abuse during the Soviet occupation. **Põide** formerly served as a site for a castle of the German knights.

Halfway between Põide and Kuressaare, along the main road, at **Valjala**, are the remains of one of the most powerful ancient forts. The fort, Estenburg, had high walls and only capitulated to the German Knights when the islanders learned of the Muhu massacre. The Estonian chiefs had to give their sons as hostages to the Livonian Order and the population was baptized en masse. The baptism ended Estonian organized resistance to the Knights. St Martin's Church is the oldest stone church in Estonia, built 1240-1270.

Near Valjala, at **Lööne**, is an old 18th century manor, and at nearby Koljala is another fine manor from the same period.

Saaremaa's southern region is also worth visiting. Leaving Kuuresaare, take the coastal road past the fine beach resort of **Mandjala** to the settlement of **Järve** where you'll see beautiful dunes and pine forests. At nearby **Tehumardi** is a monument to those killed in terrible fighting between the Soviet and German armies at the end of World War II. **Tiirimetsa** has an old Orthodox Church (1873) and windmill.

South of here you enter the Sorve peninsula — a 32km extension of the main island. **Löö** houses a fine lighthouse built in 1937 and at **Kaugatuma** a sharp cliff affords a beautiful vista of the open Baltic Sea. **Anseküla's** St Virgin Mary Church lighthouse (1864) was destroyed in World War II fighting, but a new light was erected in 1953. **Loõpollu** has a monument to the victims of World War II erected in 1974, while **Jämaja's** monument is dedicated to islanders deported to Germany in 1944. It also has a Trinity Lutheran Church (1864). At **Torgu** you'll find a monument to the terrible masssacre of 1944 when German gunners mowed down advancing Red Army troops — many of whom were Estonian conscripts. You can go by foot to view two unique Bronze Age ship burial sites (8th century BC) at **Lülle.** From **Sääre**, the southern end of the peninsula, you can see the Latvian tip of the Kurzeme peninsula on a clear day. The lighthouse was built in 1960. Ruins of German bunkers lie nearby. Beacause the Latvian-Estonian sea border has not yet been delimited, the sea nearby recently witnessed confrontations between Estonian border patrol craft and Latvian fishing boats.

Where to stay

JÜRI MITT'S TOURISM FARM, Torgu. 4 rooms, some with shared shower and WC, some with shower and WC on the floor. Sauna, bicycle rental. Located on a peninsula facilitating fishing, sailing, sea trips. Car park. Tel: (372)-45-70-421 and (372)-2-440-253 for reservations. Fax numbers are the same as the phones.

TARE HOTEL, Liikuv side 5, Pihtla Parish. Doubles, triples and quads with WC on the floor. 16 cabins for double occupancy. Field kitchen, 2 showers and 2 WCs. On a seaside, fishing, minigolf. Car park, restaurant, bar. Tel: (372)-45-909-125, 57-584.

Also, enquire at the **SAAREMAA GUESTHOUSE ASSOCIATION**, tel: (372)-45-54-991.

THE OTHER ISLANDS

A considerable Swedish population inhabited places on the west coast and islands of Estonia. First settlers started arriving in the 13th century. However, virtually all of them fled in 1944 before the Red Army occupied Estonia for the second time. Hence, the **Noarootsi peninsula** across the bay, north of Haapsalu, formerly consisted of Swedish communities. A few centuries ago, it was an island of Swedish settlers like Vormsi, but due to the gradual rise of land in West Estonia, Noarootsi has joined the mainland. In the town of **Hosby**, St Catherine's Church was built in 1500. The centre of Noarootsi is **Purksi**, which has a fine park that already had a manor built in it in 1620.

Vormsi

The other concentrated Swedish settlement, **Vormsi Island**, can be reached by ferry from the harbour of **Rohuküla**. The trip lasts about an hour. The harbour is located nine kilometres west of Haapsalu and the regular service runs to the harbour town of Sviby on Vormsi's southern coast. Vormsi is Estonia's fourth largest island, and was settled by Swedes in the 13th century, which is reflected in place names, architecture and religious artifacts. The thriving Swedish community fled during World War II and today the 400 inhabitants are Estonians. Some of the once busy 13 villages are still deserted. The largest village is **Hullo**, which has a 14th century church with a graveyard containing the largest collection of wheel-shaped crosses in Estonia. There are boarding houses on the island, so an overnight stay is possible. Travel arrangements to Vormsi can be made through: Estonian Tours, Roosikrantsi 4b, EE0106 Tallinn, Estonia, tel: (372)-2-442-034, fax: 442-034.

HIIUMAA

Hiiumaa is the second largest island (1000km^2, pop 12,000), located north of Saaremaa. It can also be reached by ferry from **Rohuküla** — the crossing takes about 1½ hours and the ferry pulls into **Heltermaa,** at Hiiumaa's eastern side. Ostensibly, it used to take about a day to go from the mainland to Hiiumaa, for the Swedish name for the island was *Dago*, meaning 'Day Island'.

Evidence suggests that it was already inhabited for centuries BC. Its soil is poor and rocky, and the islanders have always supplemented their income by fishing or by finding work on the mainland. About 60% of the island is covered with forest (lots of juniper) and because of its geographical position, the sea, the wind, and the migration of birds, its flora is very rich. It offers the botanist, ornithologist and archaeologist an interesting field to explore. The capital — and centre of the island's services — is **Kärdla** (pop 4,000), located on the northern shore. It was founded by Swedish settlers who lived by fishing and farming the sandy soil. In the 19th century the baronial Ungern-Sternberg family established a textile factory in the town. During the Soviet occupation Kärdla saw the addition of bland highrises and a large increase in population. There are no historic sites, but dramatic history is located about 7km west of Kärdla, near the main road at **Ristimägi.** Here the inhabitants, who had been free farmers, performed their last act of worship before being deported to Ukraine in the late 18th century. The dune is decked with hand-made crosses to mark the spot.

Where to stay

HOTEL PADU, Heltermaa mnt 6, Kärdla, tel: 46-98-034. Double rooms for 20. Dining room, bar, sauna and tennis courts.
HOTEL SÕNAJALA, Lautri väljak 3, Kärdla, tel: 46-99-336, fax: 46-96-305. Small and modest near the water. Two singles, four doubles. Car park.
BOARDING HOUSE KÄRDLA, Vabaduse 11, Kärdla, tel: 46-91-481.
KÕRGESSAARE VILLA, Kõrgessaare village. 12km from Kärdla. 30 beds, sauna, bar.
PRAHNU SUVILA, Nurste, tel: 46-95-508. Five rooms, 15 beds. Showers with sauna. Lounge with TV and radio. 150m to the sea. 40km from Kärdla airport; 3km from nearest bus stop.
HIIUMAA TOURISM ASSOCIATION, Leigri 5, tel: 46-91-154.

Camping
MALVESTE TURISMIKESKUS. 2½km north of Kärdla-Kõrgessaare Road. 13 cabins in a forest. Tel: (372)-46-91-525, 98-885.
RESANDE, 6km towards Lehtma. Tel: 92-694.

Where to eat

JÄÄGER, Valli 1, near Central Square, tel: 91-550. Located in a park. Decor consists of hunting trophies. Bar.
KÄRDLA, Keskväljak/Central Square, tel: 91-562. Large room. Bar.
RANNAPARGI, in Rannapark, tel: 91-287. Downstairs dining room and upstairs café-bar. On the beach. Nice views. Disco at weekends.
PRIIANKUR, on Sadama, across from the travel agency Dago.

Bars
MARDI-TRUMMI, Rookopli 8, tel: 46-91-682.
NÄKIMADAL, Vabriku valjak 1, tel: 46-96-361.
PIIBUNINA, Sadama 6, tel: 46-96-227.

Museum

HIIUMAA MUSEUM, tel: 97-121. The island's history. Offers English-speaking tours.

Post

POST OFFICE, Posti 7, Kärdla.

Shopping

Food and drink shop at north end of Keskväljak, Kärdla.
Department store, Uus 2, Kärdla.

Travel agents

ESTRESOR, Vabaduse 4, Kärdla. Offers a range of accommodations throughout Hiiumaa, bicycles, camping gear, arranges tours of the island and other parts of the Baltic states, fishing and hunting trips. Tel: (372)-46-91-093, fax: 96-350.

DAGO TRAVEL, Uus 1, Kärdla. Can provide services similar to Estresor's.
TURISTI INFORMAT, Pollu 3, tel: 46-91-377.

Service stations

Garage Lukk and Marjama, Valli 21, Kärdla. Regular repairs, welding, oil change.
Sildivend Ltd, Heltermaa mnt 4a, Kärdla, tel: 98-892.

Taxi

Tel: (372)-46-91-139.

Airport

Hiiessaare, about 6km east of Kärdla. Tel: 91-217, fax: 91-227.

North of Ristimagi follow the coastal road to **Tahkuma**. Here is a lighthouse built in 1874 in Paris which was sent by ship to the island. A nearby Soviet memorial commemorates the soldiers of the Soviet Army in World War II who were overwhelmed by advancing German forces in 1941. Thousands were either killed or captured nearby.

From Tahkuna you can go southwest to the little settlement of **Reigi** on the road to Kõrgessaare. Here you'll find a stone church built by the Ungern-Sternberg family in 1802. The Church was built in memory of a son of the family who committed suicide to escape responsibility for his large gambling debts.

Twenty kilometres west of Kärdla is the harbour village of **Kõrgessaare** which historically served as a major trading port for merchants dealing with Sweden.

Where to eat in Kõrgessaare

RESTAURANT VIINAKÖÖK, Sadama 2, tel: 93-356. In the former distillery of the manor, built in 1881. Fish and game dishes. Sauna.

Further westward is Hiiumaa's best known landmark, the **Kõpu Lighthouse** on Kõpu peninsula. At that high spot a lighthouse has stood since 1531. The present structure was built in 1845 and it is one of the oldest lighthouses in Europe. It is 37m high (it can be climbed) and can be seen from about 50km away.

Besides the sea connection, air service exists between the island and mainland.

Where to stay in Kõpu

BOARDING HOUSE LAUTRI, village of Kalana, 8km west of Kõpu. Three double rooms, bar, sauna. Camping possible.

On Hiiumaa's southern coast lies the island of **Kassari,** a beautiful unspoiled place that provides privacy, summer homes and camps to mainlanders. On the island is also Hiiumaa Museum, with a large collection of artefacts and exhibits on the island's history, nature and ethnography. Branches of the museum include **Käina,** the birthplace of composer and organist Rudolf Tobias, and the summer cottage, at Kassari beach, of Finnish-born writer, Aino Kallas, who was married to Estonian diplomat, Oskar Kallas. Many mainlanders have summer homes on the island.

Be sure to visit the southernmost tip of Kassari, the 'Sääre tipp' in which is a magnificent peninsula extending into the Baltic Sea. The peninsula becomes so thin at its end, it eventually submerges into the water. You may also wish to visit the little church at **Kiisi**, the only thatched church in Estonia.

Käina

Where to stay

HOTEL LIILIA, Hiiu maantee 22. A *Best Western* hotel. Single and double rooms with shower, WC and TV. Restaurant, bar, car park. 19km from Kärdla, tel: (372)-46-92-146, fax: 92-546.

PUULAID HOTEL, 4km outside Käina. Main building has doubles and triples, WC, showers, sauna, phone and dining room. Plus four cabins. By the sea. Water sports available. Tel: (372)-46-92-126, 97-629.

Where to eat

KÄINA at Liilia Hotel, Hiiu mnt 22. Offers Estonian and international menu. Also has a bar.

SILJA, tel: 91-152.

Another important historical monument on Hiiumaa, the Palace of the Ungern-Steinberg family, lies east of Kainaa, at the settlement of **Suuremõisa.** The palace was built in 1755-1760 by a descendant of the 16th century Swedish Governor of Estonia, Jakob de la Gardie. In 1796, the palace was purchased by the Ungern-Sternberg family which had gained much wealth in the shipping business.

In 1803, Baron Ungern-Sternberg killed one of his business partners in the palace. He was tried and deported to Siberia where he died in 1811.

MUHUMAA

The third island in size is Muhu (pop 2,200). It lies east of Saaremaa and anyone going from the mainland to Saaremaa has to go through Muhu. Muhu has a sad early history. Its castle was the site of a terrible massacre of the Estonian population which had resisted the advancing German Knights of the Sword. Bishop Albert of Rīga had his Grand

Master, Volquin, attack the Estonians in January 1227. Two-thousand Knights attacked the Estonian castle and on the seventh day great seige towers were brought up to bombard the defenders. The castle walls were breached and the Knights hacked to death all the men, women and children inside.

The ferry from the mainland pulls into **Kuivastu Harbour**. The ferry crosses frequently and the trip lasts about 30 minutes. At the harbour are a station, restaurant, hotel, post office, bar, WC and currency exchange. A car rental office is planned. Private yachts can dock.

Muhu's northern coast has many caves in its cliffs hollowed out by the sea. The northwestern shore offers peaceful, sandy beaches where visitors often set up camp.

Like other islanders, the inhabitants' lives have been historically engaged with fishing and farming. Its best known citizen is the Soviet-era writer, Juhan Smuul (1922-1971). His birthplace, in **Koguva village**, is today part of the Muhu Museum. The museum is a living, working island village, and all of its 105 buildings are protected. Thatched roof log cabins, old boats, and stone fences give it the ambience of yesteryear. Tel: (372)-45-98-616. Located on the island's western coast. It is well worth a visit, and guides are available for English, German, French, Swedish and Finnish tours (by appointment).

The only working windmill in Estonia, *Eemu*, is located on the Kuressaare road to Saaremaa before the causeway. Stop and try out the hand mill. Souvenirs are available.

The island's largest settlement and administrative centre is **Liiva.** The town has a beautifully restored (in 1993 by Swedes) 13th century church, and next to it a good restaurant. The vicarage is the birthplace of Alexander Schmidt (1831-1894) who was a rector of Tartu University. He is also known for developing a new blood coagulation theory.

Several places on the island are set up to receive farm-stay and B&B guests. For more information contact: AS Muhu Turist, tel: (372)-45-98-171.

Appendix One

Useful Words and Expressions

(In Estonian, the stress is always on the first syllable.)

Hello	Tere
Good-morning	Tere hommikust
Good-evening	Head õhtust
Good-night	Head ööd
Good-bye	Nägemiseni
Yesterday	Eile
Today	Täna
Tomorrow	Homme
Please	Palun
Thank you	Tänan väga *or* aitäh
Yes	Ja
No	Ei
You're welcome	Võtke heaks
Excuse me	Vabandage
I'm sorry	Andke andeks or andestage
My name is...	Minu nimi on...
Do you speak English?	Kas Teie räägite inglise keelt?
I don't speak Estonian	Mina ei räägi eesti keelt
Please speak slowly	Palun rääkige aeglaselt
I don't understand	Mina ei saa aru
I would like to go to..	Mina sooviksin minna .....se
Where is...	Kus on...
I would like...	Mina tahan...
How much does it cost?	Kui palju see maksab?
Cheap	Odav
Expensive	Kallis
To your health!	Terviseks! — Fast becoming the favourite way of toasting in the English-speaking world.

At a restaurant

I would like to order	Mina soovin tellida
Some more, please	Lisa, palun
That's enough, thank you	Aitab, tänan
water	vesi
coffee (with milk)	kohv (piimaga)
sugar	suhkur
salt	sool
tea	tee
juice	mahl
milk	piim
mineral water	mineraalvesi
beer	õlu
wine (red, white)	vein (punane, valge)
bread	leib
butter	või
sandwich	võileib
salad	salat
tip	jootraha

Locations

street	tänav
square	plats
hotel	hotell/võõrastemaja
castle	loss
church	kirik
restaurant	söökla/restoraan
hospital	haigla
drug store/pharmacy	apteek
movie theatre/cinema	kino
theatre	teater
museum	muuseum
post office	postimaja/postkontor
toilet	WC
railroad station	rongijaam
harbour	sadam
airport	lennujaam

Days of the week

Monday	esmaspäev
Tuesday	teisipäev
Wednesday	kolmapäev
Thursday	neljapäev
Friday	reede
Saturday	laupäev
Sunday	pühapäev

Cardinal numerals

1	üks	16	kuusteist
2	kaks	17	seitseteist
3	kolm	18	kaheksateist
4	neli	19	üheksateist
5	viis	20	kakskümmend
6	kuus	25	kakskümmendviis
7	seitse	30	kolmkümmend
8	kaheksa	40	nelikümmend
9	üheksa	50	viiskümmend
10	kümme	60	kuuskümmend
11	üksteist	70	seitsekümmend
12	kaksteist	80	kaheksakümmend
13	kolmteist	90	üheksakümmend
14	neliteist	100	sada
15	viisteist	101	sadaüks

Ordinal numerals

1st	esimene	8th	kaheksas
2nd	teine	9th	üheksas
3rd	kolmas	10th	kümnes
4th	neljas	11th	üheteistkümnes
5th	viies	20th	kahekümnes
6th	kuues	100th	sajas
7th	seitsmes		

Pronunciation guide

The Estonian language belongs to the Balto-Finnic branch of the Finno-Ugric family. It is closely related to Finnish and bears a very distant relationship to Hungarian. Estonian and Italian have been singled out by the International PEN Club as the most beautiful languages. The beauty of Estonian comes from the numerous long vowel sounds and the lack of harsh consonants. The accent is always on the first syllable. The Estonian alphabet is as follows:

a, b, (c), d, e, (f), g, h, i, j, k, l, m, n, o, p, (q), r, s, (š), (z), (ž), t, u, v, (w), ö, ä, õ, ü, (x), (y).

The letters c, f, q, š, z, ž, w, x and y are only used in loan words and foreign names. Double letters indicate both long vowels and consonants. Diphthongs always have a short first vowel.

Vowels

The letter **a** is pronounced as the English **u** in **but**;
aa is like **a** in **father**;
e as in **bet**;
ee as in the English **eh** or French **de**;
i as in **pin**;
ii as **ee** in **feel**;
o as in **off**;
oo as **eau** in the French **peau**;
u as in **put**;
uu as the oo in **food**;
ä almost as in **cat**, but with a less open mouth;
ää is the same as **a**, but with a more open mouth;
ö as **ir** in **girl**, but with rounded lips;
öö as the **oeu** in the French **voeu**;
õ is peculiar to Estonian and is pronounced with the lips in the position of a short **e** while the tongue is retracted;
õõ is the same as **õ**, but longer;
ü is produced by pronouncing **i** with a protrusion of the lips and a narrow opening of the mouth;
üü is the same as **ü**, but longer and clearer.

Consonants

The letter **b** is voiceless, almost like the **p** in **copy**;
d is voiceless as the **t** in **city**;
g is voiceless as the **ck** in **ticket**;
k, **p**, and **t** are stronger and longer than the voiceless **g**, **b**, and **d**;
h is the same as in English, but less aspirated;
j like **y** in **you**;
l as in **lily**;
m is the same as in English, but shorter;
n as in English;
r is trilled;
s is voiceless and weaker than the English **s**;
š as the **sh** in **shoe**;
v as in English;
f as in English;
z as the **s** in **was**;
ž as the **s** in **pleasure**.

Appendix Two

Travel Agents

You may find you get better rates in both airfare and hotels if you book your trip to Estonia through a travel agency that specializes in Baltic travel. Many also offer guided tours and other interesting packages. Listed below are some such agencies in the United States, Canada (two) and England. This is by no means a complete list.

In the US and Canada:
American Travel Service, 9439 S Kedzie Avenue, Evergreen Park, IL 60642. Tel: 1-800-698-1580, local tel: (708)-422-3000, fax: (708)-422-3163. Tour name: Baltic Customized Group and FIT Tours.
Blue Heart Tours, 1317 Connecticut Ave, NW, Ste 300, Washington, DC 20036. Tel: 1-800-269-4751.
East West Tours and Travel Consulting, 10 E 39th St, Ste 1021, New York, NY 10016. Tel: (212)-545-0725.
East West Travel and Tour Corp, 3614-910 Mainland Street, Vancouver, BC V6B1A9. Tel: (604)-687-3656.
EuroPlus, 226 Winchester Ave, White Plains, NY 10604. Tel: 1-800-462-2577.
Europa Tours Specialists Inc, 7301 Sepulveda Blvd, Van Nuys, CA 91405. Tel: 1-800-323-5300.
FOS Tours and Travel Inc, 15 Great Neck Rd, Suite 3, Great Neck, NY 11021. Tel: 1-800-367-3450.
FinnWay Inc, 228 E 45th St, New York, NY 10017. Tel: 1-800-526-4927.
General Tours Inc, 139 Main St, Cambridge, MA 02142. Tel: 1-800-221-2216.
Holiday Tours of America, 425 Madison Ave, New York, NY 10017-1110. Tel: 1-800-677-6454.
Its Tours and Travel, 1055 Texas Ave, Ste 104, College Station, TX 77840. 1-800-533-8688.
Inter-Tours Company, 1100 S Beverly Dr, Ste 209, Los Angeles, CA 90035. Tel: 1-800-959-4743.
LeBoat Inc Worldwide Holidays Afloat, 215 Union St, Hackensack, NJ 07601. Tel: 1-800-922-0291.
Nordique Tours, 5250 W Century Blvd, #626, Los Angeles, CA 90045. Tel: 1-800-995-7997.

Pedersen World Tours Inc, 15 Wertheim Ct, Ste 402, Richmond Hill, ON L4B3H7. Tel: 1-800-263-3274.
Scanam World Tours, 933 Highway 23, Pompton Plains, NJ 07444. Tel: 1-800-545-2204.
Scantours Inc, 1535 Sixth St, Ste 205 Santa Monica, CA 90401-0000. Tel: 1-800-223-7226.
TWA Getaway Vacations, 1 City Center, St Louis, MO 63101. Tel: 1-800-GET-AWAY
Tumlare Travel Organization, 114 Old Country Rd., Mineola, NY 11501. Tel: 1-800-223-4664.
Union Tours, 245 Fifth Avenue, #1101, New York, NY 10016. Tel: 1-800-451-9511.

In England:
Regent Holidays, 15 John Street, Bristol BS1 2HR. Tel: 0117-921-1711, fax: 0117-925-4866. Arranges discount flights and hotels. Arranges general interest group tours to the three Baltic countries during the summer.
Martin Randall Travel, 10 Barley Mow Passage, London W4 4PH. Tel: 0181-742-3355, fax: 0181-742-1066. Arranges art and architecture tours.
Explore Worldwide, 1 Frederick Street, Aldershot, Hants GU11 1LQ. Tel: 01252-319448, fax: 01252-343170. Arranges general interest tours.
ACE (Association for Cultural Exchange), Babraham, Cambridge CB2 4AP. Tel: 01223-835055, fax: 01223-837394. Arranges general interest tours.
Intourist Travel, 219 Marsh Wall, London E14 9PD. Tel: 0171-538-8600, fax: 0171-538-5967. Arranges general interest tours including Russia.

Appendix Three

Foreign Embassies

Embassies in Estonia, all in Tallinn, provide limited consular services which include advice and emergency assistance (for example, in case of theft or loss of money, passport) to their citizens. No matter what country you are from, if you are planning a long stay it is a good idea to register with consular officials of your country on your arrival.

AUSTRALIA, Office in Stockholm, Sweden: 12 Sergels Torg, Box 7003, 10386 Stockholm, tel: (46 8) 613-2900, fax: (46 8) 247-414.
AUSTRIA, Pikk 58, EE-0001, tel: 442-428, fax: 440-821.
AZERBAIJAN, Olevimägi 12, EE-0101, tel: 601-891, fax: 440-895.
CANADA, Toom-Kooli 13, EE-0100, tel: 449-056, fax: 358-298104, hours: 9am-noon, Mon-Fri.
CHINA, Haigru tn. 22, EE-0006, tel: 477-325.
DENMARK, Rävala 9-6th floor, EE-0001, tel/fax: 691-494.
FINLAND, Liivalaia 12, EE-0001, tel: 372-6-311-444, fax: 311-446. Consulate in Tartu, Uus 3-76, tel: 372-34-31-240, fax: 372-34-33-145.
FRANCE, Toomkuninga 20, EE-0100, tel: 453-682, fax: 453-688.
GERMANY, Rävala 9, EE-0100, tel: 455-606, 455-607, fax: 455-835, hours: 10am-noon, Mon-Fri.
GREAT BRITAIN, Kentmanni 20, 2nd floor, EE-0001, tel: 372-6-313-462, 313-463, fax: 372-6-313-354.
HUNGARY, Olevimägi 12, EE-0100, tel: 601-895.
ITALY, Müürivahe tn 3, EE-0104, tel: 441-577, fax: 445-919.
JAPAN, Harju 6, EE-0101, tel: 310-531.
LATVIA, Tõnismägi 10, EE-0100, tel: 372-6-311-366, fax: (2) 681-668.
LITHUANIA, Vabaduse väljak 10A, 6th floor, EE-0001, tel: 448-917, 666-634.
NORWAY, Pärnu mnt 8, EE-0100, tel: 448-014.
POLAND, Pärnu mnt 8, EE-0100, tel: 440-609.
RUSSIA, Pikk 19, tel: 443-014, fax: 443-773.
SPAIN, Estonia pst 7, EE-0026, tel: 454-769.
SOUTH KOREA, Uus tn 32/34, EE-0101, tel: 445-917.
SWEDEN, Pikk 30, EE-0001, tel: 450-350, fax: 450-676.
UNITED STATES OF AMERICA, Kentmanni 20, 3rd floor, tel: 6-312-021, fax: 6-312-025, hours: 8.30am-5pm. Consular Dept: 9am-11.30am Mon, Wed, Fri.

Appendix Four

Estonian Embassies and Consulates

AUSTRIA, 17 W. Hauthalerstrasse, A-5020 Salzburg, tel: 43-662-848-4961.
BELGIUM, Avenue de Teruren 306-4C, #1150, Brussels, tel: 32-2-770-0536.
CANADA, Consulate: 958 Broadview, Toronto, M4K 2R6, CANADA, tel: (416)-461-0764, fax: (416)-461-0448.
DENMARK, HC Anderson's Boulevard 38, DK-1553, Copenhagen, tel: 45-33-933-462.
FINLAND, Fabianinkatu 13 A2, Helsinki 13, tel: 358-0-179-528.
FRANCE, 14 Boulevard Montmartre, 75009, Paris, tel: 33-1-48-010-022.
GERMANY, Fritz-Schaffer Strasse 22, 53113 Bonn, tel: 49-228-91-490, fax: 49-228-91-47-911. Honorary Consul, Badestrasse 38, 2143 Hamburg, tel: 49-40-450-4026, fax: 49-40-450-4051.
GREAT BRITAIN, 16 Hyde Park Gate, London SW7 5D6, tel: 44-171-589 3428, fax: 589-3430.
ISRAEL, Shoham Str 525/31, Gilo93848, Jerusalem, tel: 972-2-02-767-249.
KOREA (Republic of), Cheong ahm Building 83, #3, Seosomun-dong, chung-gu, Seoul, tel: 82-2-771-43.
LATVIA, L Laicena 22, Rīga 226002, tel: 0132-611-411, fax: 8-013-2-601-068.
LITHUANIA, Turmiskiu 20, 232016 Vilnius, tel: 0122-76-48-96, fax: 370-2-22-24-00.
NORWAY, St Olavsgatan 27, Oslo 0166, tel: 47-2-11-21-48.
RUSSIA, Sobinovski per 5, 103 009, Moscow, tel: 095-290-5013, fax: 095-202-3830, Consular office: Tel: 095-290-3178, fax: 095-202-3830. Consulate: Bolshaja Monetnaja 14, St Petersburg, tel: 812-233-5548, fax: 812-233-5309.
SWEDEN, Storgatan 38, 1tr, 11455 Stockholm, tel: 46-8-665-65-50, fax: 46-8-662-99-80.
SWITZERLAND, Chemin des Aulx 8, CH-1228, Plan-les Ouates, Geneva, tel: 41-22-706-1111.
USA, 1030 15th Street NW, Suite 1000, Washington, D.C. 20005, tel: (202) 789-0320, fax: (202) 789-0471. Consular office: 630 Fifth Ave, Suite 2415, New York, NY, 10111, tel: (212)-247-2131, for visas: (212)-247-1450, fax: (212)-262-0893. In California: Consulate, 21515 Vanowen Street, Suite 211, Canoga Park, Los Angeles, CA 91303, tel: (818) 884-5850, fax: (818) 593-2973.

NOTES

NOTES

INDEX